ST. AUGUSTINE

THE PROBLEM
OF FREE CHOICE

DE LIBERO ARBITRIO

Ancient Christian Writers

The Works of the Fathers in Translation

EDITED BY

JOHANNES QUASTEN, S. T. D.
Catholic University of America
Washington, D. C.

JOSEPH C. PLUMPE, Ph.
Pontifical College Josephinum
Worthington, O.

No. 22

ST. AUGUSTINE

THE PROBLEM
OF FREE CHOICE

TRANSLATED AND ANNOTATED

BY

DOM MARK PONTIFEX

*Monk of Downside Abbey
near Bath, England*

NEWMAN PRESS

New York, N.Y./Ramsey, N.J.

Permissu Superiorum O.S.B.
 Nihil Obstat
  J. Quasten
   Cens. Dep.

Imprimatur:
  Patricius A. O'Boyle, D.D.
   Archiep. Washingtonen.
    die 6 Maii 1955

Library of Congress
Catalog Card Number: 78-62469

ISBN: 0-8091-0259-5

PUBLISHED BY PAULIST PRESS
Editorial Office: 1865 Broadway, New York, N.Y. 10023
Business Office: 545 Island Road, Ramsey, N.J. 07446

PRINTED AND BOUND IN THE UNITED STATES OF AMERICA

CONTENTS

v

ST. AUGUSTINE

THE PROBLEM
OF FREE CHOICE

DE LIBERO ARBITRIO

Augustine, *Retractationes* 1.9.1, 6: While we were still staying at Rome, we wished to debate and trace out the cause of evil. Our plan of debate aimed at understanding by means of thorough rational inquiry—so far as, with God's help, discussion should enable us—what we believed about this question on divine authority. After careful examination of the arguments we agreed that evil occurred only through free choice of will, and so the three books resulting from this discussion were called *The Problem of Free Choice.* I finished the second and third of these books, as well as I could at the time, in Africa, after I was ordained priest at Hippo Regius. . . . This work begins with the words, 'I should like you to tell me: is not God the cause of evil?'

INTRODUCTION

I. PURPOSE OF THE BOOK

Saint Augustine (354–430) wrote the *De libero arbitrio* between the years 388 and 395, thus beginning it when he was thirty-four years of age and finishing it when he was forty-one. This we know from his *Retractations*, composed towards the end of his life, in 427, and in which he reviewed all his previous writings.[1] He tells us that the *De libero arbitrio* was a record of discussions which he carried on when he was at Rome, that is to say, when he was at Rome after the death of his mother Monnica and just before his return to Africa. He adds, however, that he did not write it all at Rome, but finished the second and third books in Africa after he had been ordained priest at Hippo Regius. This, no doubt, is the reason why Evodius says very little after the beginning of the third book, leaving St. Augustine to speak almost without interruption. It is noticeable, too, that the number of theological, as opposed to philosophical, questions which are raised, increases in the third book, reflecting the development of Augustine's interests.

To appreciate the place which the *De libero arbitrio* holds among St. Augustine's writings and in the development of his thought, we must bear in mind the course of his spiritual and intellectual history. Though brought up at first as a catechumen in the Catholic Church, he joined the Manichees when he was nineteen years old, and continued as a Manichee for ten years. Two things seem to have specially attracted him in their teaching, their answer to the problem of evil and their materialist philosophy. Their belief that evil was an independent principle, the rival of good, appealed to him at this time as a solution to the difficulty of evil, and he welcomed their philosophy because he found it impossible to conceive of a spiritual substance. When the Manichaean teaching ceased to satisfy him, he went through a short agnostic phase in which he turned to Academic scepticism as the only refuge, but it was at this time that he went to Milan and came under the influence of its bishop, St. Ambrose. The teaching of Ambrose on the Old Testament greatly impressed him, and he also began to make a deep study of the Neo-Platonic philosophy, chiefly from the works of Plotinus. It was through this study of philosophy that he finally freed himself from the Manichaean influence, for he became convinced that the existence of a spiritual substance was conceivable, and that the problem of evil could be solved without supposing evil to be a positive, independent principle. He had reached this stage in the year 385, and in the next year he decided to become once more a catechumen in the Catholic Church. Henceforward Scripture and theology absorbed his attention to an increasing extent, and philosophy came to interest him only in so far as it affected theology. During the remainder of his life his writings covered almost the whole vast field of theology, his energies being focussed especially by the two chief controversies which occupied him after his return to Africa. First, there was the schism of the Donatists, which forced him to study the question of the Church and its government, and then his struggles with the Pelagians led him to study the question of grace and predestination.

These were the two main subjects on which he worked, but in addition there were numerous other questions of theology on which for particular reasons he was called upon to give his views.

With this outline before us, let us return to the *De libero arbitrio*. St. Augustine started to write it in 388, two years after his conversion to Catholic Christianity, when the problems connected with the Manichaean religion were still vividly before his mind. Thus the *De libero arbitrio* was written, as we are told in the *Retractations*, to answer the Manichaean objection to Christianity that, since the presence of evil is undeniable, it is inconceivable that God can be both almighty and infinitely good.[2] Augustine discussed the problem with Evodius and, no doubt, his other friends at Rome, and resolved to write down and publish the conclusions to which they came. They argued, as he makes clear, not merely from the motive of refuting the Manichees, but also with the aim of understanding in their own minds a truth received on faith, of finding a solution which would satisfy reason.

Being a record, at least in the earlier part, of discussions which actually took place, the book does not follow a clear logical course defining the precise subject to be examined and then working it out according to a prearranged plan. It often moves in a rather confusing way from one point to another, and, although the question of evil is the dominant idea, many other problems are introduced as the argument proceeds.

As will be remarked again below, St. Augustine continued to feel that the *De libero arbitrio* was an effective piece of work, for he mentioned it fairly frequently in his later writings. About the year 405, for example, he recommended Secundinus the Manichee to read it.[3]

2. THE DE LIBERO ARBITRIO AND MANICHAEISM

The Manichaean religion was founded by Mani about the middle of the third century A.D. Mani, born in the year 216, came from the land of Babylon, and taught in the new empire of the Sassanians with no opposition from the king. Though he was put to death (crucified) in 277 by another king who came to the throne, yet his religion spread, first all over the East, and in the next century over the Roman Empire. It continued to exist with varying fortune until the thirteenth century, when it seems to have died out almost entirely at the time of the Mongol invasions.

The religion of the Manichees was dualistic.[4] It held that there are two Principles, the Light and the Dark, and three Moments, the Past, the Present, and the Future. Light and Dark are two absolutely different eternal Existences. In the beginning they were separate, but in the Past the Dark attacked the Light, and some of the Light became mingled with the Dark, as it still is in the world around us the Present. To Mani the idea of Light was connected with all that was orderly and intelligent, and the idea of Dark with all that was anarchic and material. In the realm of Light dwelt the Father of Greatness, and in the realm of Dark a race appropriate to it. Evil began when the Dark invaded the Light. The Primal Man was called into being to repel the invasion of the Light by the Dark, but he was overcome. He called on the Father of Greatness, and the Powers of Darkness were conquered, but the damage had to be repaired, and our world is the result of that process. Adam was produced containing both Light and Dark. 'Jesus' appeared to him, and made him taste of the tree of knowledge, and so revealed to him his misery. Man can become free by continence and renunciation, and can join in the work which God is doing in the universe.

In the Present the Powers of Light have sent Prophets, of whom the most important, and the last before Mani, was Jesus Christ. Mani regarded himself as an apostle of Christ, and it seems that Manichaeism should be thought of rather as a Christian heresy than an independent religion. The world will end with the second coming of Jesus, who will judge all men by their treatment of the Manichaean Elect. To Mani, however, the ultimate antithesis was not between God and Man, but between Light and Dark. The only hope for man was that his Light particles, not his whole personality, should escape at death from the prison home of the body. The Manichees did not regard God as personal or transcendent, but as composed of the Light substance. They believed that the Fall occurred before the existence of this world, and was its cause.

The Manichaean church was made up of the Elect and the Hearers. The Elect were the true Manichees, but their renunciations were severe, and their numbers were few. All Manichees were vegetarians, but the Elect abstained also from wine, from marriage, and from property, possessing food only for a day, and clothes only for a year. Among them were women as well as men. The Elect were already Righteous, and did not practice their asceticism in order to become Righteous.

The Manichaean religion was an attempt to explain the

presence of evil in the world. It was pessimistic in so far as it held that no improvement could come until this world was abolished, but yet it maintained that in the end Light would be stronger than Darkness and that all that was good would be gathered into the domain of Light. Though there would always exist a region of Dark, it would never again invade the region of Light.

Such is the account of Manichaeism as given by Prof. Burkitt, but it seems probable that the form with which St. Augustine came in touch had more of a Christian appearance than the form just described. G. Bardy says it appeared as a kind of gnosticism, more logical and simple than its predecessors. In Africa in particular, he says, it had been influenced by its prolonged contact with Catholicism.[5]

St. Augustine was a Manichee for nine years. The Manichaean solution of the problem of evil was utterly different from that of the Catholic Church, since it accepted the principle of evil as eternal, as independent of the principle of good. When, therefore, St. Augustine left Manichaeism, he had to think out the problem of evil afresh, and to do so against the background of the Catholic conception of God as the Being upon whom all creation depends, and to whom there is no rival eternal principle of evil. How, then, if this is so, can evil arise? How can we avoid making God responsible for evil, if He is the source of all that exists? Plainly these were questions which the Manichees could use with effect against the Catholics, and Augustine set himself in the *De libero arbitrio* to answer them. A number of different problems arise in the course of the discussion, but this is the central question which gives unity to the whole work.

The *De libero arbitrio*, it should be noticed, is only one of a whole series of books which St. Augustine wrote against the Manichees. He carried on the controversy for many years, one of the most noteworthy of the series being his reply, written in the year 400 to his former associate, Faustus of Milevis.[6]

3. THE DE LIBERO ARBITRIO AND PELAGIANISM

Pelagianism takes its name from Pelagius, who was a contemporary of St. Augustine, living from ca. 360 to ca. 420. Little is known of his origin except that he came from the British Isles. He always remained a layman, but led the life of a monk, though without, as it seems, belonging to any community. He is said to have been unemotional and calculating, and to have lacked depth of character. He considered that the appeal to grace discouraged religious fervour, since it made men look only to God's help, whereas fervour was stimulated by the belief that all depended on the individual's own free will.

He came to Rome at the beginning of the fifth century, and his ideas were adopted by a younger contemporary, who was probably Italian, Coelestius. The latter expressed the views of his master more explicitly. After the sack of Rome by the Goths in 410 Pelagius and Coelestius crossed to Africa, where Pelagius once or twice met St. Augustine. Before long, however, Pelagius decided to leave Africa and go to Palestine. Coelestius, who had remained in Africa, was condemned by a local synod, and then went to Ephesus. In 415 Pelagius was accused by St. Jerome, to whom St. Augustine had written, but was acquitted by a synod of bishops who examined the case.

The African church appealed to Rome, and the pope, Innocent, supported the condemnation of Pelagianism, as also did his successor, Zosimus, after some earlier hesitation. The emperor also approved the action of the pope, and the whole church, eastern and western, agreed in denouncing Pelagianism as a heresy.

The Pelagian teaching [7] may be summed up as follows:

(a) It rejected the doctrine that through grace we are predestined to be children of God, and maintained that without the help of grace man can fulfil all divine commands.

(b) Pelagius yielded so far as to say that grace was given, but explained that it was given only that man might do right more easily; in other words, he still maintained that man could do right without grace, but in that case with more difficulty than when grace was received.

(c) He still maintained that grace was nothing else than the free will we have received from God. God helps us by His law and doctrine to learn our duty, but not to carry it out. Thus we receive knowledge from God, but not the charity whereby to live rightly.

(d) He disapproved of prayers for the conversion of sinners and similar intentions, on the ground that it is free will which makes us good, and grace is given in accordance with our merits.

(e) The Pelagians denied that children are involved in original sin. They held that baptism only had the effect of admitting children to the kingdom of God.

(f) Even if Adam had not sinned, he would, they maintained, have been subject to death.

Thus the logical consequence of the teaching of Pelagius, though he did not himself draw out this consequence in full, was the denial of the atonement and of the central doctrines of Christianity. According to Pelagius the will is free, in the sense of free to choose right or wrong on any occasion, independently of what its previous acts may have been. There is no such thing as original sin, since sin is always a matter of will and never of nature: the individual will is the ultimate determinant of conduct.

Semipelagianism was an attempt to find a way between Pelagianism and St. Augustine's doctrine of predestination, as it appeared to the Semipelagians.[8] The movement spread fairly widely in north Africa and southern Gaul. It proposed the compromise view that man's nature was damaged by the fall, but that in man's regeneration the divine will and the human will co-operated. It was condemned because it retained the essential principle of Pelagianism, that man has of himself some power to do good, and so is an ultimate determinant of his good. When Semipelagianism was condemned, so also was the doctrine of predestination to evil.

What, then, is the connection between Pelagianism and the *De libero arbitrio*, since this book was written between the years 388 and 395, and therefore before the rise of Pelagianism? The subject dealt with by the *De libero arbitrio* was bound up with the subject of the Pelagian controversy, and a number of sentences in the *De libero arbitrio* were claimed by the Pelagians as supporting their doctrine. It was natural that they should seem to have grounds for this. St. Augustine was writing to defend the Catholic doctrine that God was the source of everything outside Himself, that evil had no independent existence and yet that evil was not caused by God. He traced evil to sin, and sin to free will, and therefore stressed the individual responsibility which free will implied. He drew out his argument with no special reference to grace, because that was not the subject he was concerned with. A few years later, however, Pelagianism arose, and then the question took on a new aspect. It was no longer necessary to stress free will to explain, against the Manichees, that God was not the cause of evil, but it was now necessary to stress the limitations surrounding human free will to explain against the Pelagians, that God was the cause of all good. As a natural consequence of these circumstances certain passages in the *De libero arbitrio* appeared to support the Pelagians, and in the *Retractations* Augustine is at pains to make the situation clear, and to show that in fact his words, far from supporting Pelagianism, were compatible with all that he said later about grace.[9] There is indeed no contradiction between Augustine's earlier views as expressed in the *De libero arbitrio,* and his later views, when the Pelagian controversy had forced him to work out a theory of grace and combine it with his assertion of free will. From his earliest years as a Catholic he accepted the doctrine of grace, and he always continued to assert that the will is free. The only difference is that in his earlier writings he had no need to stress so plainly the need of grace. This is not to say that St. Augustine's solution of the problem of free will and grace is without difficulty, but only to say that there is no contradiction between his early and later views. Certainly he believed this to be so, since, even when the Pelagian controversy broke out, he found no need to retract what he had written in the *De libero arbitrio,* and indeed he claimed that in some places he and Evodius debated as though they were already arguing against the Pelagians. All he found it necessary to do in the *Retractations* was to add further explanations and cautions.

In the *Retractations* he deals very carefully with the *De Libero Arbitrio*, upon which the Pelagians had specially fastened as inconsistent with his later theories; but he does not find it necessary to add any safeguards to the definition of sin which he had given in that treatise.[10]

4. IMPORTANCE OF THE DE LIBERO ARBITRIO

Reference has already been made (5 f.) to St. Augustine's later mention and recommendation of the present work, for example, to Secundinus the Manichee. In the year 396 he writes to St. Paulinus of Nola that he is sending him the three books *De libero arbitrio*. A mutual friend, Romanianus, it seems, had been in possession of the earlier part of the treatise.[11] Almost two decades later, in 415, Augustine notes in a letter to St. Jerome: 'I wrote certain books on *The Problem of Free Choice*. These went forth into the hands of *many*, and *many* have them now.'[12] The importance attached to the treatise by the writer himself and by his contemporaries, is obvious. A very recent scholar terms it 'a work which is the highwater mark of his philosophical writing.'[13]

But another modern reader might easily take up the *De libero arbitrio* and be disappointed when he came to read it. Seeing the title, he might suppose he would find a discussion of the kind which a modern book on free will would contain—an analysis of the psychological circumstances in which choice is exercised, an examination of the conclusions to which determinism leads, an argument to show that free will involves no contradiction, and so on. The

De libero arbitrio contains little on such subjects, when considered apart from theology, and indeed its primary object is not so much to discuss free will for its own sake as to discuss the problem of evil in reference to the existence of God, who is almighty and all-good. The very opening words give us the main subject: 'I should like you to tell me: is not God the cause of evil?' Thus, though it does not seek to solve many of the questions to which free will may give rise, the *De libero arbitrio* deals, nevertheless, with a subject which lies at the heart of all theological thought, the problem of evil. Moreover the views which St. Augustine expresses in it were views which in the main he clung to throughout his life, as he is at pains to make clear even in his last years.[14]

There is another reason why the book is one of Augustine's more important works, in spite of its having been written early in his life and being comparatively short. The reason is that it contains the fullest exposition in any of his writings of an argument, based on reason and not on revelation, for the existence of God. Moreover in framing the argument he necessarily deals with some of the deepest problems of philosophy, and thus we find here much of great interest on questions of knowledge, in particular on Augustine's theory of 'illumination.' This is sufficient to rank the book high, but many other matters are mentioned, and treated with lesser, though often with considerable, thoroughness.

We may add that the *De libero arbitrio* contains several passages as fine, in their own way, as any that St. Augustine wrote. An obvious example is the praise of truth and wisdom in the second book.

5. EVODIUS

The *De libero arbitrio* is a dialogue, and, unlike many dialogues in literature, it is based on a series of discussions between real men. This is clear from Augustine's own words at the beginning of the pertinent section in the *Retractations*—'While we were still staying at Rome, we wished to debate and trace out the cause of evil'—as well as from other references which he makes elsewhere. Moreover we know a certain amount about Evodius, and it is of interest to set this down, as he plays so large a part in the book. He is referred to in the *Confessions*, when St. Augustine says that Evodius was a young man of his own city of Tagaste, and joined his circle of friends at Cassiciacum. He tells us that Evodius had been in special military service, and had been converted and baptised.[15] He mentions him again in the course of his account of Monnica's death.[16]

Evodius returned to Africa with Augustine and was made bishop of Uzala, near Utica, in 396 or 397, remaining its bishop till his death in 424. He wrote a number of letters to Augustine on theological problems, to which we have Augustine's answers.[17]

✓ ✓ ✓

The text used is that of the Benedictine edition, reprinted in Migne's *Patrologia latina* 32.1221–1310. The *De libero arbitrio* had not yet appeared in the Vienna Corpus, but is to appear soon, edited by Professor William M. Green of the University of California. Yet the present version is indebted to this recension: Professor Green most kindly and generously supplied a list of some of the

more important changes he proposes to make, even before
a selection of these appeared last year: 'Textual Notes on
Augustine's *De libero arbitrio*,' *Revue de philologie de
littérature et d'histoire anciennes* 28 (1954) 21–29 (concerning the editorial history of the present work by Augustine, see also Prof. Green's 'Medieval Recensions of
Augustine,' *Speculum* 29 [1954] 531–34). It is also a
pleasure to express my appreciation of the help I received
from Professor J. Burnaby of Trinity College, Cambridge,
and Professor A. H. Armstrong of Liverpool University.
I must record, too, the debt I owe to the French translation
and notes of P. Thonnard, in the Bibliothèque Augustinienne, *Oeuvres de Saint Augustin*, 1re Série, Opuscules
6: *Dialogues philosophiques* 3. De l'âme à Dieu (Paris
1941) 123 ff. Likewise I have seen the following modern
translations of the *De libero arbitrio:* J. H. S. Burleigh, in
The Library of Christian Classics 6: *Augustine, Earlier
Writings* (London 1953) 102–217—*On Free Will;* R.
McKeon, in Selections from Medieval Philosophers 1:
Augustine to Albert the Great (New York 1929) 11–64—
On the Free Will (2.1–46 only); C. J. Perl, in *Aurelius
Augustinus' Werke in deutscher Sprache 1: Die frühen
Werke des Heiligen Augustinus—Der freie Wille* (Pader-
born 1947). C. M. Sparrow, *St. Augustine on Free Will*
(Richmond, Va., 1947), has not been available to me.

SUMMARY OF THE DISCUSSION

Book 1

1–4   Evodius opens the discussion by asking whether
       God is the cause of evil. Augustine replies that
       God is not the cause of our doing evil, though He

is the cause of our suffering evil in just punishment; the cause of our doing evil is free will. Evodius wishes to know how a man learns to sin, and Augustine answers that, teaching and understanding in themselves being good, there can be no teacher of evil as such. This brings Evodius back to the question, how we do evil if we do not learn it. Augustine admits the difficulty, which is nothing else than the problem: If God is the Creator, why is He not responsible for sin?

5–10   We must begin by asking what sin is. Augustine argues that it does not consist in doing what you would not like done to yourself, because some sin consists in doing to others precisely what you wish done to yourself. Is passion at the root of sin? Evodius agrees that this seems true, but Augustine raises a difficulty. Passion is evil desire, and a man might commit murder in order to live without fear, thus acting through a desire which in itself is good. Why, then, is the murder wrong? Not merely because it is in fact condemned, but because the murderer wished (if this was his motive) to live without fear in order to live a bad life. Evodius can now see that passion, or blameworthy desire, is love of those things which we can lose, yet not wish to lose.

11–15   Augustine, however, feels that further discussion is necessary. Does a man act without passion, who kills another in self-defence? Is the law which permits this just? Evodius suggests that the law may have been issued without passion, to fulfil eternal justice, and in any case it may be carried

out without passion, if it is just. Yet this is not
wholly satisfactory: How can we justify killing
an assailant in order to defend temporal posses-
sions, which are not wholly in our power? May a
human law be right, and yet conflict with a higher
law? Augustine replies that a human law may be
right at one time, and cease to be right when circumstances change; such a law may be called temporal law as opposed to eternal law, which consists
in principles that never change. All that is right
in temporal law is derived from eternal law, and
eternal law is that whereby it is just that everything should have its due order.

16–22   What is due order in man? Man excels beasts
through reason and understanding, through having
a soul; he has characteristics which he shares with
the beasts, but he has others by which he excels
them, and these others are themselves of varying
grades of excellence. When reason is in control
and keeps the higher above the lower, man is in
due order, and is wise. Moreover, since the
weaker cannot overcome the stronger, the wicked
cannot make the virtuous wicked, nor can a just
soul make the virtuous wicked, because to do this
it would have to become wicked itself, and therefore weaker. Hence, since there is nothing more
excellent than a rational and wise mind except
God, nothing can make a mind the slave of passion except its own choice. A mind is justly punished for such a sin by becoming the slave of
passion.

23–30   Evodius wonders why anyone who is wise

should choose to become foolish, and how we, who have never been wise, can justly be punished for becoming foolish. Augustine replies that undoubtedly some people have a good will, though others have not: the will is in our power. Thus we can see what are the virtues of prudence, fortitude, temperance, and justice. A man, who values his own good will, has these virtues and is happy. Unhappy men do not get what they want, namely, a happy life, because they do not wish for what accompanies it, right conduct.

31-35   To return to the question of eternal and temporal law, some people love eternal things, some temporal. Happy men, loving eternal things, live under the eternal law, while the unhappy are under the temporal law, yet even so cannot escape the eternal law. The eternal law bids us love eternal, and not temporal, things, while the temporal law bids us love things we can only possess for a short time. The temporal law can inflict punishment only because we love things which can be taken away against our will. The things themselves are not to be blamed when wrongly used, but only the people who use them wrongly. We set out to discover what wrongdoing is: it is the neglect of eternal things, which we cannot lose if we love them, and the pursuit of temporal things, which can be lost. Why do we do wrong? Through the free choice of will. Why does God give us this power? We will discuss this another time.

Book 2

1–7   Evodius asks why God has given man free choice of will, and Augustine answers that it was given because man cannot live rightly without it. Evodius objects that justice is given to man that he may live rightly, and yet he cannot misuse justice: why was it right that we should be given free will, which we can misuse? Augustine asks how he would convince an unbeliever of the existence of God. Evodius says he would appeal to the evidence of those who knew the Son of God on earth. Augustine agrees that we should begin by belief through faith, but should then go on to try and understand. He puts forward three points for discussion: (1) the evidence for God's existence, (2) whether all that is good is created by God, (3) whether free will is good.

7–27   (1) Even if a man should doubt whether he exists, this proves that he exists, since otherwise he could not doubt. It is clear that we exist, that we live, and that we understand, and these are in ascending order of importance. Further, we have bodily senses, each of which has its proper object, and there must be an inner sense which distinguishes between them. The beasts have this inner sense, but they do not have rational knowledge, which we possess and which governs the senses. It is by reason that we know we have reason. The inner sense judges the bodily senses, and reason judges the inner sense; if the reason sees something eternal and unchangeable above itself, this must be God. Now each of us has his own bodily

senses, but the objects of sense are common to all
who perceive them, except when they are changed
and become the private possession of the man who
perceives them.   Is there anything which all who
reason see in common, and which remains the
same whether seen or not seen?   Evodius suggests
mathematical truths.   Augustine agrees, and goes
on to show that numbers are not seen with the
bodily senses, since the bodily senses cannot see
the meaning of 'one,' nor the law and truth which
govern numbers.   Then he turns to wisdom itself.
Though men have different views about what it is
wise to aim at, all seek a happy life, and think
wisdom consists in this.

28–39   This leads to the question whether there is one
wisdom, shared in common by all.   Such assertions as that we ought to live justly are absolutely
true, and present in common to all who see them,
and those principles in which the virtues appear
are concerned with wisdom.   This makes Evodius
ask what is the connection between wisdom and
the truths of mathematics.   Augustine replies that
it is a difficult problem, but points out that it is
certainly plain that both are unchangeably true,
and therefore that unchangeable truth exists.   The
truth, in which we see so many things, must be
higher than our minds, because it does not change,
as do our minds, and because we do not judge
truth, but judge in accordance with it.   Thus,
Augustine declares, we have found something
higher than our minds and reason, and he breaks
into an eloquent passage in praise of truth, which

is the same as wisdom. The conclusion is, since we have found in truth something higher than our minds, either this is God, or, if there is anything more excellent than truth itself, then this is God.

40–47   (2) Augustine next shows that, though we have not yet attained to wisdom, yet we have the idea (*notio*) of wisdom sufficiently before our minds to make us seek it. How is this? Because wisdom has left traces in her works by means of numbers. Every beauty in the creature reveals wisdom; yet nothing can give itself its perfection, if it does not possess it. Body and soul are given the form which perfects them by a form which is unchangeable and eternal. Whatever we observe worthy of praise, should be referred to the praise of the Creator. Evodius therefore agrees that God exists, and all good things come from God.

47–53   (3) They go on to discuss the third point, whether free will is good. Augustine argues that the bodily organs are good, although they can be used wrongly. It is better to have that without which we cannot live rightly than not to have it. There are three kinds of good things we can possess: the virtues, which we cannot use wrongly, are the great goods; bodily goods are the least; and the powers of the soul are the middle goods. These latter may be used either rightly or wrongly. The will, which is a middle good, can cling to the unchangeable good, to truth and wisdom, and thereby man can possess the happy life. Thus by the will, though it is a middle good, we can obtain the principal human goods. Evil is turning away from the unchangeable good to changeable goods, and, since this is done freely, the punishment which follows is just.

54   Finally, Augustine asks what is the cause of this turning towards evil. He answers that there is no positive cause, since it is due to defect, but nevertheless it is under our control. Though we fall by our own will, we cannot rise by our own will, and therefore believe that God will help us.

Book 3

1–3   Evodius returns to the last question: What is the cause of this movement, by which the will turns to changeable good? Augustine replies that, since the will does not turn to evil of its own nature, as can be seen from the fact that we blame it for so doing, the cause must lie only in the will.

4–8   Evodius agrees, but raises the question how the will can be free, if God foreknows what it will do. Augustine argues that our will lies in our own power, and God's foreknowledge of an action does not mean that it is not due to the will. God may foreknow that we shall be happy, but plainly we shall be happy through our own will and not against it. God has foreknowledge of our control of our own will.

9–23   Evodius admits this, but asks how it can be just for God to punish sins which He foresees will be committed. Augustine answers that to foresee a sin is not to cause it; God does not compel the will to act in a certain way by His foreknowledge, and therefore justly punishes sins. Indeed God deserves the highest praise for creating even sinners, since, even when they sin, they are higher than the bodily light for which He is rightly praised. Nor should we say that it would be better if sinners had never lived, since it is good that lesser things should exist as well as greater. We cannot truly conceive anything better in creation, which has escaped the Creator's thought. Even sinners who will not repent are more excellent than creatures which lack free will, and the beauty of created things is graduated from the highest down to the lowest. If anyone should say he prefers not to exist rather than to exist unhappily, he should remember that men do not wish to die; they wish to exist, though not to exist unhappily, and should be thankful that their wish for existence is granted. We are in our own power, and, if it is just that we should be unhappy because we have sinned, we should praise the Creator for this. All existence is good, and it is contradictory to say we prefer non-existence to unhappy existence. When a man kills himself, this is due to a natural desire for rest, not to a desire for non-existence.

24–35   Since God is almighty and good, why does He not prevent any creature from being unhappy? Creatures are arranged in fitting order from the highest to the lowest, and souls which are unhappy through their own fault, contribute to the perfection of the whole. God deserves praise for all. Are we, then, to conclude that there would be a lack of perfection if we were always happy? The perfection of the whole demands the existence of souls, but not of their sins, and unhappiness, when justly imposed as a punishment, makes the unhappy soul harmonise with the beauty of the whole. When man fell through his own sin, it was just that he should be in the power of the devil, but the devil was justly overcome. Augustine goes on to speak of God's government of creation, of His power to govern it even should the highest angels fall, and of the praise which is due to Him for the excellence of creation, and His justice towards it.

36–46 He turns to a fresh point. Every nature, that is, every substance, is good, and the Creator is praised when the creature is praised, and even when the creature is blamed, since it is blamed for not tending towards the supreme good. All vice is against nature, and by blaming the vice we praise the nature, and so praise the Creator of every nature. If a soul does not pay the debt it owes by doing what it ought to do, it will pay by suffering what it ought to suffer: whatever the issue, it is just and the Creator deserves praise.

47–59 Evodius agrees that the Creator is not responsible for our sins, but returns to the question, why some sin by their free will, while others do not, though all have the same nature. Augustine replies that perverted will is the cause of evil, and it is useless to look further. There are acts deserving blame which are done in ignorance, but these are the punishment of sin; to err unwillingly, and to be unable to refrain from acts of passion is not natural to man in his original state. Why should we suffer for the sin of Adam and Eve? We are only to blame ourselves if we fail to make use of the help God gives us, but it was not just that the first man should have descendants better than himself. In this connection Augustine discusses the origin of man's soul.

60–65   It is by practising faith in this life that we shall attain eternal truth, and it is our future destiny that is important. If we fail to make progress through our own fault, we are rightly punished, but a soul is not responsible for defects arising from its own nature. At first there must be imperfections in the soul for which it is not responsible, but God will gradually bring about its perfection, if it does not itself refuse.

66–68   What are we to say of the sufferings of young children, who die before they can gain any merit? Augustine declares that, in relation to the whole, nothing is created without a purpose. He says there is a pious belief that children who die after baptism, but before reaching the age of reason, benefit from the faith of those who have been baptised. Moreover by the suffering of their children grown-up people are corrected, and we must remember that, once suffering is past, it is nothing to the sufferer. Besides, who knows what compensation God reserves for such children?

69–70   Those who ask questions about the sufferings of animals do not understand what is the supreme good; they wish everything to be such as they suppose the supreme good is. Beasts are by nature mortal. In the suffering animal we can see how everything seeks unity, and shuns division and corruption: everything proclaims the unity of the Creator.

71–74   If the first man was wise, how did he come to sin, whereas, if he was foolish, is not God the cause of his sin? Neither of these suppositions is true. His sin was committed freely, since he was capable of recognising the command given him. When he left the heights of wisdom, during this period he was neither wholly wise nor wholly foolish.

75–76   How, then, did the devil sin? The soul can will to take pleasure in its own power, and to produce a false imitation of God. The devil fell through pride.

77   For the sake of justice, and of unchangeable truth and wisdom we should despise all temporal goods.

THE CHIEF QUESTIONS DISCUSSED

(References are given to the book and the section, omitting the chapter)

1 What is wrongdoing?

1. Wrongdoing does not consist in failing to do to another what you would like done to yourself, since in some cases we ought to fail to do so. Nor does it consist in doing what is usually condemned (1.6 f.).

2. Passion (*libido*) is the source of evil, and passion is evil desire (1.8).

3. When reason or mind or spirit controls the irrational motions of the soul, then man is governed by the eternal law (1.18).

4. Every nature as such is good, and all vice consists in going against nature (3.36–38).

5. To do wrong is to neglect eternal things and seek temporal things (1.34).

2 Is God responsible for sin? How can the created will be free, and not determined?

1. There are two kinds of evil: doing evil and suffering evil. God is the cause of the second, but not of the first, which is due to the sinner's free will (1.1).

2. We are not taught to do evil, because teaching as such is good (1.2–4).

3. Nothing equal or higher or lower can make us slaves of passion, and the cause must be free choice (1.21).

4. We have a will, and desire good things (1.25). The will is in its own power (1.26), and through the will we can gain happiness (1.29).

5. Everyone desires happiness, but if we become unhappy, it is because we do not desire what accompanies happiness, that is, a life of right conduct (1.30). We do wrong through free will (1.35).

6. Why does God give us free will? Because without it we could not do right (2.1 f.).

7. What is the cause of evil action? Evil is defect, so nothing causes evil as such (2.54).

8. Evil is not due to nature, because we only become slaves of passion through free will (3.2 f.). Every nature in itself is good (3.36–38).

9. The soul is bound to pay what is due to the Creator. If it does not pay by acting justly, it must pay by the loss of what it refuses to use well, by unhappiness (3.44). Summary (3.50).

3 Argument for the existence of God

1. One reason for accepting the existence of God is belief, based on the evidence of the New Testament (2.5).

2. Have we any reason based on understanding? To begin with, we cannot deny our own existence (2.7).

3. Man exists, lives, and understands, in ascending order of importance (2.7).

4. There must be an inner sense to distinguish between the bodily senses (2.8).

5. The inner sense ranks above the bodily senses because it governs them (2.8).
   Reason judges the inner sense (2.9, 13).

6. Reason is the highest element in man's nature (2.13). If the reason sees something eternal and unchangeable, and itself as lower, then this must be God. God, it is true, is higher than everything, but if this is not God, then what is still higher is God (2.14).

7. So we must show there is something higher than reason. Now our senses are distinct and belong to each individual, but the object perceived is common to all, if we do not change it into ourselves (2.19).

8. Is there any object perceived by the reason of each of us, yet which is common to all, and unchanged by being perceived? The truths of

mathematics (2.20). These cannot be perceived by the bodily senses, for the bodily senses perceive the changeable, while the truth of $7 + 3 = 10$ is eternal (2.21). The senses cannot perceive 'one' (2.22). Though there is no limit to number, we know what is true of all of them. We do so by 'an inner light, unknown to the bodily sense' (2.23).

9. Is the same true of wisdom? What is wisdom? We have the idea impressed on our minds from the beginning, or else we could not wish to become wise (2.26). Is wisdom the same for all men? (2.27).

10. Certain assertions (e.g. 'the better should be preferred to the worse') are true and common to all who see them (2.28). These are 'illuminations' (2.29), in which the virtues appear, and the more a man conforms to them, the more wisely he lives. Like the laws of number they are true and unchangeable (2.29).

11. Therefore there exists unchangeable truth, containing all those things which are unchangeably true (2.33). It is other than the minds of each of us (2.33), and higher than our minds because we judge in accordance with it (2.34).

12. The supreme good, happiness, is known in the truth, and this truth is wisdom (2.35 f.). Our freedom consists in submission to the truth (2.37). Truth itself is God, or if there is anything more excellent, that is God (2.39).

13. Body and soul are given their forms by a form which is unchangeable and everlasting (2.45).

4 Does evil spoil the beauty of creation?

  1. We ought not to think it would have been better
     if sinful souls had never lived (3.13). They are
     blamed in comparison with what they might have
     been. · Even the sinful soul is higher and better
     than the light which we see with our eyes (3.12).

  2. God has shown His goodness in creating that
     being whose sins He foresees (3.14). Such is
     God's goodness that He does not refrain from
     creating that being which will persist in sin
     (3.15).

  3. The creature is more excellent which sins by free
     will than that which has no free will (3.15 f.).

  4. When unhappy, a man does not wish to die, and
     should be grateful for existence (3.18). When,
     through unhappiness, a man kills himself, it is
     owing to a natural desire for rest (3.23).

  5. Creatures are arranged so fittingly in order, that
     it is wrong to wish the lower to be like the higher
     (3.24). The perfection of the whole comes from
     both lesser and greater (3.25).

  6. Provided that the souls are not lacking, in spite of
     the unhappiness of sinners the whole is perfect.
     If sinners were happy, there would be injustice
     (3.26).

  7. The Creator is praised through the blame given
     to sinners (3.37). God made creatures of every
     kind to give beauty to the whole, whether they
     sinned or not (3.32).

  8. It is the nature of some things to decay, and they
     could not exist otherwise (3.42 f.).

5 Does God's foreknowledge contradict man's free
  will?

1. God has foreknowledge of every event (3.4).
2. If God foreknows that someone will be happy, this does not mean that he will be happy against his will, but through his will (3.7).
3. Our will is in our power and is free. God's foreknowledge does not take away our freedom (3.7).
4. Foreknowledge of an event does not cause the event, though it implies that it is certain. Therefore God's foreknowledge is compatible with free action (3.10).

6 Why do children suffer?
1. When suffering is past, it is as nothing to those who have endured it (3.68).
2. Everything is created with a purpose. There is no state half-way between reward and punishment (3.66).
3. The sufferings of children may be of value in correcting their parents (3.68).
4. Who knows what compensation is reserved for the children who die before they can commit sin, yet who suffer (3.68)?

7 Why do animals suffer?
1. People who complain of this, do so because they want everything to correspond with their false notion of the supreme good (3.69).
2. It is unreasonable to wish that animals which are by nature mortal, should suffer neither death nor corruption (3.69).
3. The suffering of animals shows how everything strives for unity and against the loss of its unity,

and therefore that everything is created by the supreme unity of the Creator (3.69 f.).

8 Did the souls of men exist before joining the body?

1. Whether the souls of men pre-existed, and whether they lived in a state of wisdom is a great mystery (1.24).

2. There are four opinions about the origin of souls after Adam and Eve (3.59):
   (1) that they come by generation;
   (2) that a new soul is created when each person is born;
   (3) that God sends souls which have pre-existed elsewhere, into the bodies of those who are born;
   (4) that souls come down of their own will.
   We should not lightly accept any of these opinions.

9 Is the penalty for original sin just?

1. To err unwillingly and to be unable to refrain from acts of passion are not natural to man, but a punishment (3.52).

2. What we do against our will is not our fault (3.53).

3. Such actions are called sins because they are derived from the first sin, which was committed freely (3.54).

4. It was not right that the first man should have descendants better than himself, but it was right that his descendants, if they turned to God, should be given help (3.55).

5. The answer partly depends on the question of the origin of souls (3.56).

6. Even if a soul has at the beginning a state which another has after living wickedly, it has no small good, and can, with the Creator's help, perfect itself (3.56).

10 How can we explain evil, when it is not due to the creature's free will?

1. It is the nature of temporal things to decay, and unless this happened, one thing could not succeed another (3.42 f.).

2. Creatures are arranged fittingly in order; there is no reason for the lower to be made like the higher, for each has its proper place (3.24).

BOOK ONE

THE PROBLEM OF EVIL

1.1 *Evodius*—I should like you to tell me: is not God the cause of evil? [1]

Augustine—I will tell you, if you explain what kind of evil you mean. We use the word *evil* in two senses, one, of doing evil, and the other, of suffering evil.

E.—I want to know about both.

A.—If you know or believe God is good—and it would be wrong to think otherwise—He does not do evil. Again, if we admit God is just—and it would be wicked also to deny this—He both rewards the good and punishes the bad. Now these punishments are evils to those who suffer them. Consequently, if no one is punished unjustly—as we must necessarily believe, since we believe everything is ruled by God's providence—God is certainly not the cause of the first kind of evil, but He is the cause of the second kind.

E.—Then there is some other cause of that evil which God is not found to be responsible for?

A.—Certainly there is; it could not come about without a cause. But if you ask what it is, the question cannot be answered. There is no single cause, but everyone who does wrong is the cause of his own wrongdoing. If you are not convinced, remember what I said just now, that wrongdoing

35

is punished by God's justice. It would not be punished justly, unless it were done wilfully.[2]

2　*E.*—I should not have thought anyone sins without having learnt to do so. If this is true, I want to know who it is from whom we have learnt to sin. *A.*—Do you think that teaching is a good? *E.*—No one could say that teaching was an evil. *A.*—Might it be neither a good nor an evil? *E.*—I think it is a good. *A.*—Quite right, for knowledge is given or stimulated by it, and no one learns anything except through teaching. Do you agree? *E.*—I think only good is learnt through teaching. *A.*—Then be careful not to say that evil is learnt. Learning and teaching go together.[3] *E.*—How can man do evil, if he does not learn it? *A.*—Perhaps because he turns away from, because he abandons, his teaching, which is the same as his learning. But however that may be, it is undoubtedly clear that since teaching is a good thing, and teaching and learning go together, evil cannot possibly be learnt. If it were learnt, it would be part of teaching, and so teaching would not be a good. But you yourself grant that it is. Therefore evil is not learnt, and it is useless to ask from whom we learn to do evil. If evil is learnt, we learn what ought to be avoided, not what ought to be done. Hence to do wrong is nothing else than to disobey our teaching.

3　*E.*—I think there are really two kinds of teaching, one by which we learn to do right and another by which we learn to do wrong. When you asked whether teaching was a good, my love for the good absorbed my attention, and I only thought of that kind of teaching which is concerned with doing good. So I answered that it was a good. Now I realise that there is another kind of teaching, which I am sure is unquestionably evil, and I want to know its cause.

A.—Do you think at least that understanding is a pure good?

E.—I think it is plainly good in the sense that I do not see what can be more excellent in man. I could not possibly say that any understanding was evil.

A.—When someone is taught but does not understand, could you suppose he has learnt anything?

E.—No, of course I could not.

A.—Then, if all understanding is good, and no one learns anything unless he understands, it is always good to learn. For all who learn understand, and all who understand do what is good. So if anyone wants to find the cause of our learning anything, he really wants to find the cause of our doing good. Give up, then, your wish to discover a teacher of evil. If he is evil, he is not a teacher; if he is a teacher, he is not evil.

2.4 *E.*—Well, then, as you have succeeded in making me agree that we do not learn to do evil, tell me how it comes about that we do evil.

A.—You are inquiring into a problem which deeply interested me when I was quite a young man; it troubled me so much that I was worn out and driven right into heresy. So low did I fall, and such was the mass of empty fables which overwhelmed me, that, if God had not helped me because I longed to find the truth, I could not have

escaped, or recovered the primary freedom to
search. As I made great efforts to solve this problem, I will explain it to you in the way I finally
worked it out. God will help us, and make us
understand what we believe. We can be sure that
we are treading in the path pointed out by the
Prophet who says: *Unless you believe you will not
understand.*[4] We believe that everything which
exists is created by one God, and yet that God is
not the cause of sin. The difficulty is: if sins go
back to souls created by God, and souls go back to
God, how can we avoid before long tracing sin
back to God?[5]

WHAT IS SIN?

5   *E.*—You have now put in plain words a problem
which troubles my mind a great deal, and which
has driven me on to this discussion.
      A.—Do not let it depress you, but go on believing
what you believe. We cannot have a better belief,
even if we do not see the reason. The true foundation of a devout life is to have a right view of
God, and we do not have a right view of God
unless we believe Him to be almighty, utterly unchangeable, the creator of all things that are good,
though Himself more excellent than they, the
utterly just ruler of all He has created, self-
sufficient and therefore without assistance from any
other being in the act of creation. It follows from
this that He created all out of nothing. Of Himself He did not create, but has begotten that which
is equal to Himself. This we call the only-

begotten Son of God, whom, when we try to express ourselves more plainly, we term the Power of God and the Wisdom of God, through which He made all things which He made out of nothing. Having stated this, let us try with God's help in the following way to understand the question you wish to examine.

3.6   Your problem is to find the cause of our wrongdoing, and therefore we must first discuss what doing wrong means. Explain your view about this. If you cannot cover the whole subject in a few short words, at least give some examples of wrongdoing, and tell me what you think.

E.—Adultery, murder, and sacrilege are examples. It would take too long to make a complete list, and I could not remember everything. All agree that these are wrongdoings.

A.—First tell me why you think adultery is wrong. Because the law forbids it?

E.—No, it is not wrong because the law forbids it; the law forbids it because it is wrong.

A.—If someone tried to confuse us, dwelling on the pleasures of adultery and asking why we thought it wrong and to be condemned, surely you do not think we ought to take shelter behind the authority of the law, when we desire not only to believe, but also to understand? I agree with you, and believe most firmly, and preach the belief to all peoples and nations that adultery is wrong. But now we are endeavouring to grasp firmly with the understanding what we have received on faith. Reflect, therefore, as carefully as you can, and tell me on what grounds you regard adultery as evil.

E.—I know an act to be evil, which I should not allow in the case of my own wife. Whoever does to another what he would not like done to himself, surely does wrong.

A.—If a man's passion was so strong that he offered his own wife to another, and freely allowed her to be seduced by him because he wished to have the same licence with this man's wife, do you think he would be doing no wrong?

E.—Of course, a very great wrong.

A.—He is not sinning against the principle you mentioned; he is not doing what he would not like done to himself. You must find another reason for your conviction that adultery is wrong.

7   *E.*—I think it wrong, because I have often seen men condemned for this crime.

A.—Are not men often condemned for good deeds? To save you further reference—read history as you have it on God's own excellent authority. You will soon see what a bad impression we should get of the Apostles and all the martyrs, if we thought that condemnation was a sure proof of wrongdoing; all were condemned for confessing their faith. So if everything which is condemned is evil, it was evil at that time to believe in Christ and to confess His faith. But, if everything that is condemned is not evil, you must find another reason for teaching that adultery is wrong.

E.—I do not see any answer to this.

8   *A.*—Well, possibly passion is the evil in adultery. Your trouble is that you are looking for the evil in the outward act, that we can see. I will prove that passion is the evil in adultery. If a man has no

opportunity of living with another man's wife, but if it is obvious for some reason that he would like to do so, and would do so if he could, he is no less guilty than if he was caught in the act.

E.—Yes, that is perfectly clear. I see now that there is no need of a long argument to convince me that this is true of murder and sacrilege, and indeed of all sins. It is plain that nothing else than passion is the principal element in this whole matter of wrongdoing.

4.9   *A.*—Do you know that there is another word for passion, namely desire? [6]

E.—Yes, I do.

A.—Do you think there is any difference between this and fear?

E.—I think there is a very great difference between them.

A.—I suppose you think this because desire seeks its object, while fear avoids it.

E.—Yes.

A.—If someone kills a man, not through desire of gain, but through fear of suffering some evil, will he still be a murderer?

E.—Yes indeed, but it does not follow that this act will be free from the motive of desire. If he kills a man through fear, he certainly desires to live without fear.

A.—Do you think it is a small good to live without fear?

E.—It is a great good, but the murderer cannot possibly gain this by his crime.

A.—I am not asking what he can gain, but what he desires. [7] He certainly desires what is good if he desires to live without fear, and therefore the desire is free from blame. Otherwise we shall blame all who love what is good. So we must agree that we cannot point to evil desire as the dominant motive in every murder; it would be false to say that the dominance of passion constitutes the evil in every sin. If so, there might be a murder which was not a sin.[8]

E.—If to kill a man is murder, this may happen sometimes without any sin. When a soldier kills the enemy, when a judge or an executioner kills the criminal, or when a weapon flies from a man's hand inadvertently and by accident, I do not think they sin by killing a man.

A.—I agree, but they are not usually called murderers. Answer this question. If a slave kills his master because he is afraid of being tortured, do you think he should count among those who kill a man, without actually deserving to be called murderer?

E.—I think this is quite a different case from the other. The former act lawfully or not unlawfully; the latter are sanctioned by no law.

10 A.—Again you appeal to authority. But you must remember that the task we have undertaken is to understand what we believe. We believe in the law, and so we must try, if we possibly can, to understand whether the law which punishes this act does not punish it wrongly.

E.—It certainly does not punish it wrongly, for it punishes a man who deliberately kills his master; this is quite unlike the other examples.

A.—Do you remember you said a few minutes ago that passion was the dominant motive in every evil act, and was the cause of its being evil?

E.—Yes, I remember.

A.—Did you not also agree that the man who desires to live without fear does not have an evil desire?

E.—I remember that too.

A.—It follows that when a master is killed by his slave through this desire, he is not killed through a desire that we can blame. Therefore we have not yet discovered why this action is evil. For we are agreed that evil deeds are always evil simply because they are done through passion, that is, through a blameworthy desire.

E.—I begin to think he is condemned wrongly. I should not have the courage to say this, if I could find any other solution.

A.—Have you persuaded yourself that such a crime ought not to be punished, before considering whether the slave wished to be freed from fear of his master in order to indulge his own passions? The desire to live without fear is common both to all good and to all evil men. But the important point is that good men seek it by turning away their love from things which they cannot possess without danger of losing them, while evil men try to remove obstacles, and settle down to enjoy these things, and consequently live a life of crime and wickedness, better called death.

E.—I am coming to my senses again. I am very glad that I know clearly now what that blameworthy desire is which we call passion. I can now see it is love of those things which each of us can lose against his will.

TEMPORAL LAW AND ETERNAL LAW

5.11   So now I suggest we should inquire whether passion is also the chief motive in acts of sacrilege, which we often see committed through superstition.[9]

A.—We must not be in too much hurry. I think we ought to discuss first whether an open enemy or a secret assassin can be killed without any passion in defence of life, liberty, or honour.

E.—I cannot imagine that men act without passion when they fight for things they would be unwilling to lose. If they cannot lose them, why need they go to the length of killing a man in their defence?

A.—In that case the law is not just which authorises a traveller to kill a robber in self-protection, or any man or woman to kill an assailant, if possible before the violence has been carried out. The law also orders a soldier to kill the enemy, and if he refuses to do so he is punished by the military authorities. Can we possibly call these laws unjust, or rather no laws at all? A law which is not just does not seem to me to be a law.[10]

12   *E.*—I see pretty well that a law which gives its subjects [11] permission to commit lesser crimes in order to prevent greater ones, has a good defence against an accusation of this kind. It is a much lesser evil for the assassin than for the man who defends his own life, to be killed. It is far more dreadful that

an innocent person should suffer violence than that the assailant should be killed by the intended victim.

When a soldier kills the enemy he is enforcing the law, and so has no difficulty in carrying out his duty without passion. The law itself, which is issued to protect its subjects, cannot be convicted of passion. If its author issued it in obedience to God's will, that is, to fulfil eternal justice, he may have done so without any passion at all. Even if he issued it out of passion, it does not follow that the law need be carried out with passion, because a good law can be issued by a man who is not good. For example, if a man, having reached supreme power, should take a bribe from an interested party, and decree it unlawful to carry off a woman even for marriage, the law will not be evil because its author is unjust and corrupt. Therefore the law which, to protect its citizens, lays down that force shall be met with force, can be obeyed without passion, and the same may be said about all servants who are subject to any higher power rightly and properly.

But I do not see how the other men we mentioned can be without blame because the law is without blame. The law does not force them to kill, but leaves it to their own discretion, and so they are free not to kill anyone in defence of those things which they can lose against their will, and for this reason ought not to love. Some may perhaps doubt whether the soul's life is by any means taken away when the body perishes, but, if it can be taken away it is of no value, while if it cannot,

there is no reason for fear. And as for chastity,
everyone knows that it is rooted in the soul itself,
since it is a virtue; it cannot, therefore, be taken
away by the violence of an aggressor. Whatever
the man who is killed was going to take away is not
wholly in our power, and so I do not understand
how it can be called ours. I do not, therefore,
blame the law which allows such men to be killed,
but I do not see how I am to defend their slayers.

13 *A.*—I find it much harder to see why you try to
defend those whom no law holds guilty.[12]

E.—No law may find them guilty, if we speak of
those laws which are familiar to us and which are
made by men. I rather think they may come
under a stronger and entirely secret law, if everything is controlled by Divine Providence. How
can they be free from sin against Divine Providence, if they are stained with human blood in
defence of things which ought to be despised? So
I think that that law which is issued for the government of a people rightly allows these acts, while
Divine Providence punishes them. The law which
governs a people concerns itself with the control
of conduct sufficiently to keep the peace among a
rough population, so far as this can be achieved by
man. This other kind of fault has different punishments which are suited to it, and I think wisdom
alone can save us from them.

A.—I thoroughly approve of this distinction of
yours; although it is incomplete and imperfect, yet
it is full of faith and of ideals. The law which is
decreed to govern states seems to you to permit
much and to leave it unpunished, though it is pun-

ished by Divine Providence. Rightly so. Because a law does not do everything, it does not follow that what it does do is to be blamed.

6.14   I propose now that we examine carefully how far evil deeds ought to be punished by that law which controls peoples in this life. Then let us examine what remains to be punished necessarily and secretly by Divine Providence.

E.—Yes, I should like to do this, provided we can reach the end of such an enquiry. I think it will go on for ever.

A.—Have some courage; use your reason with confidence in God. Whatever difficulties may threaten us, they are cleared away and all becomes smooth with God's help. So raising our thoughts to Him and seeking His help, let us examine the problem before us. First, tell me whether that law which is put forth in writing, is for the good of men living this present life.

E.—Obviously it is. Peoples and states are made up of such men.

A.—Do these peoples and states belong to that class of things which cannot perish or change? Are they altogether everlasting, or are they subject to time and change?

E.—Unquestionably they belong to the class of things subject to time and change.

A.—Then, if a people is well-disciplined and observant of social good, and such that every individual puts public before private interest, is not this people rightly granted by law authority to elect its own officials to govern its affairs, that is, the affairs of the state?

E.—Certainly.

A.—If the people gradually deteriorates and prefers private to public interest, and sells its vote for bribes, and is corrupted by ambitious politicians, and puts into power criminals with no sense of honour, would not any honest man of sufficient influence who is left be justified in depriving this people of self-government, and in putting them under the authority of a few honest men or even of one? [13]

E.—Quite justified.

A.—Well then, although these two laws seem to contradict one another, one giving the people self-government, the other taking it away, and although the latter is issued in such a way that both cannot be in force at the same time in the same state, surely we shall not say that one of them is unjust, and ought not to be decreed?

E.—No.

A.—Then, I suggest we call that law temporal law, which, though just, can be justly changed in course of time.

E.—By all means.

15 *A.*—Will not any intelligent man regard that law as unchangeable and eternal, which is termed the law of reason? [14] We must always obey it; it is the law through which wicked men deserve an unhappy, and good men a happy life,[15] and through which the law we have said should be called temporal is rightly decreed and rightly changed. Can it ever be unjust that the wicked should be unhappy and the good happy, or that a well-disciplined people should be self-governing, while an

ill-disciplined people should be deprived of this privilege?

E.—I see that this law is eternal and unchangeable.

A.—I think you also see that men derive all that is just and lawful in temporal law from eternal law. For if a nation is justly self-governing at one time, and justly not self-governing at another time, the justice of this temporal change is derived from that eternal principle by which it is always right for a disciplined people to be self-governing, but not a people that is undisciplined. Do you agree?

E.—I agree.

A.—Therefore, to explain shortly as far as I can the notion which is impressed on us [16] of eternal law, it is the law by which it is just that everything should have its due order. Tell me if you disagree.

E.—I have nothing to say against this; it is true.

A.—Since there is this single law, from which all temporal laws for human government derive their various forms, I suppose it cannot itself be varied?

E.—I see that it is quite impossible. No power, no circumstances, no calamity can ever make it unjust that everything should have its due and perfect order.

A MIND IS THE SLAVE OF PASSION THROUGH ITS OWN CHOICE

7.16 *A.*—Well then, now let us see what is due order in man himself. A nation is made up of men bound together by a single law, and this law, we have said, is temporal.

Tell me: are you absolutely certain that you are alive?

E.—There is nothing more certain that I know of.

A.—Well, can you distinguish between living and knowing that you live?

E.—I know that no one, unless he is alive, knows that he is alive, but I do not know whether everyone who is alive knows that he is alive.

A.—How I wish that you knew, instead of merely believing, that animals lack reason! Our discussion would soon pass beyond this problem. Since you say you do not know, you involve us in a long argument. The point is not of such a kind that we can leave it out, and still be able to reach our conclusion with the rational precision I feel to be required.

Tell me this. We often see beasts tamed by men, not only the beast's body but its spirit so quelled that it obeys a man's will instinctively and habitually. Do you think it at all possible that any beast, whatever its ferocity and bulk and keenness of sense, should turn round and try to subdue a man to its will, though many beasts can crush his body by open or secret attack?

E.—I agree that this is quite impossible.

A.—Very good. Tell me also, since it is clear that man is far surpassed by many beasts in strength and the various functions of the body, what is the quality in which man excels, so that no beast can control him, while he can control many beasts? Is it what we usually call reason or understanding?

E.—I cannot think of anything else, since it is some-

thing in the soul by which we excel the beasts. If
they were without souls, I should say we excelled
them through having a soul. But, since they do
have souls, what better word than reason can I use
to denote what is lacking to their souls, and makes
us superior to them? For it is no insignificant
thing, as everyone realises.

A.—See how easily a task is accomplished with
God's help, which men think very difficult. I
confess I had thought that this problem, which I
find we have solved, might hold us back for as long
again as we have already taken over the discussion.
So now let me run over the argument, so that you
can keep it in mind. I think you are aware that
what we call knowledge is nothing else than perception through reason.

E.—Yes.

A.—Therefore a man who knows he is alive does
not lack reason.

E.—That follows.

A.—Beasts live, and, as has now been shown,[17] are
without reason.

E.—Yes, clearly.

A.—So now you see you know what you said you
did not know, that not everything which lives
knows that it lives, though everything which
knows that it lives necessarily lives.

17 *E.*—I have no doubt about it now; carry on with
your plan. I am satisfied that to live and to know
that we live are not the same.

A.—Which of these two do you think is the more
excellent?

E.—Plainly to know that we live.

A.—Do you think that to know that we live is better than life itself? Or do you perhaps understand that knowledge is a higher and purer form of life, since no one can know unless he has understanding? [18] What else is understanding than a life brighter and more perfect through the very light of the mind? So, if I am not mistaken, you have not preferred something else to life, but a better life to a less perfect life.

E.—You have fully grasped and explained my own view—provided that knowledge can never be evil.

A.—I think it cannot be, unless we give the word a new meaning, and use knowledge for practical experience. It is not always good to have such experience; we can, for instance, experience punishment. But how can knowledge in the proper and pure sense of the word be evil, since it is produced by reason and understanding?

E.—I follow the distinction: go on with your argument.

8.18 *A.*—What I want to say is this. Whatever it is by which man is superior to beasts, whether mind or spirit or whether either of them is the correct term [19] (we find both in Sacred Scripture), if this governs and controls all the other elements of which man is composed, then man is duly ordered. We see that we have much in common not only with beasts, but also with trees and plants, for we see that nourishment, growth, generation, health, are characteristic also of trees, which belong to the lowest grade of life. We recognise too that beasts have sight, hearing, smell, taste, touch, often more keenly than we have. Or take strength, vigour, muscular power, swift and easy movement of the body, in all of which we excel some of them, equal some, and are surpassed by some. We are certainly in a common class with the beasts; every action of animal life is concerned with seeking bodily pleasure and avoiding pain.

There are other characteristics which beasts do not seem to share, yet which are not the highest qualities of man, as for example, laughing and joking. If we judge rightly, we shall judge that this is characteristic of human nature, but of the lowest part of it. Then there is love of praise and glory, and ambition: though the beasts do not have these passions, we must not suppose that we are better than the beasts because we have them. When this craving is not subject to reason, it makes us wretched. Yet no one thinks that he ought to be preferred to someone else in wretchedness. When reason controls these motions of the soul, a man must be said to be in due order. It ought not to be called due order, or order at all, when the better is subordinated to the worse. Do you not think so? *E.*—It is clear.

A.—When reason, or mind, or spirit controls the irrational motions of the soul, then that element is ruling in man which ought to rule in virtue of that law which we have found to be eternal.

E.—I understand and agree.

9.19 *A.*—Therefore, when a man is established and ordered in this way, do you not think he is wise?

E.—If not, I do not know who else is to be thought wise.

A.—I suppose you also know that very many men are foolish.

E.—That too is quite obvious.

A.—If folly is the opposite of wisdom, since we have found out who is wise, you now know who is foolish.

E.—Everyone can see that a man is foolish, if his mind is not in control.

A.—Then what must we say, when a man is in this state? Does he lack mind, or is the mind, though present, not in control?

E.—I think, the second of these.

A.—I should like you to tell me by what evidence you are aware that a man has a mind which does not exercise its control.

E.—Please do this yourself: it is too hard a task for me.[20]

A.—At least you can easily remember, what we said a few minutes ago,[21] how beasts are tamed and broken in to serve men, and how men would suffer the same from beasts, as we have shown, unless they excelled them in some way. We did not trace this superiority to the body; it showed itself in the soul, and we found no other name for it but reason. Later we remembered it was called also mind and spirit. But if reason and mind are distinct, we certainly agree that only mind can use reason. Hence it follows that the man who possesses reason cannot lack mind.

E.—I remember this quite well, and accept it.

A.—Then do you think that those who tame beasts can be such only if they are wise? I call those wise who truly deserve the name, that is, who are controlled by mind, and who are disturbed by no power of passion.

E.—It is absurd to think that men who go by the name of animal tamers are like this, or even shepherds or herdsmen or charioteers, all of whom, as we see, control tame animals and when they are untamed break them in.

A.—There then you have plain evidence which makes it clear that a man has a mind, even when it is not in control. Such men as these have a mind, for they do things which could not be done without a mind. It is not in control,[22] for they are foolish, and, as we know, the mind is in control only in wise men.

E.—It amazes me that, when we discussed this earlier on, I could not think how to answer.

10.20   But let us continue. We have now discovered that human wisdom consists in the control of the human mind, and that it is also possible for the mind not to be in control.

A.—Do you think that passion is more powerful than mind, though we know that eternal law has granted mind control over passion? I certainly do not think so. There would not be due order if the weaker governed the stronger. So I think mind must have more power than desire, from the very fact that it is right and just for it to control desire.

E.—I think so too.

A.—Surely we do not hesitate to prefer every virtue to vice, so that virtue is stronger and more dominant, just as it is better and nobler?

E.—Undoubtedly.

A.—It follows that no wicked soul overcomes a soul which is armed with virtue.

E.—Quite true.

A.—I think you will not deny that any soul is better and stronger than any body.

E.—No one denies this, who sees—and it is obvious —that a living substance is better than a non-living substance, or one that gives life better than one that receives it.

A.—Much less, then, does any body whatever overcome a soul endowed with virtue.

E.—Plainly.

A.—Then surely a just soul, and a mind which keeps its proper and rightful control, cannot dethrone and subdue to passion another mind which keeps control with the same justice and virtue?

E.—Certainly not; not only because the same excellence is present in both, but also because the former will fall from justice, and become a wicked mind, if it tries to make another mind wicked, and by that very fact will be weaker.

21 *A.*—You have understood the point well. It remains for you to answer, if you can, whether anything seems more excellent to you than a rational and wise mind.

E.—I think nothing except God.

A.—That is my opinion too. But the problem is difficult, and now is not a suitable time to try and understand it thoroughly. Let us hold the conclusion firmly on faith, but not attempt a full and precise examination.

11   For the moment we can recognise that, whatever kind of being [23] rightly excels a virtuous mind, cannot possibly be unjust. Therefore not even this, though it may have the power, will force mind to serve passion.

E.—Everyone would at once accept that.

A.—So we conclude that, since what is equal or superior does not make a mind the slave of passion, if it is in control and virtuous, on account of its justice, while what is inferior cannot do this on account of its weakness, as our argument has shown, therefore, nothing makes a mind give way to desire except its own will and free choice.

E.—I see that this is quite conclusive.

22 *A.*—It follows that you think such a mind justly punished for so great a sin.

E.—I cannot deny it.

A.—Well, surely that punishment should not be thought a light one, which consists in the mind being ruled by passion, being robbed of its store of virtue, being dragged hither and thither, poor and needy, now judging false for true, now defending, now attacking what before it approved, and in spite of this running off into fresh falsehood, now withholding its assent, and often frightened of clear reasoning, now despairing of finding any truth at all, and clinging closely to the darkness of its folly, now striving for the light of understanding, and again falling back through exhaustion. Meanwhile the passions rage like tyrants, and

throw into confusion the whole soul and life of
men with storms from every quarter, fear on one
side, desire on another, on another anxiety, or false
empty joy, here pain for the thing which was loved
and lost, there eagerness to win what is not possessed, there grief for an injury received, here
burning desire to avenge it. Wherever he turns,
avarice can confine him, self-indulgence dissipate
him, ambition master him, pride puff him up, envy
torture him, sloth drug him, obstinacy rouse him,
oppression afflict him, and the countless other feelings which crowd and exploit the power of passion. Can we then think this no punishment at all,
which, as you see, all who do not cling to wisdom
must necessarily suffer?

JUST PUNISHMENT

23 *E.*—In my opinion this punishment is a great one,
and entirely just, if a man, being established on the
heights of wisdom, should choose to come down
and be the slave of passion; but I am doubtful
whether there can be anyone who has wished, or
wishes, to do so. We believe that man was so
perfectly formed by God and established in a life
of happiness, that only of his own will did he come
down thence to the troubles of mortal life. Yet
while I hold this firmly by faith, I have never
grasped it with my understanding. If you think
careful inquiry into this problem should be put off,
you do so against my will.

12.24   But the problem which worries me most is why

we should suffer grievous punishments of this kind, seeing that, though admittedly foolish, we have never been wise. How, then, can we be said to suffer these punishments deservedly, for having abandoned the fortress of virtue, and chosen to be slaves of passion? I should certainly not agree to your putting it off, if you can discuss this problem and explain it.

A.—You say that we have never been wise, as if it was a manifest truism. You are only thinking of the time since we were born into this life. But, since wisdom is in the soul, whether the soul lived in another life before it was joined to the body, and whether at one time it lived in a state of wisdom, is a great question, a great mystery, to be considered in its proper place.[24] Yet this does not prevent us from clearing up, so far as possible, our present problem.

25   I am asking you whether we have a will.

E.—I do not know.

A.—Do you want to know?

E.—I do not even know this.

A.—Then you must ask me nothing more.

E.—Why?

A.—Because I ought not to answer your questions, unless you want to know what you ask. Also unless you wish to become wise, I ought not to discuss the subject with you. Finally, you could not be my friend, unless you wish me well. Reflect, too, whether you do not yourself will that your life may be happy.

E.—I agree it cannot be denied we have a will.

Now go on, and let us see what you conclude from
this.

A.—I will do so; but tell me first whether you are
conscious of having a good will.

E.—What is a good will?

A.—A will by which we seek to live rightly and
virtuously and to reach the height of wisdom.
Now see whether you do not seek to live rightly
and virtuously, or whether you do not have a
strong desire to be wise, or can really venture to
deny that we have a good will when we wish for
these things.

E.—I do not deny any of this, and therefore I
agree that I have not only a will, but now that I
have a good will also.

A.—I want you to tell me how much you think this
will is worth. Do you think that riches or honours
or bodily pleasures or all these together bear any
comparison with it?

E.—God forbid anything so stupid and wicked.

A.—Should it then be only a small joy to us that
we have something in the soul, I mean this good
will, in comparison with which these things I have
mentioned are utterly worthless, yet to gain which
we see countless men accepting every toil and
danger?

E.—It ought to be a joy to us, and a very great joy
indeed.

A.—Do you think that those who lack this joy
suffer a small loss in being deprived of such a good?

E.—A very great loss.

26 *A.*—I think you now see that it lies in the power of

our will whether we enjoy or lack this great and true good. What is so fully in the power of the will as the will itself? [25]

When a man has a good will he has a possession which is far to be preferred before all earthly kingdoms and all bodily pleasures. But if a man does not possess it, then he lacks that which is more excellent than all good things not under our control, and which only the will of itself could give him. And so, when he judges himself wretched if he loses the glory of fame, great wealth, and any bodily goods, will you not judge him wretched, even though he abounds in all these things? For he clings to things which he can very easily lose and not possess while wishing to do so, but he lacks a good will which is beyond all comparison with these, and which, though it is so great a good, needs only to be desired in order to be possessed.

E.—That is very true.

A.—Therefore it is right and just that foolish men should be made wretched in this way, although they were never wise—obscure and mysterious though this latter point is.

E.—I agree.

13.27 A.—Now consider whether prudence seems to you to consist in the knowledge what to seek and what to avoid.

E.—I think it does.

A.—And is not fortitude that state of the soul in which we despise all misfortunes and the loss of things not resting in our power?

E.—I think so.

A.—Then do you agree that temperance is that state of soul which controls and checks desire in regard to those things which it is shameful to desire?

E.—That is certainly my view.

A.—And what else are we to say about justice than that it is the virtue by which each man is given his due?

E.—That is what I think about justice.[26]

A.—Then the man who has a good will, the excellence of which we have discussed at such length, will love this alone, his most precious possession, will delight in this and make it his joy and pleasure, realising fully its value, and that he cannot be robbed of it against his will. Surely we cannot doubt that he will be opposed to all that conflicts with this one good?

E.—Most certainly he must be opposed to it.

A.—Can we suppose such a man is not endowed with prudence, who sees that this good should be sought for and everything avoided which conflicts with it?

E.—I think no one can see this without prudence.

A.—Quite right. But why should we not grant him fortitude?[27] He cannot love and value highly all these things not under our control. They are loved through an evil will, and he is bound to resist an evil will as the enemy of his most precious good. Since he does not love these things, he does not grieve at their loss, but altogether despises them. We have declared and admitted that this is the work of fortitude.

E.—Yes, we must certainly grant him fortitude. I know no one who could be more truly said to have fortitude than the man who is perfectly resigned to the lack of those things of which it is not in our power to gain possession. We have concluded such a man must necessarily do this.

A.—Now consider whether we can deprive him of temperance, since this is the virtue which checks passion. What is so opposed [28] to a good will as passion? Hence you can understand that the man who loves his good will resists his passions by every means, and fights against them. Therefore he is rightly said to have temperance.

E.—Go on: I agree.

A.—There remains justice, and I certainly do not see how such a man can lack this. If he possesses and loves to possess a good will, and resists, as I have said, what is opposed to it, he cannot wish evil to anyone. It follows that he harms no one, and this can only be the case, if he gives to everyone his due. You remember, I think, that you agreed when I said this was the concern of justice.

E.—I remember. I accepted your account of the four virtues just now, and agree that all of them are present in the man who values highly and loves his own good will.

28 *A.*—What then prevents us from admitting that the life of this man is praiseworthy?

E.—Nothing at all. The whole argument points to this, and in fact requires it.

A.—Well, can you possibly help thinking that a miserable life ought to be avoided?

E.—That is emphatically my opinion; I think it certainly ought to be avoided.

A.—And you do not think a praiseworthy life ought to be avoided?

E.—No, I think decidedly that it ought to be aimed at.

A.—Therefore a life which is praiseworthy is not miserable.

E.—That follows.

A.—So far as I can see, nothing now prevents you from agreeing that that life which is not miserable is the life of happiness.

E.—Obviously.

A.—We hold, then, that a man is happy who loves his own good will, and who despises in comparison with this whatever else is called good and can be lost, while the desire to keep it remains.

E.—Yes, our former conclusions lead to this, and we must agree.

A.—You have a clear grasp of the question. But I should like you to tell me whether to love one's own good will, and to value it as highly as we have said, is itself good will.

E.—Yes, it is.

A.—But if we are right in judging the one man happy whose will is good, shall we not be right in judging the other man unhappy whose will is bad?

E.—Quite right.

A.—Then what reason is there for doubting that, even though we were never wise before, yet by our will we deserve, and spend, a praiseworthy and happy life, and by our will a life that is shameful and unhappy? [29]

E.—I agree that we have reached this conclusion by arguments which are certain and undeniable.

29 A.—Also consider another point. I think you remember our definition of a good will: it was, I believe, a will by which we seek to live rightly and virtuously.

E.—I remember.

A.—Then, if through our good will we love this good will itself, and cling to it, and prefer it before all things which we cannot be sure to keep because we want to, the result will be, as reason has shown, that these virtues will dwell in our soul. To possess them is to live rightly and virtuously. Hence it follows that whoever wishes to live rightly and virtuously, if he wishes so to wish in preference to the goods which are but passing, acquires this great possession with such ease, that to wish for it is the same as to possess what he wished. [30]

E.—Really, I can hardly keep myself from crying out for joy, when a good so great and so easy to gain is suddenly set before me.

A.—This very joy, which is caused by winning this good, if it supports the soul calmly, quietly, and steadily, is called the happy life, unless you think the happy life is different from taking joy in goods which are true and certain.

E.—That is my opinion.

14.30 A.—Quite right. But do you think that anyone does not by every means desire and long for a happy life?

E.—Undoubtedly everyone desires it.

A.—Why then does not everyone gain it? We agreed that men deserve a happy life by their will, and also an unhappy life by their will, and deserve it in such a way as to receive it. But here a difficulty arises, and unless we scrutinise it carefully, it will tend to upset the clear reasoning we worked out before. For how does anyone of his own will endure an unhappy life, though no one at all wishes to live unhappily? Or how does a man through his own will gain a happy life, if so many are unhappy, and all wish to be happy?

Does it come about because to desire good or evil is different from deserving something through a good or bad will? For those who are happy and who ought also to be good, are not happy because they wished to live happily—the wicked also wish this—but because they wished to live rightly, which the wicked do not wish. Therefore it is not surprising that unhappy men do not get what they want, namely, a happy life. They do not also want that which accompanies it, and without which no one is worthy of it or gains it, that is to say, a life of right conduct.

For the eternal law, to the consideration of which it is now time to return, has settled this with unchangeable firmness; it has settled that merit lies in the will, while reward and punishment lie in happiness and misery.[31] And so, when we say that men are wilfully unhappy, we do not mean that they wish to be unhappy, but that their will is such that unhappiness is the necessary result, unwilling though they are. Hence this does not contradict our former conclusion, that all wish to be happy, but not all are able so to be. Not all wish to live rightly, which is the only state of will that deserves a happy life. Have you any objections to this? *E.*—No, I have none.

SIN IS THE NEGLECT OF ETERNAL THINGS

15.31 But now let us see how this is connected with the problem we were going to discuss about the two laws.

A.—Very well. But first tell me about the man who loves to live rightly, and so delights in it that not only is it right for him but also pleasant and agreeable. Does he not love this law, and hold it most dear to him? For by it he sees that a happy life is given to a good will, and an unhappy life to an evil will.

E.—He loves it with all his heart and strength since he lives as he does in obedience to this law.

A.—Well, when he loves this law, does he love something which is changeable and temporal, or something which is firm and everlasting?

E.—Certainly, something which is everlasting and unchangeable.

A.—Do those who persist in their evil will, at the same time desire to be happy? Can they love that law by which such men rightly earn unhappiness?

E.—I think they cannot.

A.—Do they love nothing else?

E.—They love very many things, those things in gaining or keeping which their evil will persists.

A.—I suppose you mean wealth, honours, pleasures, physical beauty, and all the other things which they may be unable to gain though they want them, and may lose against their will.

E.—Yes, those are the things.

A.—You do not think these last for ever, do you, for you see they are subject to time and change?

E.—It would be sheer madness to think so.

A.—Then, since it is clear that some men love eternal things while others love temporal things, and since we agree that there are two laws, one eternal and the other temporal, if you have a sense of fairness, which of these men do you think should be subject to the eternal law, and which to the temporal law?

E.—Your question seems easy. I think that happy men through their love of eternal things live under the eternal law, while the temporal law is laid upon the unhappy.

A.—You judge rightly, provided you keep constantly in view what reason has very clearly shown, that those who serve the temporal law cannot escape the eternal law. Through it we have maintained that every just effect, every just change is brought about. You understand no doubt that those who cling to the eternal law with a good will do not need the temporal law.

E.—Yes, I understand.

32 *A.*—So the eternal law bids us turn away our love

from temporal things, and turn it back, when purified, towards things that are eternal.

E.—Yes, it bids us do this.

A.—What else then do you think the temporal law
orders but that, when men cling with their desire
to those things which can be called ours for a short
time, they shall possess them by that same right by
which peace is maintained in human society, so far
as is possible in such affairs?

The things I mean are, first, the body and what
are called its goods, such as sound health, keen
senses, strength, beauty, and so on, some of which
are necessary for the useful arts, and therefore of
more value, others of which are of less value.
Then there is freedom, though indeed there is no
true freedom except for those who are happy and
cling to the eternal law; but here I mean that freedom by which men think they are free, when they
do not have other men as their masters, and which
is desired by those who wish to be released from
any human masters. Then parents, brothers, wife,
children, relations, connections, friends, and all
who are joined to us by some bond. Or again the
state itself, which is usually regarded as a parent;
honours, too, and distinctions, and what is called
popular favour. Lastly, money, under which
single term is included everything of which we are
rightful masters, and which we are regarded as
having the power to sell and give away.

How this law assigns to each man his share, it
would be a long and difficult matter to explain,
and one plainly not necessary for our purpose.

We need only notice that the power of this law to enforce itself does not extend further than to take away and confiscate as a punishment those things or a part of them. Hence it brings pressure to bear through fear, and to gain its end turns and twists the souls of the unhappy people for whose government it is fitted. For, while they fear to lose these things, they exercise in their use a certain restraint suitable to hold together such a society as can be composed of men of this kind. This law does not punish the sin which consists in loving the above objects, but the sin which consists in taking them wrongfully from other people.

So consider whether we have now finished the task you thought would be endless. We set out to inquire how far the right of punishment extended of that law by which earthly peoples and states are governed.

E.—I see we have finished the task.

33 *A.*—Do you see also that there would not be any punishment, whether wrongly inflicted, or inflicted by the sanction of the above law, unless men loved those things which can be taken away against their will?

E.—I see that too.

A.—Now, one man makes good use and another bad use of the same things. The man who makes bad use, clings to them and is attached to them by his love, that is to say, is subject to things which ought to be subject to him. He makes those things of service to himself, for the control and good management of which he himself ought to be of service. On the other hand, the man who uses them rightly shows indeed their value, but not for himself. They do not make him good or better, but rather are made good by him. Therefore he is not attached to them by love of them, and does not make them, as it were, members of his own soul—as would happen if he loved them—lest, when the time comes for their amputation, they may infect him with painful corruption. He is fully their master, ready to possess and control them when there is need, and still more ready to lose them and not possess them. This being so, surely you do not think silver or gold are to be condemned because some men are avaricious,[32] or food because some men are greedy, or wine because some men are drunkards, or beautiful women because some men are fornicators and adulterers, and so on, especially as you see that a doctor makes a good use of heat, and a poisoner a bad use of bread?

E.—It is quite true that not the things themselves are to be blamed, but the men who make a bad use of them.

16.34 A.—Very well. I think we now begin to see what is the power of eternal law, and how far temporal law can go in inflicting punishment. We have distinguished precisely enough the two classes of things, eternal and temporal, and the two classes of men, those who love and seek for eternal things, and those who love and seek for temporal things. We have agreed that it lies in the will what each man chooses to seek and attach himself to,[33] and that the mind is not cast down from its position of control, and from its right order, except by the will. It is plain too that the thing is not to be condemned when a man uses it wrongly, but the man himself who uses it wrongly. Let us return now, I suggest, to the question proposed at the beginning of this discussion, and see whether it has been solved. We set out to ask what wrongdoing is, and with this end in view we have conducted the whole discussion.

Therefore we are now ready to turn our minds to the question whether wrongdoing is anything else than the neglect of eternal things, which the mind enjoys of itself and perceives of itself, and which it cannot lose when it loves them, and the pursuit, as though they were great and wonderful, of temporal things, which are perceived by the body, the lowest part of man, and the possession of which can never be assured. In this one class all wrongdoing, that is, all sin, seems to me to be included. I am anxious to know what you think about it.

35   *E.*—What you say is true, and I agree that all sins are included in this one class, and consist in turning away from godly things which are truly lasting, and in turning towards things which are changeable and insecure. Although these latter things are constituted rightly in their own order, and attain a certain beauty of their own, nevertheless it shows a corrupt and disordered soul if we are given over to their pursuit, seeing that by divine disposition and right the soul is given power to control them at its will.

And now I think that other problem is also cleared up and settled, which we decided to consider after the question what wrongdoing is, namely, the question why we do wrong. Unless I am mistaken, the argument has shown that we do wrong through the free choice of our will. But I want to know whether that very free choice, by which we have concluded that we have power of sinning, ought to have been given us by Him who created us. Without it apparently we should not have sinned, and there is danger that through this line of argument God may be thought the cause even of our wrongdoing.

A.—Have no fear of this. We must, however, find some other opportunity of examining the question more carefully: now it is time to bring the present discussion to an end. I want you to believe that we have, as it were, knocked at the door of great and hidden questions which we must search out. When with God's help we begin to enter their sanctuaries, you will certainly recognise what a difference there is between this discussion and those which follow, and how far more excellent are the latter, not only in the intelligence required to examine them, but also in the profundity of their content and in the clear light of their truth. Only let us have a right spirit, so that Divine Providence may allow us to keep to the course we have marked out, and to reach the end.

E.—I will do what you wish, and willingly fall in with your proposal.

BOOK TWO

WHY HAS MAN BEEN GIVEN FREE CHOICE?

1.1   *E.*—Now explain to me, if you can, why God has given man free choice of will. For if man had not received this gift, he would not be capable of sin. *A.*—Do you know for certain that God has given man this gift, which you think ought not to have been given?

E.—As far as I thought I understood in the first book, we have free choice of will, and we only sin as a result.

A.—I remember too that this became clear to us. But my present question is whether you know that God gave us the gift which plainly we have, and as a result of which plainly we can sin.

E.—No one else gave it, I think. We are created by God, and from Him we deserve punishment if we sin, or reward if we act rightly.

A.—I should like to be told whether you know this also because it is evident or whether you believe it freely on authority without knowing it.

E.—I agree that at first I accepted authority on this question. Yet it is surely true that whatever is good comes from God, and that whatever is just is good, and that sinners are justly punished, and those who do right justly rewarded. The conclusion from this is that God makes sinners unhappy and those who do right happy.

74

2   *A.*—I do not deny this, but I ask the second question, how you know we are created by God. You have not explained this, but only that from Him we deserve punishment or reward.

E.—I see that this other point also is clear, only because we have already established that God punishes sins. For indeed all justice comes from Him. It is not the work of justice to punish strangers, in the same way that it is the work of goodness to help strangers. Hence it is clear that we belong to Him, because not only is He supremely kind in giving us help, but also supremely just in punishing us. So, from what I asserted and you agreed, namely, that all good comes from God, we can also conclude that man is created by God. Man himself is something good in so far as he is man, for he can live rightly when he so wills.[1]

3   *A.*—Obviously, if this is true, the question you proposed is solved. If man is something good and cannot do right except when he so wishes, he ought to have free will, without which he could not do right. Because sin occurs through free will, we must not suppose God gave man free will for the purpose of sinning. It is a sufficient reason why it ought to be given, that man cannot live rightly without it.

We can understand that it was given for this purpose, because, if anyone uses it to sin, God punishes him. This would be unjust if free will had been given not only that man might live rightly, but also that he might sin. How could a man be punished justly, if he used his will for the very purpose for which it was given? Since, however, God punishes the sinner, what else do you think He says but: Why did you not use your free will for the purpose for which I gave it you, that is, to do right? Then, if man lacked free choice of will, how could that good be brought about, which consists in the due maintenance of justice by the condemnation of sins and the honouring of good deeds? It would not be a sin or a good deed, unless it was done wilfully. Hence punishment and reward would be unjust, if man did not have free will. There must be justice both in punishment and in reward: it is one of the good things which come from God. Therefore it was right that God should give free will to man.

2.4 *E.*—I agree now that God gave it. But I ask you: do you not think that, if it was given for the purpose of good conduct, it ought not to have been possible to misuse it for sin? It is not possible to misuse justice itself which has been given to man that he may live rightly. Can anyone live wrongly through justice? And in the same way no one would be able to sin through his will, if his will had been given for the purpose of good conduct.

A.—I hope God will grant that I may be able to answer you, or rather that you may answer yourself, instructed by that truth within you, which is the source of all instruction.[2] I want you to tell me shortly—if you know for certain that God gave us free will, the matter about which I asked you—whether we should say that the gift ought not to have been given us, which we agree has been given by God. For, if it is doubtful whether He has given it, we are justified in asking whether it is a good gift. Then, if we find it is a good gift, we shall find also that it is the gift of Him who is the giver of all good things to man.[3] If, however, we find it is not a good gift, we shall realise that He did not give it, since it is wicked to blame Him. On the other hand, if it is certain that He gave it, we must agree that, in whatever form it has been given, it ought not to have been withheld or given in any other way than that in which it has been given. For He gave it, whose act we cannot by any means be justified in blaming.

5   *E.*—I hold this firmly by faith, but, as I do not hold it as a matter of knowledge, let us examine it as though it were altogether doubtful. In view of the fact that it is doubtful whether free will has been given for the purpose of good conduct, since by means of free will we can sin, I see it becomes doubtful whether it ought to have been given us. For, if it is doubtful whether free will was given for the purpose of good conduct, it is also doubtful whether it ought to have been given. Hence it will be doubtful too whether God gave us free will. For, if it is doubtful whether it ought to have been given, it is doubtful whether it has been given by Him whom it is wrong to suppose gave anything which ought not to have been given.

A.—At least you are certain that God exists.

E.—Even this I hold for certain not through direct perception, but through belief.

A.—Then, if one of those fools of whom Scripture

records, *the fool said in his heart: there is no God,*[4] should say this to you, and should refuse to believe with you what you believe, but should want to know whether your belief is true, would you have nothing to do with this man, or would you think you ought to convince him in some way of what you hold firmly—especially if he should seriously wish to know, and not obstinately to dispute it?

E.—Your last remark tells me clearly enough what answer I ought to make to him. Though quite unreasonable, he would certainly admit that I ought not to argue with a crafty and obstinate man about so great a matter, or indeed about anything at all. Granting this, he would first beg me to believe that he was an honest inquirer, and in the present affair concealed no trickery or obstinacy.

Then I should show, what I think is easy for anyone, that he wishes another person, who does not know it, to believe what he himself knows concerning the secrets of his own soul, and therefore that he in his turn would be much more reasonable if he believed in God's existence on the authority of all those writers who have testified that they lived with the Son of God. They have recorded that they saw things which could not possibly have happened, if there were no God. He would be very foolish if he blamed me for believing these writers, seeing that he wished me to believe him. He would find no reason for refusing to imitate what he could not rightly blame.

A.—So, on the question of God's existence, you think it is sufficient that our decision to believe these witnesses is a prudent one. Why, then, I want to know, do you not think that we ought similarly to accept the authority of these same men with regard to those other matters, which we resolved to examine as being uncertain and quite unknown, without troubling about further investigation?

E.—The reason is that we want to know and understand what we believe.

6   *A.*—You remember rightly what we cannot deny we asserted at the beginning of our former discussion.[5] Unless belief and understanding were distinct, and unless we ought to start by believing any important question of theology which we wish to understand, the Prophet would have been wrong in saying, *unless you believe, you will not understand.*[6] Our Lord Himself also by word and deed urged those whom He called to salvation, first to believe. Afterwards, when He spoke of the gift itself which He would give to believers, He did not say, 'This is eternal life, that they may believe,' but, *This is eternal life, that they may know Thee, the only true God, and Jesus Christ, whom Thou hast sent.*[7] Then He says to those who already believe, *Seek and you shall find,*[8] for what is believed without being known cannot be said to have been found, nor can anyone become capable of finding God, unless he has first believed what afterwards he is to know.

Therefore in obedience to the Lord's commands let us seek earnestly. What we seek at His exhortation we shall find also from His teaching, so far as these matters can be found in this life and by persons such as ourselves. We must believe that these things are seen and grasped more clearly and perfectly by better men even while they dwell in this world, and certainly by all good and devout men after this life. We must hope that so it will happen to us, and we must desire and love these things, despising what is earthly and human.

THE EVIDENCE FOR GOD'S EXISTENCE

3.7   Let us then, I suggest, examine the question in the following order: first, how it is clear that God exists; [9] secondly, whether whatever is good, in whatever degree it is good, is created by Him; thirdly, whether free will is to be counted among good things. When we have decided these questions, it will be plain enough, I think, whether it has been given rightly to man.

So, in order to start from what is clearest, I ask you first: Do you yourself exist? Are you perhaps afraid that you may be mistaken, when asked this question? If you did not exist, you could not possibly be mistaken.[10]

E.—Go on rather to the next point.

A.—Then, since it is clear that you exist, and since this would not be clear to you unless you were alive, it is clear also that you are alive. Do you understand that these two statements are quite true?

E.—Yes, I understand that at once.

A.—Then this third point too is clear, namely, that you understand.

E.—It is clear.

A.—Which of these three do you think is the most important?

E.—Understanding.

A.—Why do you think so?

E.—There are these three, existence, life, understanding: a stone exists, and an animal lives. I do not think a stone lives or an animal understands, but it is quite certain that a person who understands, also exists and lives. Therefore I do not hesitate to judge that in which all three are present as more important than that which lacks one or two of them. For what lives, certainly exists, but does not necessarily understand: such, I think, is the life of an animal. It certainly does not follow that what exists also lives and understands, for I can agree that corpses exist, but no one would say that they lived. Far less does what is not alive understand.

A.—We hold, therefore, that of these three two are lacking in a corpse, one in an animal, and none in a man.

E.—True.

A.—We hold also that in these three that is most important which man has in addition to the two others, namely, understanding. Since he has this, it follows that he exists and lives.

E.—Yes, we hold this.

8 *A.*—Now tell me whether you know you have the

ordinary bodily senses, sight, hearing, smell, taste, and touch.

E.—I do.

A.—What do you think is the proper object of the sense of sight? That is, what do you think we perceive when we see?

E.—Any bodily thing.

A.—Surely we do not perceive the hard and the soft when we see?

E.—No.

A.—What then is the proper object of the eyes, which we perceive through them?

E.—Colour.

A.—What is it of the ears?

E.—Sound.

A.—What of smell?

E.—Odour.

A.—What of taste?

E.—Flavour.

A.—What of touch?

E.—Soft or hard, smooth or rough, and many other such things.

A.—Do we not perceive by touch and sight the shapes of bodily things, that they are large or small, square or round, and so on? Does it not follow that these cannot be assigned specially to sight or touch, but must be assigned to both?

E.—I understand.

A.—Then do you understand also that the different senses have their proper objects which they report, and that some have objects in common?

E.—I understand this too.

A.—Surely, therefore, we cannot distinguish by any of these senses what is the proper object of any sense, and what all or some of them have in common?

E.—Certainly not; they are distinguished by an inner perception.

A.—Can this be reason, which beasts lack? It seems to me that by the reason we grant this, and know that it is so.

E.—I think rather we grasp with our reason that there is an inner sense, to which everything is referred by the five ordinary senses. The faculty by which the beast sees is different from that by which it shuns or seeks what it perceives by sight. The one sense resides in the eyes, but the other is within, in the soul itself. By the latter animals are either enticed to seek and seize, or are warned to shun and reject, not only what they see but also what they hear, and what they perceive with the other bodily senses. This, however, can be called neither sight, nor hearing, nor smell, nor taste, nor touch, but is something else which presides over all the rest together. While, as I have said, we grasp this with our reason, I cannot precisely call it reason, for plainly the beasts possess it.

9   *A.*—I recognise this, whatever it may be, and do not hesitate to call it an inner sense. But unless that which is conveyed to us by the bodily senses, passes beyond the inner sense, it cannot become knowledge. Whatever we know we grasp with our reason. We know, for example—to say nothing of other facts—that colours cannot be perceived

by hearing nor sounds by sight. This knowledge does not come to us from the eyes or ears, nor from that inner sense which even the beasts do not lack. We must not suppose that they know that light is not perceived with the ears or sound with the eyes: we distinguish these only by rational reflection and thought.

E.—I cannot say I am convinced about this. Might not they recognise that colours cannot be perceived by hearing or sound by sight, through that inner sense which you admit they possess?

A.—You do not think, do you, that they can distinguish between the colour they perceive, and the power of sense in their eye, and the inner sense in their soul, and the reason which marks out exactly the limits of each?

E.—No, certainly not.

A.—Well, could reason distinguish and define these four unless colour was presented to it by the sense of sight, and again that sense by that inner sense which presides over it, and again that inner sense by its own act, if there were no other intermediary?

E.—I do not see how else it could be.

A.—Do you observe that colour is perceived by the sense of sight, and that the sense of sight is not perceived by itself? You do not see that you see by the same sense by which you see colour.

E.—Certainly not.

A.—Try also to distinguish these. I think you do not deny that colour is different from seeing colour, and again from possession of a sense by which, when colour is not present, we could see it, if it were present.

E.—I distinguish between these, and agree they are distinct.

A.—You do not see with your eyes, do you, any of these three except colour?

E.—No.

A.—Tell me then how you see the other two; you could not distinguish them if you did not see them.

E.—I only know that a means exists; I know nothing more.

A.—So you do not know whether it is reason or the vital principle, which we call the inner sense and which presides over the bodily senses, or something else?

E.—I do not know.

A.—Yet you know that these elements cannot be defined except by the reason, and the reason can only define what is presented for its examination.

E.—That is certain.

A.—Therefore whatever else the faculty may be by which we perceive everything that we know, it is the servant of reason. It presents and reports to the reason whatever it comes upon, so that what is perceived may be able to be distinguished in its proper sphere, and grasped not only by sense perception but also by knowledge.

E.—That is so.

A.—The reason itself distinguishes between its servants and what they present to it, and also recognises what comes between these and itself, and it asserts itself to be their governor. Surely it does not grasp itself except by means of itself, that is, by the reason? Would you know that you possessed reason unless you perceived it by reason?

E.—Perfectly true.

A.—Then, since, when we perceive colour we do not likewise by the same sense perceive the fact that we perceive it, nor when we hear a sound do we also hear our hearing, nor when we smell a rose do we smell our smelling, nor when we taste something do we taste in the mouth our tasting, nor when we touch something can we touch the actual sense of touching: it is clear that the five senses cannot be perceived by any of the five senses, though they perceive all bodily things.

E.—That is clear.

4.10   *A.*—I think it is clear also that the inner sense not only perceives what is presented by the five bodily senses, but also perceives the bodily senses themselves. A beast would not move itself by seeking or shunning something, unless it perceived that it perceived; and this it does not do in such a way as to know, for this is the work of reason, but only in such a way as to move, and it does not have this perception by any of the five senses.

If this is still obscure, it will become clear if you notice, for example, what takes place in any one sense, say, in the sense of sight. A beast could not possibly open its eye, and move it to look at what it wants to see, unless it perceived that it did not see with the eye closed or turned in the wrong direction. But if it perceives that it does not see when it does not see, it must necessarily perceive that it sees when it sees. It shows that it is aware of both situations, because, when it sees, it does not turn the eye as a result of that desire through which it turns the eye when it does not see.

Whether this vital principle, which perceives that it perceives bodily things, also perceives itself, is not so clear, except in so far as everyone who asks himself the question realises that all living things shun death. Since death is the contrary of life, the vital principle must necessarily perceive itself, seeing that it shuns its contrary. If this is still not plain, leave it alone; we must not try to reach our goal except by clear and certain proofs.

These facts are clear: bodily things are perceived by a bodily sense; this sense cannot be perceived by itself; but an inner sense perceives both that bodily things are perceived by a bodily sense and also the bodily sense itself; and, finally, all this and reason itself is made known by reason, and grasped by knowledge. Do you not agree?

E.—Yes indeed.

A.—Well then, tell me how the problem comes in, which we wish to solve and have been working at for all this time.

5.11 *E.*—As far as I remember, of those three questions which we proposed just now so as to put this discussion into order, the first is now under consideration, namely, how it can become evident to us that God exists, even though we must believe it with all possible firmness.

A.—You are quite right. But I want you also to notice carefully that, when I asked you whether

you knew that you yourself existed, it became
clear that you knew not only this but also two
other things.

E.—I notice that too.

A.—Now observe to which of these three you recognise that every object of the bodily senses belongs: I mean, in what class of things you think
should be placed whatever is the object of our
senses through the agency of the eyes or any other
bodily organ. Should it be placed in the class
which merely exists, or in that which also lives, or
in that which also understands?

E.—In that which merely exists.

A.—In which of these three classes do you think
the sense itself should be placed?

E.—In that which lives.

A.—Then, which of these two do you think is
better, the sense itself or its object?

E.—Undoubtedly the sense itself.

A.—Why?

E.—Because that which also lives is better than that
which merely exists.

12 *A.*—Well, do you hesitate to rank that inner sense,
which we have already discovered to be below
reason, and yet common to us and the beasts, as
higher than the sense by which we perceive bodily
things? You have already said the latter sense
should be ranked above bodily things themselves.

E.—I should not hesitate for a moment.

A.—Again, I should like to hear why you do not
hesitate. You could not say that the inner sense
should be placed in that class of the three which

includes understanding, but you must place it in that class which exists and lives, without understanding. Even the beasts which lack understanding have that sense. This being so, I ask why you rank the inner sense above the sense which perceives bodily things, though both are in that class which lives. You have ranked the sense whose object is bodily things, above such things just because they are in that class which only exists, while the sense which perceives bodily things is in the class which also lives. Since the inner sense is also found to be in this class, tell me why you think it is better.

If you say it is because the inner sense perceives the other sense, you will not, I think, find any principle which we can follow,[11] that every percipient is better than the object it perceives. We might have to conclude in that case that everything which has understanding is better than the object it understands. This, however, is false, since man understands wisdom, but is not better than wisdom itself. So consider why you think the inner sense should be regarded as superior to the sense by which we perceive bodily things.

E.—Because I know it somehow controls and judges the other sense. If the latter fails in its duty, the inner sense exacts a kind of debt from its servant, as we discussed a little time ago. The sense of sight does not see that it sees or does not see, and, because it does not see this, it cannot judge what is lacking to it or what satisfies it. The inner sense can make this judgment, for it warns

the soul of the beast to open its eye when shut, and
to do what it perceives needs to be done. Undoubtedly that which judges is better than that
which is judged.

A.—Then do you notice that the bodily sense in
some way also judges bodily things? It is affected
by pleasure or pain when it comes in contact with
a bodily thing gently or harshly. Just as the inner
sense judges what is lacking to, or what satisfies,
the sense of sight, so too the sense of sight judges
what is lacking to, or what satisfies, colour.[12]
Moreover, as the inner sense judges the hearing,
whether it is sufficiently attentive or not, so the
hearing in its turn judges sound, whether it is
gentle or loud.

We need not go through the other bodily senses,
for I think you realise now what I mean. The
inner sense judges the bodily senses; it approves
them when they respond normally, and exacts
what they owe it. In the same way the bodily
senses judge bodily things, welcoming a gentle
touch and resisting the opposite.

E.—Yes, I see this and agree it is quite true.[13]

6.13 *A.*—Now consider whether reason in its turn
judges the inner sense. I am not asking now
whether you hesitate to call it better than the inner
sense, because I am sure you do call it better. Yet
I think now we should not even ask whether reason
judges this inner sense. For in regard to those
things which are below reason, that is, bodily
things and the bodily senses and the inner sense,
what else but the reason tells us how one is better

than another, and how reason is nobler than any of them? This could not possibly happen, unless it judged them.

E.—That is obvious.

A.—So that kind of thing which not only exists, but also lives, yet does not understand, such as the soul of a beast, is nobler than that kind of thing which only exists without living or understanding. Again, that which includes existence, life, and understanding, such as the rational mind of man, is nobler still. I am sure you do not think that anything nobler can be found in us, among those faculties which make up our nature, than that which we have placed third among the three? It is clear we have a body and a vital principle which stirs and quickens the body, both of which we recognise to be present in beasts. It is also clear that we have something else, the head or eye, so to speak, of our soul, or whatever more suitable expression can be used to describe the reason and understanding. The beast does not have this in its nature. So I beg you to consider whether you can find anything which is higher than reason in man's nature.

E.—I see nothing at all which is better.

14 *A.*—Well, if we can find something which you are certain not only exists but also is nobler than our reason, will you hesitate to call this, whatever it is, God?

E.—If I could find something better than the best in my nature, I should not necessarily call it God. I should not like to call that which is above my

reason, God, but rather that which is above everything else.

A.—That is plainly right. God granted to your
reason this reverent and true opinion of Himself.
But I ask you: if you find there is nothing above
our reason except the eternal and unchangeable,
will you hesitate to call this God? You know that
bodily things change, and clearly the life which
animates the body has various moods and is subject
to change. Reason itself at one time strives after
the truth, and at another does not strive, sometimes
reaches it and sometimes does not; it is manifestly
proved to be changeable. If without using any
bodily means, if neither by touch, nor taste, nor
smell, neither by the ears, nor the eyes, nor any
sense lower than itself, but by its own self, the
reason sees something eternal and unchangeable,
and itself as lower than this, then it must confess
that this is its God.

E.—I will confess clearly that to be God, which all
agree to be higher than anything else.

A.—Very well. All I need do is to show that there
is a being of such a kind, and either you will admit
this being to be God, or, if there is anything higher,
you will grant that the higher being is God.[14] So,
whether there is something higher or whether
there is not, it will be clear that God exists, when,
with His help, I shall show, as I promised, that
there exists something higher than reason.

E.—Show, then, what you promise.

7.15 *A.*—I shall do so. But I first ask whether my
bodily sense is the same as yours, or whether mine

is only my own, and yours only your own. If this were not so, I could not see anything with my eyes which you would not see.

E.—I entirely agree that each of us have our own senses, of sight or hearing and so on, though they are in a common class. One man can both see and hear what another does not hear, and with all the other senses each man's perceptions can be different. So it is clear that your sense is only yours, and my sense only mine.

A.—Will you make the same reply about the inner sense, or will you not?

E.—Yes indeed, the same reply. My inner sense perceives my bodily sense, and yours perceives yours. I am often asked by a man who sees something whether I see it also. The reason is simply that I am conscious of my seeing or not seeing, while my questioner is not.

A.—Then I suppose each of us has his own reason? It may be that I understand something which you do not understand, and you may be unable to know whether I understand, though I myself know.

E.—It is clear that each of us has his own distinct rational mind.

16 *A.*—You surely could not say that we each have our own suns or moons or morning stars or such like, though each of us sees them with his own sense?

E.—I certainly should not say so.

A.—Many of us can at the same time see the same thing, though the senses of each of us are our own distinct senses: with these distinct senses we see the one object, and we all see it at the same time. It may happen, therefore, although your sense and mine are distinct, that we may not each see distinct objects; one and the same thing may be presented to each of us, and may be seen at the same time by each of us.

E.—That is perfectly clear.

A.—We can also hear the same sound at the same time, so that, although my hearing is distinct from yours, yet the sound which we hear at the same time is not distinct to each of us, nor is one part of it received by my hearing and another by yours. When a sound is made, the same sound and the whole of it is present to the hearing of both of us.

E.—That also is clear.

17 *A.*—You may now notice what we say about the other bodily senses too: as far as our present subject is concerned, they are not quite in the same position as the two senses of sight and hearing, nor are they quite different. You and I can breathe the same air, and perceive what it is like from the smell. We can both taste the same honey or any other food or drink, and can perceive what it is like from the taste, though this is one and the same, while the senses of each of us, yours and mine, are distinct to each of us. Though we both perceive the same smell or the same taste, yet you do not perceive it with my sense nor I with yours, nor by any faculty which can be common to us both: my sense is entirely mine, and yours is entirely yours, even though we both perceive the same smell or

taste. It follows that those other senses are found to have a characteristic similar to that of the senses of sight and hearing. They are unlike them, so far as our present subject is concerned, in that, though we both breathe the same air with our nostrils, or take the same food when we taste it, yet I do not draw in the same part of the air as you, nor do I take the same part of the food as you, but we take different parts. Therefore, when I breathe, I draw from the whole air as much as is sufficient for me, and you draw another part, as much as is sufficient for you. The same food is wholly taken by each of us,[15] yet the whole cannot be taken both by you and me in the same way that you and I both hear the whole of a word simultaneously, and both see exactly the same sight: different parts of food and drink must pass into each of us. Is this not quite clear?

E.—I agree it is perfectly clear and certain.

18 *A.*—You do not think, do you, that the sense of touch is comparable with the senses of sight and hearing in that respect we are now considering? Not only can we both perceive by touch the same bodily thing, but we can also both touch the same part; we can both perceive by touch not only the same bodily thing but the same part of it. It is not the same with touch as with food, for you and I cannot both take the whole of the food put before us, when we are both eating it. You and I can touch the same thing and the whole of it, not merely different parts—we can each touch the whole.

E.—I agree that in this respect the sense of touch is very much like the two senses mentioned before. But I see that they are unlike in this, that both of us can see and hear the whole of the same thing at exactly the same time, while, though we can touch the whole of a thing at the same time, we can only touch different parts—the same part only at different times. I cannot touch the part which you are touching, unless you move your hand.

19 *A.*—Your answer is very acute, but you must see this. Of all the things we perceive there are some we both perceive together, and others we each perceive separately. We each perceive separately our own senses: I do not perceive your sense, nor you mine. We each separately, and not both together, perceive objects of the bodily senses, that is, bodily things, only when they become our own in such a way that we can make them change completely into ourselves. Food and drink are examples, for you cannot have a perception of the same part as I have. Nurses may chew food and give it to children, but, when they do so, if the food is tasted and consumed and changed into the nurse's body, it cannot possibly be brought back and offered as food for the child. When the palate tastes something it enjoys, it claims for itself irrevocably a part, however small, and makes this conform to the nature of its body. Otherwise there would remain no taste in the mouth, after the food had been chewed and spat out again.

The same can be said of the parts of the air which we breathe. For, though you may be able to draw in some part of the air which I breathe out, yet you cannot draw in that which has actually nourished me; this cannot be given up. Doctors tell us that we take nourishment even with our nostrils. When I breathe, I alone can perceive this nourishment, nor can I breathe it out and give it up, so that you may draw it in with your nostrils and perceive it.

When we perceive other sensible objects we do not, by perceiving them, break them up and change them into our own body. Both of us can perceive them either at the same time or at different times, in such a way that the whole, or the part which I perceive, is also perceived by you. Examples of this are light or sound or bodily things with which we come in contact, but which we do not alter.

E.—I understand.

A.—It is clear, therefore, that those things which we perceive with our bodily senses but do not change, do not share the nature of these senses, and consequently are common to us, for the very reason that they do not suffer change and become our personal and, so to speak, private possession.

E.—I quite agree.

A.—By our personal and, so to speak, private possession, I mean that which belongs to each individual and to no one else,[16] that which he alone perceives in himself, that which belongs to his own peculiar nature. But that which is common and, so to speak, public, is what is perceived by all who have perception, with no alteration or change in itself.

E.—That is true.

8.20 *A.*—Well, listen now, and tell me whether anything can be found which all who reason see in common, each with his own reason and mind. An object which is seen is present to all and is not changed for the use of those to whom it is present, as in the case of food or drink, but remains incorrupt and entire, whether seen or not seen. Do you perhaps disagree with this?

E.—No, I see there are many examples, though it is enough to mention one. The law and truth of number is present to all who reason. All calculators try to grasp their truth by reason and understanding; one man can do so more easily, one less easily, one not at all. However, their truth presents itself equally to all who can grasp it. When a man perceives it, he does not change it and make it into his food of perception, as it were; and when he makes a mistake about it, the truth does not fail but remains entirely true, while he is in error in proportion to his failure to see it.

21 *A.*—Quite right. You are not unpractised in these things, and I see you have quickly found your answer. Yet, if someone were to tell you that these numbers were impressed on our minds, not as a result of their own nature but as a result of those things we experience with the bodily sense, and were, so to speak, images of visible things, what would you answer? Do you agree with this?

E.—No, I could not agree.[17] Even if I perceived

numbers with my bodily sense, I should not as a result be able to perceive with my bodily sense the meaning of division or addition of numbers. By the light of my mind I check the man who reaches a wrong result in addition or subtraction. Whatever I become aware of with my bodily sense, whether heaven or earth or any bodily thing they contain, how long they will last I do not know. But seven and three are ten, not only now, but always. There has never been a time when seven and three were not ten, nor will there ever be. Therefore I have said that this incorruptible truth of number [18] is common to myself and to everyone who reasons.

22   *A.*—I do not dispute your answer; it is perfectly true and certain. But you will easily see that the numbers themselves are not perceived through the bodily senses, if you reflect that every number connotes a given amount of units. For example, if one is doubled it is two, if trebled three, if it has ten units it is ten. Any possible number is named according to the units it possesses, and is called this number.

But if you have a true notion of 'one,' you certainly find that it cannot be perceived by the bodily senses. Whatever is the object of a bodily sense is proved to be many, and not one, because it is a bodily thing and so has countless parts. I need not dwell on each small and indistinct part; however small such a bodily part may be, it certainly has one part on the right, another on the left, one above and another below, one on the far side and another on the near side, parts at the ends and a part in the middle. We are bound to admit this is so, on however small a scale. Consequently we grant that no bodily thing is perfectly one, yet all these many parts could not be counted, unless they were distinguished through knowledge of 'one.'

I look for 'one' in a bodily thing, and undoubtedly do not find it. I know indeed what I am looking for, and what I do not find there; and I know that it cannot be found, or rather, that it is not there at all. While I know that a bodily thing is not one, I know what 'one' is. If I did not know 'one,' I could not count 'many' in a bodily thing. From whatever source I get my knowledge of 'one,' I do not get it through a bodily sense, for through a bodily sense I only know a bodily thing, which we can prove is not perfectly one.

Moreover, if we do not perceive 'one' by a bodily sense, we perceive no number by that sense, none at least of those numbers we distinguish with the understanding. All of these are made up of a given quantity of units, and the bodily sense cannot perceive a unit. Half of any small bodily thing, whatever size the half may be, itself has a half. Thus there are two halves in a bodily thing, yet they themselves are not perfectly two. But, since the number we call two is twice what is perfectly one, its half, namely that which is perfectly one, cannot in its turn have a half, or a third, or any fraction, because it is perfectly one.

23   Then, if we keep the order of the numbers, after one we see two, and this number, compared

with one, is found to be double. Twice two does not come next, but three comes next, and then four, which is twice two. This pattern runs through all the other numbers by a sure and unchangeable law, so that after one, that is, after the first of all numbers (not counting the number itself) the next is that which doubles it, for the next is two. After the second number, that is, after two (not counting this number itself), the second is that which doubles it, for after two the first is three, while the second is four, which doubles two. After the third number, that is, after three (not counting this number itself), the third is its double, for after the third, that is, after three, the first is four, the second is five, and the third is six, which is double three. Similarly, after four (not counting this number itself), the fourth is its double, for after the fourth, that is, after four, the first is five, the second is six, the third is seven, and the fourth is eight, which is double four. Through all the other numbers you will find what you found in the first two numbers, that is, in one and two: whatever the number may be, counting from the beginning, this same number being added to it the number you reach is its double.[19]

How, then, do we recognise that this fact, which we recognise throughout all numbers, is unchangeable, sure, and certain? No one is aware of all numbers with any bodily sense, for they are innumerable. How, then, do we know that this holds good throughout them all? By what idea or image do we see so sure a truth so confidently throughout innumerable instances, unless we do it by an inner light, unknown to the bodily sense?

24 By these and many other such proofs those to whom God has given the gift of reasoning and who are not darkened by obstinacy, must admit that the law and truth of number do not concern the bodily sense, that they are unalterably sure, and are perceived in common by all who reason.

Many other things may suggest themselves which are presented in common and, as it were, publicly, to those who reason, and which are distinguished by each man's mind and reason individually, and yet remain entire and unchangeable. Nevertheless I was glad to hear that the law and truth of number were the first to suggest themselves to you, when you wished to answer my question. It is not without significance that in the Sacred Books number is joined to wisdom, where it is said: *I and my heart went round about to know and consider and seek wisdom and number.*[20]

9.25 However, I ask you: what, in your opinion, should we think of wisdom itself? Do you suppose that each individual has his own individual wisdom, or that one wisdom is present to all in common, so that each man is wiser the more fully he shares in it?

E.—I do not yet know what you mean by wisdom. I see that men have different views as to what constitutes wise action or speech. Soldiers think they are acting wisely. Those who despise war and devote their energies to farming, regard this as preferable and believe they are wise. Those who are clever at money-making think they are wise. Those who pay no attention to, or set aside, all this and all such temporal interests, and devote themselves entirely to the search for truth that they may know themselves and God, judge this the great work of wisdom. Those who refuse to surrender themselves peacefully to seek and contemplate the truth, but rather endure the laborious cares of public office in order to help their fellowmen, and take their part in the just management and direction of human affairs, think they are wise. Those who do both of these things, and engage themselves partly in the contemplation of truth, and partly in active works which they regard as a debt to society, think they are supremely wise. I leave aside countless groups, each of which prefers its members to others, and would like them alone to be wise.

So, since our purpose is not to say what we believe, but what we hold with clear understanding, I could not possibly make any reply to your question unless besides holding by belief what wisdom itself is, I know this by contemplation and by the light of reason.

26 *A.*—You do not think, do you, that there is any other wisdom but the truth, in which we distinguish and grasp the supreme good? All those, whom you have mentioned as following different aims, seek the good and shun evil, but they follow different aims because they have different opinions about the good. If a man seeks what ought not to be sought, he errs, even though he would not seek

it unless he thought it was good. But the man who seeks nothing cannot err, nor can he who seeks what he ought to seek.

Therefore, in so far as all men seek a happy life, they are not in error. In so far, however, as anyone does not keep to the way of life which leads to happiness, even though he confesses and professes that he wishes only for happiness, to that extent he is in error. For error comes about when we follow an aim which does not lead us where we wish to go. The more a man errs in his way of life, the less wise he is, for to this extent he departs from the truth, in which the supreme good is distinguished and grasped. When the supreme good is sought and gained, a man is happy, and this we all undoubtedly desire.

Therefore, just as we agree that we wish to be happy, so we agree that we wish to be wise, for no one is happy without wisdom. No one is happy without the supreme good, which is distinguished and grasped in that truth which we call wisdom. So, as, before we are happy, the idea of happiness is nevertheless impressed on our minds—for through this idea we know and say confidently and without any doubt that we wish to be happy—so too, before we are wise, we have the idea of wisdom impressed on the mind. It is through this idea that each of us, if asked whether he wishes to be wise, replies without any shadow of doubt that he does so wish.

27   So, if we agree what wisdom is, I want you to tell me whether you think wisdom is presented in common to all who reason, as is the law and truth

of number, or whether you think there are as many different wisdoms as there could be different wise men. For each man has a different mind, so that I can see nothing of your mind, nor you of mine. It may be that you cannot explain the nature of wisdom in words, yet, if you did not see it with your mind in any way, you would not know at all that you wished to be wise, and that you had a duty so to wish—a fact I think you will not deny.

E.—If the supreme good is the same for all, the truth in which it is distinguished and grasped, that is to say, wisdom, must be the same, shared in common by all.

A.—Do you doubt that the supreme good, whatever it is, is the same for all men?

E.—Yes, I am doubtful about this, because I see men taking pleasure in different things as their supreme goods.

A.—I should like no one to doubt about the supreme good, just as no one doubts that, whatever it is, no man can become happy unless he gains it. Since, however, this is a large question, and may demand a long discussion, let us by all means suppose that there are as many supreme goods as there are different objects sought as supreme goods by different men. Surely it does not follow that wisdom itself is not the same, shared in common by all men, because those goods which they distinguish through it and choose, are many different goods? If this is your opinion, you may doubt that the light of the sun is one, because we see in it many different things. Of these many things each man chooses what to enjoy with his sense of sight. One man likes to look at a high mountain and enjoy its view, another a flat plain, another a curving valley, another green woods, another the level, restless sea. Another takes together all or several of these beautiful [21] things for the joy of looking at them.[22]

The objects are many and varied which men see in the light of the sun and which they choose for their enjoyment, yet the light of the sun is itself one in which the gaze of each beholder sees and grasps an object to enjoy. So too the goods are many and varied from which each man chooses what he wants, and, seeing and grasping his choice, constitutes it rightly and truly the supreme good for his enjoyment. Yet the very light of wisdom, in which these things can be seen and grasped, may be one light shared in common by all wise men.

E.—I agree that this is possible, and nothing prevents the same wisdom being common to all, even though the supreme goods are many and varied; but I would like to know whether it is so. Because we grant it is possible, we do not necessarily grant it is so.

A.—Meanwhile we know that wisdom exists. Whether there is one wisdom shared in common by all, or whether each man has his own wisdom, just as he has his own soul or mind, we do not yet know.

E.—That is true.

IN TRUTH WE FIND GOD

10.28 *A.*—Well then, where do we see this fact which we know—that wisdom or wise men exist, and that all men wish to be happy? I certainly should not doubt that you do see this and that it is true. Do you, therefore, see this is true in the same way that you see your thoughts, which I am entirely ignorant of unless you inform me? Or do you see it to be true in such a way that you understand it can be seen to be true by me also, though you do not tell me?

E.—Certainly in such a way that I do not doubt you also can see it, even against my will.

A.—Hence, is not the one truth common to both of us, which we both see with our individual minds?

E.—Quite clearly so.

A.—I think you do not deny that we should devote ourselves to wisdom. I think you grant this is true.

E.—I certainly do not doubt it.

A.—Can we deny that this is true, and one, and common to the sight of all who know it, although each sees it with his own mind, and not with yours or mine or anyone else's? For that which is seen is present in common to all who see it.

E.—This is undeniable.

A.—Will you not also agree that the following propositions are absolutely true, and are present in common to you and me and all who see them: we ought to live justly; the better should be preferred to the worse; like should be compared with like; every man should be given his due?

E.—I agree.

A.—Could you deny that the incorrupt is better than the corrupt, the eternal than the temporal, that which cannot be injured than that which can be injured?

E.—No one could deny it.

A.—So everyone can call this truth his own, though it is present without change to the sight of all who are able to behold it?

E.—No one could truthfully say it was his own property, since it is one and common to all, just as much as it is true.

A.—Again, who denies that we should turn the heart away from what is corrupt and towards what is incorrupt, that is, that we should love not what is corrupt but what is healthy? When a man admits a truth, does he not also understand that it is unchangeable and present in common to all minds which are able to see it?

E.—That is perfectly true.

A.—Will anyone doubt that a life is better, if no difficulty can move it from a firm, virtuous purpose, than if it is easily shaken and upset by the troubles of this life?

E.—Undoubtedly.

29 A.—I will not ask any more questions about this. It is enough that you see, as I do, and admit to be quite certain that those principles and illuminations, so to speak, in which the virtues appear, are true and unchangeable and, whether separately or

all together, are present in common to the sight of those who can see them, each with his own reason and mind. But I do ask this question, whether you think these are concerned with wisdom. I believe that in your opinion a man is wise who has gained wisdom.

E.—That is certainly my opinion.

A.—Well, could a man, who lives justly, so live unless he saw what were the higher things he should prefer to the lower, what were the like things he should put together, and what were the things he should assign as due to each?

E.—No, he could not.

A.—You will not deny, will you, that the man who sees these things sees them wisely?

E.—No.

A.—Well, does not the man who lives prudently choose the incorrupt, and judge that it should be preferred to corruption?

E.—Clearly.

A.—Then I suppose it cannot be denied that he chooses wisely, when he chooses to turn his soul to what no one doubts ought to be chosen?

E.—I certainly should not deny it.

A.—So when he turns his soul to a wise choice, he does so wisely.

E.—Most certainly.

A.—And the man who is deterred by no threat or penalty from that which he chooses wisely, and to which he is wise in turning, undoubtedly acts wisely.

E.—Beyond any doubt.

A.—So it is quite clear that those principles and illuminations, as we have called them, in which the virtues appear, concern wisdom. The more a man uses them in living his life, and the more he passes his life in conformity with them, the more wisely he lives and acts. But nothing which is done wisely can rightly be called distinct from wisdom.

E.—Certainly not.

A.—Therefore the principles of number are true and unchangeable; their law and truth are, as you said, present unchangeably and in common to all who see them. In the same way the principles of wisdom are true and unchangeable. When I asked you about a few instances of these, you replied that they were manifestly true, and you grant that they are present to the sight of all in common who are able to behold them.[23]

11.30 *E.*—I cannot doubt it. But I should very much like to know whether these two, wisdom and number, are contained in any one class, because you mentioned that they are coupled together in Holy Scripture. Does one depend on the other, or is one included in the other; does number, for example, depend on wisdom, or is it included in wisdom? I should not dare to say that wisdom depends on number or is included in number. Because I know many mathematicians, or accountants, or whatever they should be called, who make wonderfully clever calculations, but very few, if any, wise men; somehow or other wisdom appears to me far nobler than number.

A.—You speak of something at which I also often

wonder. When I meditate on the unchangeable truth of number, and, so to speak, its home or sanctuary, or whatever word is suitable to describe the place where number resides, I am carried far away from the body.²⁴ Finding, it may be, something which I can think of, but not finding anything I can express in words, I return, worn out, to familiar things in order to speak, and I express in ordinary language what lies before my eyes.

The same thing happens to me when I concentrate my thoughts with the fullest attention that I can, on wisdom. I wonder much, since both of these are established in the most secret and certain truth, and in view also of the witness of Scripture, which, as I have mentioned, couples them together, I wonder very much indeed, as I say, why number is of little value to most men, while wisdom is precious to them.

The fact, however, surely is that somehow they are one and the same thing. Yet, since Sacred Scripture says about wisdom that *she reacheth from end to end mightily and ordereth all things sweetly*,²⁵ that power by which *she reacheth from end to end mightily* perhaps signifies number, and that by which *she ordereth all things sweetly* refers directly to wisdom, though both belong to one and the same wisdom.

31 Wisdom has given numbers to all things, even the lowest and those ranked least of all; all bodily things, though they are below everything else, possess these numbers. But it has not given the power to be wise to bodily things, nor to all souls, but

only to rational souls. It is as if it has made its dwelling among them, so that from there it may set in order all those things, even the lowest, to which it has given numbers. Therefore, since we judge easily about bodily things as things belonging to a lower rank than ours, and see the numbers impressed on them are lower than we are,[26] for this reason we hold numbers of little value. But, when we begin, as it were, to mount upward, we find that numbers pass beyond our minds and abide unchangeably in truth itself.

Because few can be wise, while it is granted even to fools to count, men admire wisdom but despise number. Learned students, the further they are removed from the grossness of earth, the more clearly they see number and wisdom in truth itself, and hold both precious. Compared with the truth, not only gold and silver and the other things for which men strive, but even they themselves appear worthless.

32   Number seems of little value to men, and wisdom precious, because they can count numbers more easily than they can acquire wisdom. Do not be surprised at this, for you see that men regard gold as more precious than the light of a lamp, though it is absurd to value gold in comparison. But they honour more highly a thing much lower because even a beggar lights his lamp, and only a few have gold. I do not suggest for a moment that wisdom is found lower when compared to number, since it is the same; but it demands an eye capable of discerning it.[27]

Light and heat are perceived, fused together, so to speak, from one fire, and cannot be separated from each other; yet heat is communicated to what is put near the fire, while light is diffused far and wide. So too the power of understanding which wisdom contains, heats what is closer to it, such as a rational soul, but does not affect what is more distant, such as bodily things, with the warmth of wisdom; it only shines on them with the light of number. Perhaps this is obscure to you, but no analogy from a visible thing can be made applicable in every respect to what is invisible.

Only notice this point, which is sufficient for our problem and is apparent even to more lowly minds such as our own. Although we cannot be clear whether number resides in wisdom or is derived from wisdom, or whether wisdom itself is derived from number or resides in number, or whether both terms can be shown to refer to the same thing, yet it is certainly plain that both are true, and true unchangeably.

12.33 Therefore you would by no means deny that there exists unchangeable truth, containing all those things which are unchangeably true. You could not call this yours or mine or any man's, but it is present and offers itself in common to all who behold unchangeable truths, like a light which in a wonderful fashion is both secret and public. No one could say that anything which is present in common to all who have reason and understanding belongs to the nature of one individual.

You remember, I think, our discussion a little

while ago about the bodily senses.[28] We decided that the common objects of the sense of sight or of hearing—colours and sounds, for instance, which you and I both see at the same time—do not share the nature of our eyes or ears, but are common objects of perception.

So you would certainly not say that what you and I perceive in common, each with his own mind, shares the nature of the mind of either of us. You could not say that what the eyes of two people see at the same time is the eyes of either of them; it is something else to which both of them direct their sight.

E.—That is manifestly true.

34 *A.*—Do you think that this truth, about which we have been talking for such a long time, and in which, though one, we see so many things, is higher than our minds, or equal to them, or lower? If it were lower, we should make judgments about it, not in accordance with it. We make judgments about bodily things because they are lower; we often say not only that such and such is true of them, but also that it ought to be. Similarly, not only do we know that our souls are in a particular state, but often that they ought to be. And in the same way we judge about bodily things, and say, 'It is not so bright as it ought to be,' or 'not so square,' and so on; and of souls, 'It is not so ready as it ought to be,' or 'not so gentle,' or 'not so vigorous,' according to the nature of our character. In making these judgments we follow the principles of truth within us, which we see in common.

No one ever makes these the object of a judgment. When a man says that the eternal is superior to the temporal, or that seven and three are ten, no one asserts that it ought to be so, but, knowing it is so, we rejoice to make the discovery without scrutinising and trying to correct it.

If this truth were on an equality with our minds, it would itself be subject to change. Sometimes our minds see it more clearly, sometimes less clearly, and as a result they admit themselves to be subject to change. The truth, however, abiding in itself, gains nothing when we see it more clearly, and loses nothing when we see it less clearly, but, whole and sound, it gladdens with its light those who are turned towards it, and punishes with blindness those who are turned away from it. Again, we judge about our own minds according to the truth, though we can by no means judge about the truth itself. We say, 'our mind understands less than it ought,' or, 'it understands as much as it ought.' But the mind ought to understand more in proportion as it approaches, and clings to, the unchangeable truth. Hence if the truth is neither inferior to nor equal to our minds, it can only be higher and more noble.

13.35   I had promised, you may remember, to show you something higher than our mind and reason. This thing is truth itself. Embrace it if you can, and enjoy it; and *delight in the Lord, and He will give thee the requests of thy heart.*[29] What more do you ask than to be happy? What is happier than the man who enjoys the firm, unchangeable, most excellent truth?

Men declare they are happy when they embrace the fair bodies, ardently desired, of wives and even of harlots, and can we doubt of our happiness in the embrace of truth? Men declare they are happy when with parched throats they reach an abundant and healthful spring of water, or when they are hungry and discover a dinner or supper, richly furnished. Shall we deny our happiness when we are given the food and drink of truth? We often hear men declare they are happy if they lie amid roses and other flowers, or enjoy the sweet smell of ointments. What is more fragrant, what more delightful, than the inspiration of truth? Do we hesitate to call ourselves happy, when so inspired? Many place their lives' happiness in song, in the music of lyre and flute: when these are missing, they count themselves wretched; when these are present, they are transported with joy. When the truth, tuneful and eloquent in its silence, falls noiselessly, as it were, upon our minds, shall we seek elsewhere for a happy life, and not enjoy that which is so sure and so near at hand? Men take delight in gleaming gold and silver, in glittering gems and colours, in the light itself which our eyes perceive in fire upon the earth, or in the stars, the moon, or the sun; men take delight in the splendour and graciousness of these things. When neither poverty nor trouble keeps them from such enjoyment, they count themselves happy and for these things they wish to live forever. Are we afraid to set the happiness of life in the light of truth?

36 Since the supreme good is known and grasped in the truth, and since that truth is wisdom, let us see in wisdom the supreme good, and grasp and enjoy it. The man who enjoys the supreme good is indeed happy.

The truth shows men all the things which are truly good, and each man, understanding these according to his capacity, chooses for his enjoyment one or several of them. Among those who choose an object to look at in the light of the sun and who take pleasure in the sight, some may possess strong, healthy, vigorous eyes, and these men are perfectly ready to gaze at the sun itself, which also illuminates other objects in which weaker eyes take pleasure. So too a strong, vigorous, mental gaze, when it sees with certainty many unchangeable truths, turns to the truth itself in which all things are shown; to this it clings as though forgetful of all else, and in it enjoys all things together. For whatever is delightful in other truths, owes its delightfulness to the truth itself.[30]

37 Our freedom consists in submission to the truth, and it is our God Himself who frees us from death, that is, from the state of sin. For truth itself, speaking as a man with men, says to those who believe in Him: *If you continue in my word, you shall be my disciples, indeed, and you shall know the truth, and the truth shall make you free.*[31] The soul enjoys nothing with freedom unless it enjoys it securely.

14   No one, however, possesses securely those goods, which he can lose against his will. But no one loses truth and wisdom against his will, for no one can be separated from them physically. That which we call separation from truth and wisdom is a perverted will, which loves lower things. No one wishes for something against his will.

We have, therefore, in the truth a possession which we can all enjoy equally and in common; there is nothing wanting or defective in it. It receives all its lovers without stirring their envy; it welcomes all, and is chaste with each. One man does not say to another: go back and let me come; take away your hands and let me embrace it. All cling to it; all touch it at the same time. It is a food which is never divided; you drink nothing from it which I cannot drink. When you share in it, you make nothing your private possession; what you take from it still remains whole for me too. I do not wait until you surrender the inspiration it gives you before I can be inspired; no one ever takes any part of it for his private use, but it is wholly common to all at the same time.[32]

38   Therefore what we touch, or taste, or smell, are less like the truth than what we hear and see. Every word is heard wholly by all who hear it, and wholly by each at the same time, and every sight presented to the eyes is seen as much by one man as by another at the same time. But the likeness is a very distant one. No voice sounds wholly at the same time, since its sound is lengthened out and protracted, and some comes earlier, some later.

Every sight offered swells, as it were, over space, and is not wholly everywhere. Certainly all those things are taken away from us against our will, and there are obstacles which prevent us from being able to enjoy them.

For instance, even if the music of a singer could last forever, his admirers would struggle and vie with each other to hear him; they would crowd each other, and the more numerous they were, they would fight for seats, each one anxious to get nearer to the singer. They would retain nothing lastingly which they heard, and sounds would only touch them and die away. If I wished to look at the sun, and could continue to do so, it would leave me when it sets, and so too a cloud would veil it from my sight; and there are many other obstacles through which I should lose the pleasure of this sight against my will. And, granted I could see forever the beauty of light and hear forever the beauty of sound: what great thing would it be to me, since I should share it in common with the beasts?

But no thronging crowd of hearers keeps others from approaching the beauty of truth and wisdom, provided only there is a constant will to enjoy them. Their beauty does not pass with time, nor move from place to place. Night does not interrupt it, nor darkness hide it, and it is not subject to bodily sense. It is close to all its lovers throughout the world who turn towards it, and for all it is everlasting. It is in no place, yet nowhere is it absent; from without it admonishes us, within it instructs us. It changes all its beholders for the better; it is itself never changed for the worse. No one is its judge; without it no one judges rightly.

Clearly, therefore, and undoubtedly it is more excellent than our minds, for it is one, and yet makes each separate mind wise and the judge of other things, never of the truth.

15.39   If I showed there was something above our minds, you admitted you would confess it to be God, provided there was nothing else higher. I accepted your admission, and said it was enough that I should show this. For if there is anything more excellent, it is this which is God, but, if there is nothing more excellent, then truth itself is God. Whichever is the fact, you cannot deny that God exists, and this was the question we set ourselves to debate.[33]

If you are influenced by what we have received on faith through the most holy teaching of Christ, namely, that there is a Father of Wisdom, remember that we have also received this on faith—that Wisdom, begotten of the eternal Father, is His equal. We must ask no further questions about this, but hold it firmly by faith.

God exists, and He exists truly and supremely. We not only hold this, I think, by our faith as certain, but we also attain to it by a sure, though very feeble, kind of knowledge. This suffices for the question we have undertaken, and enables us to explain the other matters connected with it. Or have you any objections to raise?

E.—I accept this with a joy past belief, which I

cannot express to you in words. I declare it to be most certain. My inner voice declares this, and I desire to be heard by the truth itself, and to cling to it. This I grant to be not only good, but the supreme good, and the source of happiness.

EVERY PERFECTION COMES FROM GOD

40 *A.*—Quite right. I too rejoice greatly. But, I ask you, are we already wise and happy, or are we still on the way towards this?

E.—I think rather we are on our way towards it.

A.—How then do you understand those things which you declare that you rejoice in as true and certain? You grant that wisdom consists in understanding them. Can a foolish man know wisdom?

E.—He cannot, so long as he is foolish.

A.—Then you must be already wise, or you do not yet know wisdom.

E.—I am certainly not already wise, yet I should say I was not foolish, so far as I know wisdom. I cannot deny that what I know is certain, and that wisdom consists in this knowledge.

A.—Tell me, please: will you not admit that the man who is not just is unjust, and the man who is not prudent is imprudent, and the man who is not temperate is intemperate? Can there be any doubt about this?

E.—I admit that when a man is not just, he is unjust, and I should make the same answer about the prudent and the temperate man.

A.—Why, then, is a man not foolish when he is not wise?

E.—I admit this too, that when a man is not wise, he is foolish.

A.—Now, which of these are you?

E.—Whichever you call me, I do not dare to say I am yet wise. From what I have admitted, I see I must draw the conclusion that I should not hesitate to say I am foolish.

A.—Therefore a foolish man knows wisdom. As we have said, he would not be sure that he wished to be wise, and that this was his duty, unless the idea of wisdom was established in his mind. It is thus that you have in your mind the ideas of those things about which you answered each of my questions, the things in which wisdom consists, and in the knowledge of which you rejoiced.

E.—What you say is true.

16.41 *A.*—What else, then, do we do when we endeavour to be wise, but concentrate, as it were, our whole soul with all the energy we can upon the object we reach with our mind, and set our soul there, and fix it firmly? We do this that the soul may not now rejoice in its own individual self which has entangled it in passing interests, but that, setting aside all inclination to things of time and space, it may grasp that which is always one and the same. Just as the whole life of the body is the soul, so the happy life of the soul is God. While we are engaged in this work, and before we have finished it, we are on the way.

We are allowed to rejoice in those true and certain goods, which gleam even in the darkness of our present path. Is not this what Scripture tells us about the conduct of Wisdom towards its lovers, when they come and seek for it: *she shall show herself to them cheerfully in the ways and shall meet them with all providence?* [34] Wherever you turn she speaks to you by means of the traces she has left on her works, and calls you back within, when you are slipping away into outward things, through the very forms of these outward things. She does this so that you may see that whatever bodily thing delights you and attracts the bodily senses, is subject to number, and that you may ask whence it comes, and may return to yourself, and understand that you could not approve or disapprove what you perceive with the bodily senses, unless you possessed within yourself certain laws of beauty to which you refer all the beautiful things you perceive outside. [35]

42   Look at the sky and the earth and the sea, and whatever shines brightly above or creeps below or flies or swims. They have forms because they have numbers. Take these away, and nothing will be left. What is their source, but the source of number? For, so far as they have being, they have numbered being.

Artists, in whatever bodily forms they work, have in their art numbers to which they adapt their work. They move their hands and tools in their art until that which is formed externally, conforming to the inward light of number, is perfected so far as possible, and, after being expressed by the

senses, pleases the inner judge who gazes upwards
upon number. Ask, then, who moves the limbs of
the artist himself. It is number, for they too are
moved according to number. If you take away
the work from his hands and take from his mind
the intention of exercising his art, and if you say
that pleasure moves his limbs, it will be a dance.
Ask what is pleasant in dancing, and number will
answer, It is I.

Look at the beauty of a graceful body: numbers
are held in place. Look at the beauty of bodily
movement; numbers alter in time. Go to the art
from which they come, search in it for time and
place; there is no time, no place. Yet number lives
in it. Number has no position in space nor dura-
tion in time. When those who wish to become
artists set themselves to learn their art, they move
their bodies in space and time, and their souls in
time; with the passage of time they become more
skilful.

Then pass beyond the soul of the artist, to see
everlasting number. Wisdom will now shine from
its inner dwelling, and from the very sanctuary of
truth. If your sight is still too weak and is re-
pelled, turn your mind's eye to that path where
she showed herself cheerfully. But remember that
you have put off the vision, to return to it when
your strength is greater.

43   Alas for those who abandon you as leader and
who stray in what are but your footprints, who
love the signs which you show but not yourself,
who forget your meaning, O wisdom, most gra-

cious light of a purified mind! You tell us without ceasing your name and your greatness. Every excellence in a creature reveals you. By the very beauty of his work the artist, as it were, suggests to its admirer not to be wholly absorbed in it, but so to glance at the work produced that he may reserve his attention for the artist who made it. Those who love your works instead of yourself are like those who hear a wise and eloquent speaker, who listens too eagerly to the pleasant voice and the carefully uttered syllables, but lose that which matters most, the meaning of the speaker, whose words are spoken only as signs.

Woe to those who turn away from your light, and love to linger in their darkness! It is as if they turned their backs upon you, they are held fast in the shadow cast on them by their works of the flesh, and yet what delights them even there they still receive from the brightness shed by your light. But love of the shadow makes the soul's eye too lazy and weak to endure your sight. Then a man is wrapped more and more in darkness, while he is inclined to seek whatever his weakness can endure more easily. Gradually he is unable to see what is supreme, and to think evil whatever deceives his blindness or attracts his poverty,[36] or pains him when held captive. In this he suffers the punishment of his defection, and what is just cannot be evil.

44   You cannot grasp with bodily sense or attention of the soul any changeable thing you see which is not possessed by some form of number: take this

away, and it falls back to nothing. Therefore
have no doubt that there is some eternal and unchangeable form, in order that changeable things
may not cease, but, with measured movement and
distinct and varied forms, may pass through their
temporal course.[37] This eternal form is neither
contained, nor, as it were, spread in space, nor prolonged nor altered in time; it enables those other
things to receive their forms, and according to
their nature to realise and use the numbers proper
to place and time.

17.45   Every changeable thing must necessarily be able
to realise its form. Just as we call what can change
changeable, so I should call what can receive its
form 'formable.' Nothing can give its form to
itself, since nothing can give itself what it does not
possess, and indeed a thing is given its form, that it
may possess its form. Hence, if anything possesses
a form, there is no need for it to receive what it
possesses, but, if it does not possess a form, it cannot receive from itself what it does not possess.
Nothing, then, as we have said, can give itself a
form. What more can we say about the changeable character of body and soul? We said enough
earlier on. So we conclude that body and soul are
given their forms by a form which is unchangeable and everlasting. To this form it was said:
*Thou shalt change them, and they shall be
changed. But thou art always the selfsame, and
thy years shall not fail.*[38] By years which shall not
fail the inspired writer means eternity. It is also

said of this form that *remaining in herself the same, she reneweth all things.*[39]

From this, too, we understand that all things are ruled by providence. If everything which exists would become nothing, were the form wholly withdrawn, the unchangeable form itself is their providence. For it makes all changeable things subsist, and realise themselves and act through the numbers proper to their forms. They would not be, if it were not present. Every man advancing on the way to wisdom, perceives, when he attentively reflects on the whole of creation, that wisdom shows herself to him cheerfully on his way, and comes to meet him in every act of providence. He becomes the more eager to finish his journey, as the journey becomes more delightful through that wisdom, which he ardently longs to reach.

46   If, besides that which exists and does not live, and that which exists and lives but does not understand, and that which exists and lives and understands, you find some other kind of creature, only then may you say there is something good, which does not come from God.

These three kinds of thing can be expressed by two words, by calling them body and life. For that life which is only life and has no understanding—of animals, for example—and that life which has understanding—such as that of men—are both rightly called life. But these two kinds of thing, that is, body and life, when regarded as creatures (the Creator Himself has life, and this is supreme life)—these two created things, body and life, be-

cause, as we explained above, they are able to receive forms and because they fall to nothing if the
form is altogether lost, show well enough that they
derive their existence from that form which is always the same.

Therefore all good things, great or small, can
only come from God. What is greater among
creatures than the life which has understanding,
and what can be less than body? However defective they may become, and however near they may
approach towards non-existence, some form always remains if they are to exist at all. But whatever form remains to a thing which is defective,
comes from that form which can have no defect,
and which does not allow even the movements of
things, whether the things are growing worse or
better, to escape the law of their numbers. Hence
whatever we observe in the nature of things to be
worthy of praise, whether we judge it worthy of
little or great praise, should be referred to the most
excellent, unutterable praise of its Creator. Have
you any objection to this?

FREE WILL IS GOOD

18.47 *E.*—I confess I am sufficiently convinced. There
is evidence, so far as is possible in this life and for
beings such as ourselves, that God exists and that
all good things come from God. Everything
which exists comes from God, whether it has
understanding and life and existence, or whether

it has only life and existence, or whether it only has existence.

Now let us turn to the third question, whether it can be shown that free will is to be counted among good things. If this is proved, I shall not hesitate to grant that God has given it to us and that it ought to have been given.

A.—You have remembered correctly what we proposed to discuss, and have been quick to notice that the second question has already been settled. But you should have seen that the third is also solved.

You said you thought free choice of will ought not to have been given, because by it we sin. Against your view I argued [40] that we could not act rightly except by this free choice of will,[41] and I claimed that God had given it rather for this purpose. You replied that free will ought to have been given us in the same way that justice has been given, for we can only use justice for its right purpose. This reply of yours forced us into that complicated discussion in which I tried to prove to you that good things, great and small, only come from God. This could not be shown so clearly, unless we first refuted the wicked opinion of the fool who said in his heart, *There is no God.*[42] We argued on so great a matter according to our poor ability, but God Himself helped us over the dangerous passage.

These two propositions, that God exists and that all good things come from Him, we already held with firm faith, but we have examined them so carefully that the third point also becomes most clear, that free will is to be counted among good things.

48   In a former discussion we decided it was plain that the body is a lower kind of thing than the soul, and therefore that the soul is a greater good than the body. If, then, we find among bodily goods some which man can use wrongly, yet if we do not say for this reason that they ought not to have been given us, because we agree that they are good, it will not be surprising if there are also goods in the soul which we can use wrongly, but which, being good, cannot have been given except by the source of all good.

You see how much good the body lacks when it has no hands; nevertheless a man uses his hands wrongly if he does cruel or shameful acts with them. If you saw someone without feet, you would agree that an important good was lacking to bodily perfection, and yet you would not deny that a man used his feet wrongly if he used them to harm someone or to dishonour himself. We see the light with our eyes, and with them we distinguish bodily forms. This is the element of greatest beauty in the body, and hence the eyes are given the highest position, the position of honour, and their use serves to guard the health and to assist life in many other ways. Yet men often act shamefully through their eyes and make their eyes minister to their lust. You see what good the face lacks without the eyes, but when we possess them, who else gave them than God, the giver of all good things?

You value these bodily organs, and, disregarding those who use them wrongly, you praise Him who has given as such good things. So too free will, without which no one can live rightly, must be a God-given good, and you must admit rather that those who use this good wrongly are to be condemned than that He who gave it ought not to have given it.

49 E.—First, I should like you to prove to me that free will is a good, and then I should grant that God gave it us, because I agree that all good things come from God.

A.—Did I not prove this to you with much labour in our first discussion, when you agreed that all beauty and every bodily form are derived from the form which is supreme over all things, that is, the truth, and when you agreed they are good? Truth itself says in the Gospel that our very hairs are numbered.[43] Have you forgotten what we said about the supremacy of number and about its power extending from end to end? It would be sheer folly to count as good our hairs, which are least in size and importance, and not to trace them to their cause. God is the source of all good things; the greatest and the least good things come from Him, from whom comes every good thing. It would be sheer folly in view of this to hesitate about free will, without which even those who live the worst lives grant that it is impossible to live rightly.

Now answer, please, which you think is the better in us, that thing without which we can, or that thing without which we cannot, live rightly.

E.—Please forgive me; I am ashamed of my blindness. As everyone knows, that without which there is no good life is far nobler.

A.—Will you deny that a one-eyed man can live rightly?

E.—I am not so utterly mad.

A.—Since, then, you grant that the eye is a good to the body, but that its loss does not prevent us from living rightly, will you not hold that free will is a good, since without it no one lives rightly?

50 Take justice, which no one uses wrongly. This is counted among the highest goods proper to man, and among all the soul's virtues which go to make up a right and worthy life. No one uses wrongly either prudence or fortitude or temperance. In all these, as in justice itself which you mentioned, right reason reigns, without which no virtues can exist. And no one can use right reason wrongly.

19 These are great goods, but you ought to remember that, not to speak of great goods, not even the least can exist except as coming from Him from whom comes all good, that is, from God. That was the conclusion of our earlier discussion, and you willingly agreed many times.

The virtues, then, by which we live rightly, are great goods, but all kinds of bodily beauty, without which we can live rightly, are the least goods. The powers of the soul, without which we cannot live rightly, are the middle goods. No one uses the virtues wrongly, but anyone can use the other goods, the middle and the least, wrongly as well as rightly. No one uses virtue wrongly, because the work of virtue is the good use of those things which we are capable of using wrongly. No one makes a bad use when he makes a good use. Hence the magnificent abundance of God's goodness has furnished us not only with great goods, but also with the middle and the least. His goodness should be praised more highly for great than for middle goods, more for middle than for least, but for all more than if He had not given all.

51 E.—I agree. But, since we are discussing free will, and since we see that it uses other things either rightly or wrongly, I am puzzled by the question, how free will is to be counted among those things which we use.

A.—In the same way that we know by reason all those things of which we have exact knowledge,[44] and yet reason itself is counted among the things we know by reason. Have you forgotten that when we inquired what is known by the reason, you agreed that reason itself is known by reason? Do not be surprised, therefore, if we use other things by means of free will, that we can also use free will itself by means of itself. The will, which uses other things, in a certain way uses itself, just as the reason, which knows other things, knows itself. Memory not only grasps all other things which we remember, but it also, since we do not forget that we have a memory, in a certain way retains itself within us; it remembers not only other

things, but also itself, or rather through memory
we remember other things, and also memory itself.

52   So, when the will, which is a middle good, clings
to the unchangeable good, not as a private possession but as common to all—in the same way as the
truth, about which we have said much, however
inadequately—then man possesses the happy life.
This happy life itself, which consists in the disposition of the soul when it clings to the unchangeable good, is the proper and principal good for
man.   In this lie all the virtues which no one can
use wrongly.   We understand sufficiently that,
though these are important and principal goods in
man, they are not held in common, but individually, by every man.

It is through clinging to truth and wisdom,
which is common to all, that all become wise and
happy.   One man does not become happy through
the happiness of another man.   When one man
imitates another in order to become happy, he
seeks to become happy by the same means by
which he sees the other has become happy, that is,
by means of the unchangeable truth which is common to all.

Nor is one man prudent through another's prudence, nor brave through another's bravery, nor
temperate through another's temperance, nor is a
man made just through another's justice.   But he
becomes such by conforming his soul to the unchangeable principles and illuminations of the virtues,[45] which have incorruptible life in truth itself
and wisdom which is common to all.   The model

this man has set up for himself, is endowed with these virtues, and he has conformed and attached his soul to their principles.

53   The will, then, if it clings to the unchangeable good which is common to all, obtains the principal and important human goods, though the will itself is a middle good. But the will sins, if it turns away from the unchangeable good which is common to all, and turns towards a private good, whether outside or below it. It turns towards a private good when it wishes to be its own master—outside, when it is anxious to know the private affairs of someone else, or whatever is not its own concern, and below it, when it loves bodily pleasure. Thus a man who becomes proud, curious, and self-indulgent, is caught up in another life, which compared to the higher life is death. This life, however, is under the rule of Divine Providence, which puts everything in its proper place and assigns to everyone his due.

So it comes about that those goods which are sought by sinners are by no means evil, nor is free will evil, which we have found must be counted among certain middle goods. Evil is the turning of the will away from the unchangeable good, and towards changeable good. Since this turning from one to the other is free and unforced, the pain which follows as a punishment is fitting and just.

THE CAUSE OF SIN IS NOT POSITIVE BUT NEGATIVE

20.54   Perhaps you will ask, since the will moves when it turns from the unchangeable to the changeable good, how this movement arises. The movement is certainly evil, though free will must be counted as a good, since without it we cannot live rightly. The movement, the turning away of the will from Lord God, is undoubtedly a sin—but surely we cannot call God the cause of sin? This movement cannot therefore come from God. What, then, is its source?

When you ask this question, if I answer that I do not know, you will perhaps be disappointed, but yet I shall be answering truly. For that which is nothing cannot be known. Only keep firm your sense of reverence towards God, so that no good may occur either to your senses, your intelligence, or your thoughts in any way, which you do not acknowledge to be from God. Nothing of any kind is to be found which does not come from God.[46] Recognise God at once as author of everything in which you see measure, number, and order. If you take these entirely away, nothing whatever will be left. You may say there remains some incipient form, where you find neither measure nor number nor order. But, since, when these are present, the form is perfect, you must not speak even of an incipient form: it seems to stand only as material to be perfected by the artist. For, if the perfection of the form is a good, the beginning of the form must already be a good. When all good is completely taken away, there will remain not even a trace—absolutely nothing.⁴⁷ [47] All good is from God; therefore no kind of thing exists which is not from God. Hence that movement of turning away, which we agree to be sin, is a defective movement, and a defect comes from nothing. Notice, then, what is its source and be sure it does not come from God.

Yet, since the defect lies in the will, it is under our control. If you fear it, you must simply not desire it; if you do not desire it, it will not occur.⁴⁸ [48] What greater security can you have than to live that life in which nothing you do not desire can happen to you? But, though man fell through his own will, he cannot rise through his own will. Therefore let us believe firmly that God's right hand, that is, Our Lord Jesus Christ, is extended out to us from on high; ⁴⁹ [49] let us await this help with sure hope, and let us desire it with ardent charity.

If you still think any further question should be asked about the source of sin—I myself think there is no need at all—if you really think there is, we must put off the discussion to another time.

E.—I quite agree with your wish to put off the further problems to another time. I should not admit your view that the question is finished.

BOOK THREE

THE CAUSE OF SIN LIES IN THE WILL

1.1 *E.*–It is fairly clear to me that free will must be counted among goods, and not among the least of them, and therefore we are bound to agree that God gave it, and that it was rightly given. If you think this is a convenient time, I should like you to tell me what is the cause of that movement by which this will turns away from the unchangeable good which is common to all, and turns towards private goods, whether belonging to others or below it, indeed to all changeable goods.[1]

A.–What need is there to know this?

E.–Because, if the will which we are given, of its very nature moves as it does, it cannot help turning in this direction. There cannot be any fault, if nature and necessity compel it.

A.–Do you like this movement, or dislike it?

E.–I dislike it.

A.–Then you blame it.

E.–Yes, I blame it.

A.–So you blame an inculpable movement of the soul.

E.–I do not blame an inculpable movement of the soul. I do not know whether there is any fault when it leaves the unchangeable good, and turns to changeable goods.

A.–Then you blame what you do not know.

E.—Do not quibble about a phrase. Though I said: 'I do not know whether there is any fault,' yet I really meant that undoubtedly there is a fault. By my way of saying it I ridiculed any doubt about a matter so clear.[2]

A.—You see what a certain truth it is, since it makes you forget so quickly what you just said. If that movement is due to nature or necessity, it cannot deserve any blame whatever; but you hold so firmly that it does deserve blame, that you think doubt is absurd about a matter so clear. Why then do you think you ought to assert, even perhaps with some doubt, what you yourself demonstrate to be plainly false? You said: 'If the free will we are given of its very nature moves as it does, it cannot help turning in this direction. There cannot be any fault if nature and necessity compel it.' You should have known for certain that the movement is not due to the will's nature, since you are certain it deserves blame.

E.—I said that the movement deserved blame, and therefore that I disliked it, and I have no doubt it ought to be blamed. But I deny that the soul deserves blame, when this movement draws it from the unchangeable good to changeable goods, if its nature is such that the movement is necessary.

2 *A.*—Whose is that movement, which you agree is certainly worthy of blame?

E.—I see it is in the soul,[3] but I do not know whose it is.

A.—Do you deny that the soul moves with that movement?

E.—No.

A.—Then do you deny that a movement by which a stone moves is a movement of the stone? I am not speaking of the movement by which we move it, or by which any other force moves it, as for instance if it is thrown up in the air, but I am speaking of the movement by which of its own accord it falls back on the ground.

E.—I do not deny that the movement by which, as you say, it turns and comes down to the ground again is a movement of the stone, but I say it is due to its nature. If the soul has the same kind of movement, it is certainly natural, and it cannot rightly be blamed for a natural movement. Even if the movement leads to its destruction, this is forced by necessity of nature. Thus, since we do not hesitate to call this movement culpable, we must absolutely deny that it is natural. Therefore it is not like the natural movement by which the stone moves.

A.—Have we established anything in our two earlier discussions?

E.—Certainly, we have.

A.—I think you remember we were fairly satisfied in the first discussion that the mind becomes the slave of passion only through its own will.[4] It cannot be forced to a shameful act by anything above it, nor by anything equal, for this would be unjust, nor by anything below it, for this would be impossible. The movement, therefore, must be due to itself, by which it turns its will to enjoyment of the creature from enjoyment of the Creator. If this movement is called culpable—and to doubt this is, in your opinion, absurd—it is certainly not natural, but voluntary.   In one respect it is like the movement by which the stone comes down to the ground again, because, as the one belongs to the stone, so the other belongs to the soul; but in another respect it is unlike, because the stone is not able to check the movement by which it comes down, whereas the soul does not move against its will to leave the higher and choose the lower.[5] Hence the movement is natural to the stone, but voluntary to the soul.

Consequently if anyone says the stone sins because it falls down through its own weight, he is not perhaps more stupid than the stone but he is certainly considered mad.   But we convict the soul of sin, when we prove that it abandons what is higher and prefers the enjoyment of what is lower.

So what need is there to ask the source of that movement by which the will turns from the unchangeable good to the changeable good?   We agree that it belongs only to the soul, and is voluntary and therefore culpable; and the whole value of teaching in this matter consists in its power to make us censure and check this movement, and turn our wills away from temporal things below us to enjoyment of the everlasting good.[6]

3   *E.*—I see; I almost feel and grasp the truth of what you say.   I am aware of nothing more surely and deeply than that I have a will, and by it move to enjoy something.   Indeed I do not know what I

can call my own, if the will is not mine by which I assert myself for or against something. So, if I do wrong through my will, who is responsible except myself? Since a good God has made me, and I cannot do any good action except by my will, it is fairly clear that it was given for this purpose by the good God.

If the movement by which the will turns in different directions were not voluntary and under our control, a man would not deserve praise or blame, when he, as it were, turns the hinge of his will up or down.[7] Nor would it be at all necessary to warn him to leave temporal and gain eternal good, or to try to live well and not ill. Yet whoever thinks that such advice should not be given to men, ought to be banished from among men.

GOD'S FOREKNOWLEDGE

2.4   This being so, I am troubled exceedingly by the question how God can have foreknowledge of all future events, and yet how there can be no necessity for us to sin. If anyone says an event can happen contrary to God's foreknowledge, he is attempting to destroy the foreknowledge of God, and this is most inane and blasphemous.

Hence, if God foreknew that the first man would sin—and this must be granted by anyone who agrees with me that God has foreknowledge of all future events—if, therefore, this is so, I do not say that God should not have created him, for He created him good, nor that his sin could in any way be prejudicial to God, seeing that He created him good. No, in creating him God showed His goodness, and in punishing him He showed His justice, and in saving him He showed His mercy. So I do not say God should not have created him, but I say this: since God had foreknowledge that he would sin, it must have happened of necessity, because God foreknew it would happen. How, then, is the will free, when the necessity seems so inescapable?

5   A.—You have knocked vigorously. I hope God in His mercy will come to the door and open it as we stand knocking.[8] I think, however, that the greater part of mankind is troubled by this question only because they do not inquire in the right spirit, and are quicker to excuse their sins than to confess them.

Some [9] are glad to suppose that no divine providence presides over human affairs, and, abandoning soul and body to mere chance, they deliver themselves to be buffeted and torn by passions. They deny divine justice and cheat the justice of man; they think they can get rid of their accusers through the help of Fortune. Yet they are accustomed to mould or paint Fortune as blind, so that they may be superior to her whom they believe is their ruler, or may admit that these words and feelings of theirs are equally blind. We can agree without absurdity that all their actions fall out by chance, since each is indeed a fall. However, I think we argued sufficiently in our second discussion against this foolish and unbalanced error.[10]

Others, on the other hand, while not daring to deny that God's providence governs men's lives, prefer to commit the crime and the blunder of supposing it is weak or unjust or evil, rather than humbly to confess their sins.

All these people should let themselves be persuaded, when they think of that Being who is most good, just, and powerful, that the goodness, justice, and power of God are far greater than anything they can conceive. They should understand, when they reflect on themselves, that it would be their duty to thank God, even if He had willed them to be a lower kind of being than they are, and they should cry out from the very depths of their hearts: *I said, O Lord, be Thou merciful to me. Heal my soul, for I have sinned against Thee.*[11] Thus they would be led to wisdom by the sure paths of God's mercy; they would not be puffed up by success, nor depressed by failure in their inquiries; knowledge would make them more capable of seeing,[12] and ignorance more restrained in the search.

I am sure that you are already persuaded of this; but notice how easily I answer so profound a problem, after you have made a few answers to my questions.

3.6   This is no doubt what puzzles and troubles you, the apparent contradiction between saying that God has foreknowledge of all future events, and that we sin freely and not of necessity. If God has foreknowledge that man will sin, then, you say, man must necessarily sin. But if he must do so, his sin is not a result of choice, but is rather a fixed and inevitable necessity. You fear that the conclusion of this reasoning will be either blasphemous denial of God's foreknowledge of all future events, or, if this is impossible, admission that we sin of necessity and not freely. Is there any other point which troubles you?

E.—Nothing else at present.

A.—So in your opinion everything foreknown by God comes about of necessity, and not freely.

E.—I certainly think so.

A.—Pay attention, then, reflect and tell me, if you can, what will be your will tomorrow—to do wrong or right?

E.—I do not know.

A.—But do you think God does not know?

E.—Certainly not.

A.—Then, if He knows what you will will tomorrow, and foresees what all men will will in the future, whether they exist now or will exist, far more does He foresee what He will do to the just and to the unjust.

E.—Of course, if I say God foreknows my actions, I should say much more confidently that He foreknows His own actions, and foresees clearly what He will do.

A.—Then are you not afraid of the retort that He too will act of necessity and not freely, if everything that God foreknows happens of necessity and not freely?

E.—When I said that everything happened of necessity which God foreknew, I was referring only to what happens in creation, not to what happens in God Himself. Things do not happen in God, but have eternal being.

A.—So God does nothing in His creation?

E.—He has fixed once for all the order of events in the created universe; He does not make new decisions.

A.—Does He not make anyone happy?

E.—Certainly He does.

A.—Then He is responsible, when the man becomes happy.

E.—Yes.

A.—Then, if, for instance, you will be happy a year from now, He will make you happy a year hence.

E.—Yes.

A.—So He foreknows now what He will do in a year.

E.—He has always foreknown it. Now again I agree that He foreknows this, if this is what will happen.

7 *A.*—Tell me, please: are you not His creature, or will your happiness not occur in you?

E.—Of course I am His creature, and my happiness will occur in me.

A.—Therefore your happiness will occur in you of necessity and not freely through God's action.

E.—His will is my necessity.

A.—So you will be happy against your will.

E.—If it was in my power to be happy, I should be happy now. I wish to be happy now, and am not, because it is not I but God who makes me happy.

A.—The voice of truth speaks clearly in what you say. You could not be aware of anything in our power, if not of our actions when we will. Nothing is so fully in our power as the will itself, for it is ready at once and without delay to act as we will.[13] We can truly say, we grow old [14] of necessity and not of our own will; or, we are ill of necessity and not of our own will; [15] or, we die of necessity and not of our own will; and so in other matters of the sort; but no one would be so mad as to venture to say, we do not will of our own will.

Therefore, though God foreknows what we shall will in the future, this does not imply that we do not make use of our will. With regard to happiness, you said you do not make yourself happy, as if I denied it. I say that when you will be happy, you will be happy through your will and not against it. Because God foreknows your future happiness, and because nothing can happen otherwise than as He has foreknown—to deny this would be to deny His foreknowledge—it does not follow that we must suppose you will not be happy through your own will. This would be absurd, and very far from true.

The foreknowledge of God, which is certain even to-day of your future happiness, does not take away your will to be happy, when you begin to be happy. So too, if your will in the future is sinful, it will not cease to be your will, because God has foreknown what will happen.

8   I want you to realise how blind we should be if

we said: If God has foreknown my future will, because nothing can happen contrary to His foreknowledge, I must necessarily will what He has foreknown. But, if this is necessary, I must admit that I will of necessity, and not through my will. How utterly foolish this would be! How could it be true that nothing happens contrary to God's foreknowledge, if He foreknows that something will be willed, when nothing will be willed?

I pass over the equally monstrous assertion, which I attributed just now to the same speaker: I am bound to will in this way. He assumes necessity, and tries to eliminate will. If he is bound to will, how can he will, if there is no will?

If, instead of saying this, he says his will itself is not in his power, because he is bound to will, we shall confront him with your own words, when I asked whether you would be happy against your will. You replied that you would be happy already, if it were in your power, for you said you willed it, but could not yet achieve it. I pointed out that the voice of truth spoke in you, for we cannot deny that we have the power, unless the will is absent. But when we will, if the will itself is absent, we do not will. If it is impossible that we should not will when we will, the will must be present when we will. Nothing else is in our power, if not what is present to us when we will. Our will would not be a will, if it were not in our power. Moreover, since it is in our power, it is free. What is not in our power, or may not be in our power, is not free to us.

Hence we do not deny that God has foreknowledge of all future events, and yet that we will what we will. Since He has foreknowledge of our will, that will must exist, of which he has foreknowledge. It will be a will, because He has foreknowledge of a will. Nor could it be a will, if it were not in our power. So He has foreknowledge also of our power over it. My power is not taken away by His foreknowledge, but I shall have it all the more certainly because He whose foreknowledge is not mistaken has foreknown that I shall have it.[16]

E.—I do not deny any longer that all God has foreknown comes about necessarily, and that He forethat our will remains free and in our power.

TO FORESEE SIN IS NOT TO CAUSE IT

4.9 A.—What, then, is your difficulty? Have you forgotten what we decided in our first discussion? Will you deny that no one compels us to sin, either above us or below us or equal to us, but that we do so through our own will?

E.—I do not venture to deny any of this. Yet, I admit, I do not yet see how these two, God's foreknowledge of our sins and our free will in sinning, knows our sins, yet at the same time in such a way do not contradict one another. We must admit God is just and has foreknowledge. But I should like to know how it can be just to punish sins which are bound to occur, or how future events which He has foreknown, are not bound to occur, or how we can avoid holding the Creator responsible for what is bound to happen in His creature.

10 *A.*—On what grounds do you think our free will contradicts God's foreknowledge? Because it is foreknowledge or because it is God's foreknowledge?

E.—More because it is God's foreknowledge.

A.—Is that so? If you foreknew someone would sin, would he be bound to sin?

E.—Yes, he would be bound to sin. I should not have foreknowledge, unless what I foreknew was certain.

A.—Then it is not because God foreknows it that what He foreknows is bound to happen, but only because it is foreknowledge. If what is foreknown is not certain, there is no foreknowledge.

E.—I agree. But what does this imply?

A.—It implies, unless I am mistaken, that you would not necessarily compel a man to sin by foreknowing his sin. Your foreknowledge would not be the cause of his sin, though undoubtedly he would sin; otherwise you would not foreknow that this would happen. Therefore these two are not contradictory, your foreknowledge and someone else's free act. So too God compels no one to sin, though He foresees those who will sin by their own will.

11 Why, then, should not one who is just punish what he does not compel, though he foreknows it? When you remember past events you do not compel them to have happened, and in the same way God does not compel future events to happen by

His foreknowledge of them. You remember actions you have performed, but you have not done all the actions you remember, and in the same way God foreknows everything of which He is the cause, but He is not Himself the cause of everything He foreknows. He is not the cause of evil actions, but He is their just avenger.

So you may now understand how justly God punishes sin, for He does not do what He knows will happen. If He ought not to punish sinners because He foresees they will sin, neither ought He to reward those who act rightly, because equally He foresees they will act rightly. Let us then admit that His foreknowledge is such that He is aware of all future events, and His justice is such that sin, being voluntarily committed and not brought about by His foreknowledge, is judged and punished.

5.12   Let us turn to the third point you raised, why we must not hold the Creator responsible for what happens necessarily in His creation.[17] We should remember that principle of religion which tells us clearly that we ought to give thanks to our Creator.[18] It would be most just to praise His profuse generosity, even if we had been placed in a lower rank of creation. Our soul, though corrupted with sin, is higher and better than if it were changed into the light seen by our eyes. And yet you see how greatly souls, even when they have surrendered to the bodily senses, praise God for this glorious light.

Therefore, do not be troubled by the blame

accorded to sinful souls, and do not say in your heart it would have been better had they never existed. They are blamed in comparison with themselves, when it is realised what they would be, if they had chosen not to sin. God, their Creator, deserves the highest praise that men can render, not only because He treats them justly when they sin, but also because He has created them with so noble a nature that, even when stained with sin, they are in no way surpassed in dignity by bodily light, for which He is also justly praised.

13   I want you to be careful, too, while perhaps not going so far as to say that it would have been better had they not lived, not to say that they ought to have been made differently. For whatever reason shows you with truth to be better, be assured that God has made this, He who is the Creator of all good things.[19] It is not good reason but the vice of envy, if you wish that the lower should not exist, because you think something higher should be created. It is as though, because you saw the heavens, you wished there should be no earth. This would be utterly wrong. You would rightly complain, if you saw the earth had been created and the heavens left out, because then you might say that it should have been made in accordance with the idea you could form of the heavens. Having seen that the design you wished to produce for the earth has been carried out, but is called the heavens instead of the earth, I think that, as you have not been deprived of something better, you should by no means feel envious, when a lesser thing is made, and earth exists.

Again there is such variety in the different parts of the earth that we can think of no earthly beauty, in its full extent, which God the Creator of all has not produced. From the fairest and richest land to the most barren and infertile, we pass so gradually from one to another, that none can be called bad except in comparison with that which is better. So you climb through all the degrees of excellence, until you reach the supreme kind of land, yet you would not wish this to exist alone.[20] Now, what a difference there is between the earth in all its expanse and heaven! Between them come liquid and air, and from these four elements are composed all the many kinds and forms of things, countless to us, but all numbered by God.

There may be something in nature which your reason cannot conceive, but it is impossible that a thing should not exist which you conceive truly. You cannot conceive anything better in creation, which has escaped the Creator's thought. The human soul is by nature in contact with the divine types on which it depends. When it says, this would be better than that, it sees this in the type with which it is in contact, provided it tells the truth and sees what it says it sees. It should believe, therefore, that God has done what through true reason it knows He ought to have done, even though it does not see this in actual fact. Even though man could not see the heavens with his eyes, and yet by true reason concluded that a thing of this kind ought to have been made, he should believe this had happened, though he did not see it with his eyes. He would not see in his thoughts that it ought to have been done, unless he saw it in those types through which all is accomplished. What does not exist in them, one can no more truly see in his thoughts than it can have true existence.

14   It is a common mistake, when something better is conceived in the mind, not to look for it in the right place. It is as though a man, grasping with his reason perfect roundness, should be annoyed not to find it in a nut, having never seen any round object except this fruit. In the same way some people see with perfect truth that a creature is better if, while possessing free will, it remains always fixed upon God and never sins; then, reflecting on men's sins, they are grieved, not because they continue to sin, but because they were created. They say: He should have made us such that we never willed to sin, but always to enjoy the unchangeable truth.

They should not lament or be angry. God has not compelled men to sin just because He created them and gave them the power to choose between sinning and not sinning. There are angels who have never sinned and never will sin. If you are pleased by the creature which perseveres in the will not to sin, you must not doubt that you are right in preferring this creature to that which is sinful. But, just as you prefer it in thought, so God the Creator has preferred it in His ordering of things. You must believe that such a being exists on high in heaven. For if the Creator has shown His goodness in creating that being whose future sins He foresees, He will certainly have shown His goodness in creating a being whom He foreknew would not sin.

15   A sublime creature such as this has everlasting happiness, enjoying forever its Creator, and deserving this by its constant will to uphold justice. Then too the sinful creature has its appointed place, for, though it has lost happiness through its sin, it has not given up the power to recover happiness. It excels indeed the creature possessed forever by a will to sin; between the latter and that other which is constant in its will for justice, this stands in the middle, recovering its position through the humility of penance.

Such is the generosity of God's goodness that He has not refrained from creating even that creature which He foreknew would not only sin, but remain in the will to sin.[21] As a runaway horse is better than a stone which does not run away because it lacks self-movement and sense perception, so the creature is more excellent which sins by free will than that which does not sin only because it has no free will. I should praise wine as a thing good of its kind, and I should blame a man who was drunk with this wine, and yet, while praising the wine through which he was drunk, I should rank higher the man whom I had blamed and while he was drunk. So that which has been created a bodily thing, deserves praise in its proper rank, while those deserve blame who, through immoderate use of it, turn away from the perception of truth. Yet even these, depraved and drunken, are nobler than this other thing, laudable in its own rank, greediness for which caused their ruin; but not owing to their vices, but to the dignity of their lasting nature.

16   Therefore the soul is always superior to the body, and no sinful soul, whatever its fall, is ever changed into a body; its nature as a soul is never entirely taken away, and so it never ceases to be superior to a body. Among bodies light holds the first place. Consequently the lowest soul should be ranked above the highest body, and while it is possible that some other body ranks higher than the body united to a soul, no body ranks higher than the soul itself.

Why, then, should not God be praised, praised indeed beyond utterance, since He has made souls which will abide by the laws of justice, and has made other souls which He has foreseen will sin or even persevere in sin, for even these latter are better than those creatures which cannot sin because they have no rational and free choice of will? These latter again are better than the brightest splendour of any bodily thing whatever, a splendour which some men worship, most erroneously, as the substance of Almighty God Himself.[22]

In the order of bodily creatures, from the choirs of the stars to the number of our hairs, the beauty of these good things is so graduated that it would be foolish to ask why this or that exists. All things are created in their proper order. How much more foolish would it be to ask the same question about a soul, since, in whatever degree its beauty is lessened or maimed, without doubt it will always [23] surpass in dignity any bodily thing!

17 Reason and utility have different standards of judgment. Reason judges by the light of truth, and with right judgment it puts the lesser below the greater. Utility is influenced for the most part by habitual convenience, and judges that to be higher which truth proves to be of less value. Reason ranks the heavenly bodies far above the earthly bodies. Yet what carnal man would not prefer that many stars should be lacking in heaven, rather than that a single bush should be lacking in his field or a single cow in his herd? Grown-up people either disregard, or at least patiently await the correction of, the judgments of children who prefer the death of anybody and everybody, with the exception of some few near and dear to them, to the death of their sparrow; and that all the more if the person in question frightens them, and a sparrow is beautiful and sings. So too those who judge ignorantly, praise God for lesser creatures, since they appreciate them better with their bodily senses, and praise Him little, if at all, for higher and better creatures, or even try to blame Him and suggest improvements, or believe He is not their Creator. When men, who with the growth of the soul have advanced towards wisdom, find this, they should accustom themselves either to disregard such judgments altogether, if they cannot correct them, or to endure them calmly until they can correct them.

6.18 This being so, we are far from the truth if we

hold the Creator responsible for the sins of the creature, even though what He foreknows is bound to happen. You say you do not see how you can help holding Him responsible for what is bound to happen in His creature: but I on the contrary do not find any ground—and I assert none can be found, indeed, none exists—for holding Him responsible for what is bound to happen in His creature, coming about as it does through a sinful will.

If anyone should say, I should prefer to have no existence rather than an unhappy existence, I answer: That is a lie. You are unhappy now, yet you do not wish to die, only because you wish to exist. Though you do not wish to be unhappy, nevertheless you wish to exist. Be thankful that you have your wish to exist, in order that you may be delivered from the existence you have against your wish. You exist according to your will, and you exist unhappily against your will. But if you are ungrateful for being granted your wish to exist, you are rightly compelled to exist as you do not wish. Therefore I praise the goodness of the Creator because you have what you wish, though you are ungrateful for it; I praise the justice of what He ordains, in that you endure ungratefully what you do not wish.

19   If he should say, I do not wish to die because I prefer to exist unhappily than not to exist at all, but because I do not wish to be still more unhappy after death, I reply: If this is unjust, you will not

be unhappy; but if it is just, let us praise Him by whose law this will be the case.

If he says: How am I to know that I shall not be unhappy, if this is unjust, I answer: If you have power over yourself, either you will not be unhappy, or you will be unhappy justly, because you have governed yourself unjustly. Or else, having the will and not the strength to govern yourself justly, you are not in your own power, but in that of no one at all or of someone else. If you are in no one's power, this is either against your will or according to your will; but it cannot be against your will, unless some force has conquered you, yet no force can conquer you if you are in no one's power. And if through your own will you are in no one's power, again we must conclude that you are in your own. Thus, either you are unhappy justly by governing yourself unjustly, or whatever happens to you is according to your will, and you have cause to give thanks to the goodness of your Creator. If you are not in your own power, either a stronger power or a weaker controls you. If a weaker, it is your own fault, and your unhappiness is just, for you could overcome a weaker power if you wished. If a stronger power controls you and you are weaker, by no means will you be right in thinking so rightful a disposition unjust.

Hence it is quite true to say: If this is unjust, you will not be unhappy; but if it is just, let us praise Him by whose law this will be the case.

7.20   Let us suppose that he says: I prefer to be unhappy than not to exist at all, because I already exist. But if I could have been consulted before I existed, I should have chosen not to exist rather than to exist unhappily. Now it contributes to my unhappiness that, although unhappy, I am afraid of not existing. I am actually not wishing what I ought to wish, for I ought to wish not to be rather than to be unhappy. I admit that now I prefer to be unhappy than not to exist; but the more foolish this wish is, the more unhappy it is, and the more unhappy, the more clearly I see I ought not to wish it. I reply: Be all the more careful not to make a mistake when you think you see the truth. If you were happy, you would certainly prefer to exist rather than not to exist. Now, however, when you are unhappy, you prefer even to exist unhappily than not to exist at all, while at the same time not wishing to be unhappy.

So do your best to consider how great a good is existence, which both the happy and the unhappy desire. If you consider this carefully, you will realise that you are unhappy in the degree in which you fail to approach that which exists supremely, that you prefer non-existence to unhappy existence in the degree in which you fail to see that which exists supremely, and therefore that you wish to exist in spite of this because you depend upon Him who supremely is.

21　　　If, then, you wish to avoid unhappiness, love within yourself this wish to exist. The more you wish to exist, the closer you will approach to that which exists supremely; so give thanks now that you exist. Granted that you are lower than the happy: but you are higher than those things which do not have even the will to be happy, though many of these are praised by the unhappy. Everything is rightly praised for the very fact that it exists, for from the very fact that it exists, it is good.

The more you love to exist, the more will you desire eternal life and the more you will wish to be so disposed that your inclinations be not temporal, be not marked and branded with love for temporal things. These temporal things have no existence before they exist, and while they exist they pass away, and when they have passed away they will exist no more. When they are still in the future, they do not yet exist, and when they are past, they are now no more. How then shall we hold them lastingly, seeing that the beginning of their existence is their passage into non-existence? [24] But he who loves existence appreciates these things so far as they exist, and loves that which has eternal existence. If his love of the former rendered him unstable, he will be given constancy through his love of the latter; and if he was weak through the love of passing things, he will be made strong in the love of what is lasting. He will stand firm, and he will gain that very existence which he desired when he feared non-existence, and when he could not stand firm, being caught in the love of passing things.

You should, therefore, be very pleased, and by no means displeased, when you prefer even to be unhappy than not to be unhappy, because then you

would cease to exist.   If to this elementary will to
exist little by little you add further existence you
will rise upwards towards that which exists supremely, and thus you will check any such fall as
that by which the lowest in the scale of existence
passes into non-existence, carrying with it the
strength of its lover.   Hence he who prefers not to
exist rather than to exist unhappily, since his non-
existence is impossible, must exist unhappily.   But
he who has more love for existence than hatred for
unhappiness, should get rid of what he hates by
adding to it what he loves.   When he begins to
exist in the perfection of his nature, he will not be
unhappy.

8.22   Notice how absurd and contradictory it is to
say: I should prefer not to exist rather than to exist
unhappily.   A man who says, I should prefer this
to that, chooses something.   But non-existence is
not something; it is nothing.   Therefore you cannot possibly make a real choice, when there is
nothing for you to choose.   You say you wish to
exist, though you are unhappy, but that you ought
not to have this wish.   What, then, should you
wish?   Rather, you say, non-existence.   If this is
what you should wish, it is better; but what does
not exist, cannot be better.   Therefore you ought
not to wish it; and the feeling by which you do not
wish it, is truer than the supposition by which you
think you ought to wish it.   Moreover, that which
a man chooses rightly as an object of desire, when
attained, must make him better.   But he cannot

become better if he does not exist, so that no one can be right in choosing non-existence.

Nor should we be troubled by the judgment of those who through the stress of unhappiness have killed themselves. Either they have sought to find refuge where they supposed they would be better off, and this is not unreasonable, whatever view they may have held; or if they thought they would cease to exist altogether, the false choice of people choosing nothing will concern us much less. How am I to follow a man who makes a choice, and when I ask what he chooses replies, nothing? If he chooses non-existence, he is certainly proved to choose nothing, even though he be unwilling to make this answer.

23 However, let me try to tell you my view on this whole matter. No one, when he kills himself or wishes to die by any other means, really feels, I think, that he will not exist after death, even though he may have some kind of opinion in the matter. But opinion is derived from the error or truth of reasoning or belief, whereas feeling takes its strength from custom or nature. We can see at once that a man's opinion may be different from his feeling, because we often think we ought to do one thing, while we should like to do something else. Further, sometimes feeling is truer than opinion, when the latter is derived from error and feeling is based on nature. For example, often a sick man likes cold water and finds it a relief, but believes it will do him harm to drink it. Sometimes opinion is truer than feeling, as when he believes

the doctor's warning that cold water is harmful, and yet likes to drink it. Sometimes both are true, when something is good for you and you not only believe this, but also like to have it. Sometimes both are wrong, when something is harmful and you believe it is good for you and you like to have it. Right opinion usually corrects a wrong custom, and wrong opinion usually harms what is naturally right; such is the power of the control and supremacy of reason.

So when a man believes that he will not exist after death, yet unbearable troubles make him long heart and soul for death and he is determined to embrace death, his opinion is false and utterly wrong, but his feeling is a natural desire for rest. But what is restful is not nothing; indeed it has truer being than what is restless. Restlessness changes our inclinations, so that one inclination destroys another. But rest brings permanence, and this is especially implied by saying a thing exists. Thus when a man wills to die, all that he desires is not non-existence after death, but rest. Though he falsely believes he will cease to exist, his nature seeks rest, that is, increase of existence. Hence, just as it is utterly impossible that anyone should take pleasure in non-existence, so it is utterly wrong that anyone should be ungrateful to the Creator's goodness for his existence.[25]

WHY DOES GOD NOT PREVENT UNHAPPINESS?

9.24   A man says: It would not have been difficult or laborious for Almighty God to see to it that everything He created should possess what its nature requires, and no creature should be rendered unhappy. Being almighty, He did not lack the power to do this, and being good, He would not grudge it. I answer that creatures are arranged so perfectly in order from the highest to the lowest, that envy alone would cause a man to say: That creature should not exist; and it is envy if he says: That should be different. For if he wishes it to be like a thing of higher rank, it already exists, and is such that nothing ought to be added, for it is perfect. If he says, I should like this too to have that excellence, either he wishes to add to the higher creature, though it is already perfect, and then he will be extravagant and unjust; or he wishes to destroy it, and then he will be evil and envious.

But if he says, I wish this did not exist, he will still be evil and envious, since he wishes a thing not to exist, though he is forced to praise what is lower.[26] He might as well say, I wish there were no moon, while he must admit that even the light of a lamp, though far inferior, is beautiful of its own kind, pleasant in the surrounding darkness, convenient for use at night, and in view of all this excellent in its own small way. To deny this would be folly or obstinacy. How then can he rightly go so far as to say, I wish there were no moon, when he knows he would be making himself absurd were he to say, I wish there were no lamp? If instead of saying, I wish there were no moon, he said the moon ought to have been like the sun, he fails to realise that he is only saying, I wish there were no moon, but two suns. In this he makes a double mistake: he wishes to add to the perfection of things by desiring a second sun, and to detract from their perfection by wishing to do away with the moon.

25   Here he may remark that he makes no complaint about the moon, because its lesser degree of brightness does not make it unhappy; but in the case of souls he is distressed not by the darkness of them, but by their unhappiness. Let him carefully consider that while the brightness of the moon does not involve unhappiness, the brightness of the sun is not concerned with happiness either. For though they are heavenly bodies, yet bodies they are in respect to this light, light which can be seen by bodily eyes. But no bodily things in themselves can be happy or unhappy, though they may be the bodies of happy or unhappy people.

The comparison drawn from the heavenly bodies nevertheless teaches this lesson. When you reflect on the difference in these bodies and see that some are brighter than others, you are wrong to wish the darker to be removed or made equal to the brighter. If you look at each thing in its relation to the perfection of the whole, you find that this very variety of brightness helps you to see the existence of everything. You find the perfection of the whole is derived from the presence of both great and small. So too consider the differences between souls. You will find the unhappiness which grieves you has this value: that those souls which have rightly become unhappy because they willed to be sinful, are not lacking to the perfection of the whole. It is wrong to say that God ought not to have made them unhappy; indeed He deserves to be praised for making other creatures far lower than unhappy souls.

26   But one may not understand fully what I have said and make this objection: If our unhappiness completes the perfection of the whole, there would be a lack of perfection if we were always happy. Hence, if the soul only becomes unhappy through sin, our sins must be necessary for the perfection of the whole creation which God has made. How then is it just that He punish sins when without these sins God's creation would not attain its full perfection?

The answer is as follows. The sins themselves or the unhappiness itself are not necessary for the perfection of the whole; but the souls are necessary as souls. If they so will, they sin; if they sin, they become unhappy. If their unhappiness continues after their sins have been removed, or if it even precedes their sins, the proper order and direction of the whole is truly said to be impaired. Again, if sins are committed and there is no unhappiness, the order of things is also stained with injustice. When those who do not sin enjoy happiness, the whole is perfect. When sinners are unhappy, the whole is perfect in spite of this. Provided that souls themselves are not lacking, whether those which are made unhappy when they sin or those which are made happy when they do right, the whole, having beings of every kind, is always complete and perfect. For sin and the punishment of sin are not themselves substantial things, but they are states of substantial things, the former voluntary, the latter penal. Now the voluntary state when sin is committed is a shameful state. Therefore to this is applied a penal state, to set it where such may fitly be, and to make it harmonise with the beauty of the whole, so that the sin's punishment may make up for its shamefulness.

27   Hence it comes about that the higher creature which sins is punished by lower creatures, because these latter are so low that they can be raised in honour even by wicked souls, and so can harmonise with the beauty of the whole. What is so noble in the house as man? And what so ignoble and low as its drain? Yet a slave, found guilty of some fault and set as a punishment to clean the drain, gives it honour by his disgrace. Both of these things, the slave's disgrace and the cleaning of the drain, thus joined together and reduced to a special kind of unity, have their part in the proper management of the house, and combine to give the whole the beauty of good order. If the slave had not willed to do wrong, the work of the house would have been carried on by other means, and the necessary cleaning would have been done.

There is nothing lower in the scale of things

than an earthly body. Yet even a sinful soul gives such honour to corruptible flesh that it conveys to it a becoming beauty, and living movement. Such a soul on account of its sin is not fit to dwell in heaven, but is fit to dwell on earth for its punishment. Whatever choice the soul makes, the whole is beautiful and well ordered, each part fitting its own place, whose Creator and Governor is God. The noblest souls, when they dwell in the lowest created things, honour them not by being unhappy, for this they are not, but by their good use of them. But if sinful souls were allowed to dwell on high, it would be wrong, for they are not fitted for things of which they cannot make a good use and on which they cannot confer honour.

28 Therefore, though this orb of the earth is appointed to be the place of corruptible things, yet it preserves as far as possible the image of what is higher, and continues to show examples and traces of this. If we see some great and good man, obeying the call of honour and duty, allow his body to be burned by fire, we do not call this a penalty for sin, but a proof of courage and endurance. Though the most horrible corruption consumes the members of his body, we love him more than if he suffered nothing of the kind. We are amazed that the nature of his soul is not changed with the changing body. When, however, we see the body of a cruel robber consumed as a punishment in the same way, we approve the lawful enforcement of public order. Both men make these sufferings

honourable, but one does so by his virtue, the other by his sin.

If we saw the good man, after being consumed by fire or even before it, rendered fit to dwell in heaven and raised to the stars, we should certainly rejoice. But if we saw the robber and criminal, whether before or after his punishment, still keeping his evil will, raised to dwell in eternal glory in heaven, should we not all be shocked? Hence both of them can give honour to lower creatures, but only one to creatures which are higher.

This bids us to notice that our mortal flesh has been honoured both by the first man when he suffered the punishment his sin deserved, and by Our Lord, when in His mercy He delivered us from sin. The just man, still abiding in justice itself, could have a mortal body, but the wicked man cannot, if he remains wicked, gain the immortality of the saints, which is that of the angels in heaven. I do not mean those angels of whom the Apostle says— *Know you not that we shall judge angels*,[27] but those about whom Our Lord says—. . . *for they shall be equal to the angels* of God.[28] Those who desire to be equal with the angels through vainglory, wish the angels to be equal with them, not themselves with the angels.[29] If they persist in so willing, their punishment will be equal to that of the apostate angels, since they love their own power more than that of Almighty God. Because such men have not sought God by the gate of humility which the Lord Jesus Christ has shown in Himself, but have lived in pride and without mercy, they will be set upon the left side and it will be said to them: *Depart . . . into everlasting fire which was prepared for the devil and his angels.*[30]

10.29   Sins arise from two sources, from a man's own thoughts and from the persuasion of another, and to this I think the words of the Prophet refer: *From my secret ones cleanse me, O Lord, and from those of others spare thy servant.*[31] Both are voluntary, for our own thoughts do not lead to sin against our will, while our consent to the evil persuasion of another is also due to our own will. Yet to sin as a consequence of our own thoughts without the persuasion of someone else, and, still more, to persuade another to sin through envy and treachery is graver than to be led into sin by another's influence.

The justice of the Lord is observed when both sins are punished. The matter was weighed in the balance of justice when man was given into the power of the devil himself, after the devil had subdued him by his evil persuasion. It would have been unjust that he should not rule over his captive.[32] The perfect justice of the supreme and true God, which extends everywhere, could not possibly leave fallen sinners outside the scope of its government. Because man sinned less grievously than the devil, his salvation and restoration were furthered by the very fact that he was delivered to the prince of this world, that is, the lowest and mortal part of creation to the prince of all sinners and the lord of death, unto the mortality of the flesh. Thus, frightened by his consciousness of mortality, in fear of trouble and death from vile and miserable beasts, even the very smallest, and uncertain of the future, man has accustomed himself to check unlawful joys, and especially to crush pride, by the seduction of which he was cast down and which is the only vice to prevent the healing power of mercy. What indeed has such need of mercy as one who is unhappy, and what is so unworthy of mercy as one who is at once unhappy and proud?

30   Hence it has happened that the Word of God, through whom all things have been made, and in whom all the happiness of the angels consists, has stretched forth His mercy to our unhappiness, and that the Word has become flesh and has dwelt among us.[33] Thus it was to be possible for man to eat the bread of angels, though himself not yet equal to the angels, if the bread of angels should itself deign to become equal with men. Nor did it abandon the angels when it came down to us: at the same time wholly theirs and wholly ours, it feeds them from within by that which God is, and teaches us from without by that which we are. Thus we also are made fit by faith to receive it like them as our food in the vision face to face.

The rational creature finds in the Word its most excellent food and feeds upon it. The human soul is rational. But it was held in mortal bonds in punishment of sin, and was reduced to such low condition that it strives to understand invisible things by conclusions drawn from visible things. The food of rational creatures has been made visible, not by changing its nature, but by putting on ours, that it may recall us, who pursue visible things, to itself invisible. Thus the soul which in its inward pride had deserted Him, finds Him outside in His humility. By imitating His visible humility it will return to Him invisible and on high.

31 The Word of God, God's only Son, clothed with man's nature, has subdued under man the devil whom He has ever held, and ever will hold, under His law. He has wrested nothing from the devil by force, but has overcome him by the law of justice. Having deceived the woman and overthrown the man by the woman, the devil claimed all the descendants of the first man as sinful, and therefore as subject to the law of death. He did this from the wicked desire to harm them, yet by lawful right. He claimed them so long as his power held, until he slew the Just Man, in whom he could point to nothing which deserved death, not only because He was slain in spite of His innocence, but also because He was born free from passion. To passion the devil had made his prisoners slaves, so that he might keep in his power whatever was born of it, as the fruit of his own tree, through a wicked desire to hold them, but by a genuine right of possession.

Therefore he is compelled with full justice to let free those who believe in Him and whom he has most unjustly killed. By temporal death they pay their debt, and by everlasting life they live in Him who paid on their behalf a debt He himself did not owe. The devil, however, could justly have, as sharers with him in his everlasting damnation, those whom he had persuaded to persist in infidelity.

Thus man, who had become the devil's captive by persuasion, and not by force, was not snatched away from the devil by force; and man had justly to endure the further humiliation of serving him to whom he had given a wicked consent, but was justly set free by him to whom he had given a good consent. Man sinned less greatly by consenting than the devil by persuading him to evil.

11.32   God therefore made all natures, not only those which were to abide in virtue and justice, but also those that were to sin. He created them not that they might sin, but that they might add beauty to the whole, whether they willed to sin or not. If there had been no souls at the very summit of the whole created order, such that if they chose to sin, they would weaken and shatter the whole, a great element would be lacking in creation; for that would be lacking which would upset, if taken away, the stability and harmony of things. Such are the excellent, holy, sublime creatures, the powers of heaven or above it, whom God alone commands, and to whom the whole world is subject. If these creatures did not perform their just and perfect duties, the whole could not exist. Again, if there were no souls whose decision to sin or not to sin would in no way alter the order of the whole, an important element would also be lacking. So there are rational souls, lower than the higher souls in their function, but equal in nature.

There are many ranks still lower than these, but worthy of praise, among the creatures of God most high.

33   Therefore that kind of being has a higher function, whose sin and also whose non-existence would impair the whole. That has a lower function, whose non-existence, but not whose sin, would impair the whole. To the former is given power to maintain all things, as its special function necessary for the order of the whole. It does not possess unchanging good will because it has been given this function; but it has been given the function because He who gave it foresaw that its good will would persist. It does not maintain everything by its own authority, but by fidelity and scrupulous obedience to the authority and commands of Him from whom and through whom and in whom all things have been made.[34]

To the latter was also given, provided it did not sin, the great function of maintaining all things. But it was given this function, not as peculiar to itself, but as shared with the former, since its own future sin was foreknown. All spiritual beings can join together without gain and separate without loss. Thus the higher being would not find its action made easier by this partnership, nor made more difficult, should the other desert its function by committing sin. Spiritual creatures, though each may possess its own body, cannot be joined or separated by position and physical association, but by likeness or unlikeness of their inclinations.

34   The soul which is given its place, after sinning,

among the lower, mortal bodies, governs its body, not altogether at its own choice, but so far as the laws of the whole permit. Yet such a soul is not for this reason lower than the heavenly body to which even earthly bodies are subject. The ragged garment of a condemned slave is much inferior to the garment of a slave who has served well and is highly regarded by his master; but the slave himself is better than any fine garment, for he is a man.

The higher being, then, keeps close to God, and in a heavenly body, through its angelic power, it also honours and governs an earthly body, obeying the order of Him whose will it beholds in a manner beyond expression. The lower being, burdened with mortal limbs, directs with difficulty within itself the body by which it is pressed down, and yet honours it as much as it can. Upon other bodies with which it comes in contact, it exercises from outside a far weaker power, so far as it can.

12.35 We conclude from this that the lowest bodily creature would not have lacked fitting adornment, even though the being of which we have just spoken, had not willed to sin. For that which can govern the whole, governs also a part; but that which can do less, cannot necessarily do more. The skilful physician cures even the scab thoroughly; but, because he can deal with the scab effectively, it does not follow that he can heal every human ailment. Indeed, if we see a cogent reason for holding that there ought to have been a creature which never sinned and never will sin, this same reason shows us also that it abstains from sin through its free will, of its own accord and unforced. Nevertheless, if it should sin—though it has not sinned, in accordance with God's foreknowledge of its sinlessness—yet, should it sin, the inexpressible force of God's power would be strong enough so to govern the whole that, by rendering to all what is due and fitting, He would allow nothing shameful or unbecoming to exist in His whole dominion.

For, if the whole angelic creation had fallen by sinning against His commands, without using any of the powers created for this purpose, God would govern all things by His own authority in a supremely befitting way. He would not on this account view with hatred the existence of a spiritual creature. Even towards bodily creatures, far lower than spiritual creatures even when sinful, He has shown such profusion of goodness that no one can reasonably contemplate heaven and earth and all visible things, so harmoniously formed and ordered according to their natures, without believing God to be their author, and confessing that He deserves ineffable praise.

On the other hand, even though there is no better government for creation than when by the excellence of their nature and the goodness of their will the power of the angels governs all things, even so the fall of all the angels would not have deprived the Creator of the angels of means to govern His dominion. His goodness would not find it wearisome nor His omnipotence find it hard to create others to set in the places deserted by those who had sinned. If spiritual creatures, whatever their number,[35] were justly condemned, this could not disturb that order of things which allows for the condemnation of all who deserve it, in the manner which is right and proper. Therefore, wherever we turn our thoughts, we find that God deserves ineffable praise—the most good Creator of all beings and their most just Ruler.

HAPPINESS AND UNHAPPINESS IN THE END ARE BOTH JUST

36 Finally, let us leave the contemplation of the beauty of things to those to whom God has granted the power to see it, and let us not presume by mere words to bring them[36] to contemplation of the ineffable. And yet, because of men who are loquacious or weak or deceitful,[37] let us examine briefly this important question.

13 Every nature which can become less good, is good. A nature becomes less good when it is corrupted. Either corruption does not harm it and it does not become corrupt; or, if it is corrupted, corruption harms it. If it harms, it takes away some of its goodness and makes it less good. If it deprives it entirely of all its good, what remains of it cannot be corrupted, because there will be no good left which corruption can remove; corruption cannot harm it in this way. That which corruption cannot harm cannot become corrupt. That nature which does not suffer corruption is incorruptible, and hence there will be a nature,

absurd though this is, which corruption makes incorruptible.

Therefore it is true to say that every nature, so far as it is a nature, is good. For, if it is incorruptible it is better than the corruptible, while, if it is corruptible, since corruption makes it less good, undoubtedly it is good. Every nature is either corruptible or incorruptible. Hence every nature is good. By a nature I mean what we usually call substance. Therefore every substance is either God or derived from God, for every good thing is either God or derived from God.

37 Having firmly established this as the principle of our reasoning, listen to what I have to say. Every rational nature, created with free will, if it abides in the enjoyment of the supreme, unchangeable good, is undoubtedly worthy of praise, and every nature which strives to so abide is also worthy of praise. But every nature which does not abide in this and does not will to aim at this end, in so far as it does not attain the end and does not aim at it, is worthy of blame.

If, therefore, a created rational nature is praised, no one doubts that its Creator deserves praise; and if the creature is blamed, no one doubts that its Creator is praised when it is blamed. For when we blame the creature, because it does not will to enjoy the supreme and unchangeable good, its Creator, without any doubt we praise the Creator. What a good, then, is God! How far beyond expression should every tongue, and how far beyond expression should every thought, extol and

honour Him, the Creator of all, without praise of
whom we can neither be praised or blamed! We
cannot be blamed for not abiding in Him, unless
to abide in Him is our great, supreme, and principal good. How can this be so unless it is because
He is beyond expression good? What cause can
be found in our sins to blame Him, when there is
no blame for our sins which is not praise for Him?
38   Again, in the very things which are blamed it is
only the vice which is blamed; and there is no
blaming a vice without praising its nature. If what
is blamed is according to nature, it is not vice; it is
you who should be corrected, rather than what
you wrongly blame, that you may learn to give
blame rightly. Or if it is a vice and can be rightly
blamed, it must be against nature. All vice, from
the very fact that it is vice, is against nature. If it
does not harm nature, it is not vice; if it is vice
because it does harm, it is vice because it is against
nature.

But, if a nature is corrupted by another's vice,
and not by its own, it is unjustly blamed, and we
must ask whether that other nature is not corrupted by its own vice, when its vice could corrupt
another's nature. What else is it to be vitiated
than to be corrupted by vice? A nature which is
not vitiated is free from vice, but that which corrupts by its vice another's nature certainly has vice.
That nature is vicious, and is corrupted by its own
vice, by the vice of which another nature can also
be corrupted.

Hence we conclude that all vice is against

nature, even against the nature of that thing which has the vice. Therefore, since it is only vice that is blamed in anything, and since it is vice because it is against the nature of that thing which has the vice, nothing is rightly blamed for vice, unless its nature is praised. Vice is only rightly displeasing to you, because it makes vicious what pleases you in the nature.

14.39   We must also notice this question: is it true that a nature is subject to corruption by the vice of another nature without any vice of its own? If a nature with its vice approaches another nature with a view to corrupting it, and finds in it nothing corruptible, it does not corrupt it. But if it does find something corruptible it effects the corruption of the other nature by the vice it finds in it. The stronger is not corrupted by the weaker if it refuses to be corrupted, but if it wills to be corrupted its corruption begins from its own vice rather than another's. Nor can an equal be corrupted by an equal if it refuses. When a vicious nature approaches another which is without vice in order to corrupt it, by that very fact it does not approach as equal, but as weaker on account of its vice.

But if a stronger corrupts a weaker, either this occurs through the vice of both, if it occurs through the evil desire of both; or through the vice of the stronger, if such is the superiority of its nature that, even though vicious, it is still superior to the lesser nature which it corrupts. Who would be right in blaming the fruits of the earth, because men do not use them well, but corrupted by their own vice corrupt them by abusing them for the purpose of luxury? Nevertheless it would be folly to doubt that human nature, even when vicious, is nobler and stronger than any fruit, even when free from vice.

40   It is possible too for a stronger to corrupt a weaker nature, and for this to happen through no vice of either of them—if by vice we mean what is deserving of blame. Who, for instance, would dare to blame a thrifty man who sought nothing more from the fruits of the earth than support of nature, or to blame these fruits themselves for being corrupted when used as his food? We do not, as a rule, use the word 'corruption' to express this, because 'corruption' is a term used to denote a vice.

It is easy to note this as of common occurrence, that the stronger nature corrupts the weaker without using it to satisfy its own needs. A case in point is when in the order of justice guilt is punished. This is the principle expressed by the Apostle when he says: *If any man violate the temple of God, him shall God destroy.*[38] Or, again, in the order of changeable things one gives way to another according to the most suitable laws given to the whole and adapted to the strength of each part. If a man's eyes were too weak by nature to bear the light and the sun's brightness should injure them, we should not suppose the sun did this in order to make up any deficiency in its own light, or through any vice on its part. Nor would the eyes themselves deserve blame because they obeyed their master and were opened in face of the light, or because they succumbed to the light itself and were injured.

Therefore, of all forms of corruption only that which is vicious is rightly blamed. Other forms either should not be called corruption, or, not being vicious, certainly ought not to be blamed. As a matter of fact, the word *vituperatio* (blame) is thought to be derived from the words *vitium* and *paratum*, and to mean, what is prepared for, that is, suitable for, and due to, vice alone.[39]

41 Vice, I began to say, is only evil because it is opposed to the nature of the thing which has the vice. Hence it is clear that the nature of this same thing whose vice is blamed is worthy of praise. Thus we must agree that to blame the vice is nothing else than to praise the nature of that thing whose vice is blamed. Because vice is opposed to nature, the malice of vice increases in proportion to the decreased soundness of the nature. Therefore, when you blame vice, you obviously praise the thing whose soundness you wish for. And to what should the soundness belong except to the nature? A perfect nature, far from deserving blame, deserves praise in accordance with the kind of nature it is. What you see to be lacking in the perfection of a nature, you call vice, showing plainly enough that the nature pleases you, since you blame its imperfection on account of your will for its perfection.

15.42 So, if to blame vices is also to commend the beauty and dignity of the natures which have the vices, how much more is God, the Creator of all natures, worthy of praise even in their vices! From Him they derive their possession of a nature; they are vicious in so far as they depart from the art with which He made them, and they are rightly blamed in so far as he who blames them sees the art with which they have been made, and blames them for what he does not see in them. And if the very art by which all things have been made, that is, the supreme unchangeable Wisdom of God, truly and supremely exists—as in fact it does—you can see whither that thing is bound which departs from His art.

The defect, however, would not deserve blame, unless it were voluntary. Please consider whether you are right in blaming what is as it ought to be: I think not; but rather what is not as it ought to be. No one owes as a debt what he has not received,[40] and to whom does the debtor owe anything, except to him from whom he has received it, and to whom he therefore owes it? What is paid when money is transferred to the heirs, is paid to him who made the will. And what is paid to the lawful heirs of creditors, is paid to the creditors themselves to whom the heirs lawfully succeed. Otherwise it would not be a payment, but a transfer or grant, or something of this kind.

Consequently it would be most absurd to say that temporal things ought not to decay. They are placed in an order of things such that, unless they decay the future cannot follow the past, nor can the beauty of the ages unfold itself in its natural course. They act in accordance with what they have received, and they pay their debt to Him to whom they owe their being, in accordance with the measure of their being. If anyone expresses grief at their decay, he should notice what he is saying—yes, what he is saying in making that complaint—if he thinks it is just and prudently said. In pronouncing those words, if he takes pleasure in one part of the sound and refuses to let it go and make the way for the rest (it is by sounds which die out and are followed by others that speech is composed), he will be considered a sheer madman.

43 Therefore no one rightly blames a failure in these things which thus decay. They have received no further being, in order that everything may occur at its proper time. No one can say: It ought to have lasted longer; for it could not pass the limits assigned to it.

But it is in rational creatures that the beauty of the whole creation reaches its fitting climax, whether they sin or not. Now either they do not sin, which it is quite absurd to say, for a sin is committed even by condemning as a sin what is no sin; or their sins do not deserve blame, which is equally absurd, for then we shall be on the way to praise wrong actions and the whole purpose of the human mind will be upset and life thrown into confusion; or we shall blame an action performed as it ought to be performed, and execrable madness will overtake us, or, in milder language, most unfortunate error; or, if we are forced, as we are, by true reasoning to blame sins, and to blame a thing rightly only because it is not as it ought to be, then ask what a sinful nature owes and you will find it owes right action; ask to whom it owes this, and you will find it owes it to God. For He who has given it the power to act rightly if it wishes, has also given it the power to be unhappy if it does not act rightly, and to be happy if it does.

44   Since no one is above the laws of the almighty Creator, the soul is bound to pay what is due. Either it pays this by the good use of what it has received, or else by the loss of what it refuses to use well. Hence if it does not pay by acting justly, it will pay by suffering unhappiness, for the word 'debt' applies to both. Thus what has been said could also have been formulated as follows: If a soul does not pay by doing what it ought to do, it will pay by suffering what it ought to suffer.

There is no interval of time between these two; the soul does not do what it ought at one time, and suffer what it ought at another time. The beauty of the whole must not be impaired even for a moment; it must not contain the shame of sin without the beauty of punishment. But the manifestation of what is now punished in secret, and the terrible sense of unhappiness this involves, is reserved for the future judgment. Just as one sleeps if he is not awake, so the man who does not do what he ought to do, suffers immediately what he ought to suffer, because so great is the happiness derived from justice that to depart from it is to enter upon unhappiness. There is no alternative.

Therefore, when as a result of deficiency of being things decay, either they have not received any further being and there is no fault (in the same way that there is no fault if, while they exist, they receive no further being), or else they refuse to be what they had the power to be if they chose. Since what they might have possessed is good, they are guilty if they refuse it.

16.45 God owes no debt to anyone, because He gives everything freely. If anyone should say God owed him a debt for his merits, certainly existence is not owed to him, for he did not exist to be owed a debt. And what merit is there in turning to Him from whom you derive your being, in order that you may obtain further perfection from the source of your very being? What payment have you made beforehand, which you can demand back as a debt? If you refuse to turn towards Him, He loses nothing, while on your part, unless you turn to Him and pay back the existence you have received from Him, you lose Him without whom you would be nothing and from whom you receive your existence. If this happens, though you will not cease to exist, will you not suffer unhappiness? Everything owes to Him—first, its existence as a nature; secondly, the further perfection it can gain if it wills what it has received the power to will, all that it ought to be. No one is responsible for what he has not received; but he is justly responsible for not doing what he ought to do, and he has a duty to perform if he has received a free will and sufficient powers.

46 Therefore, when a man does not do what he ought, this certainly is no fault of the Creator;

rather, it is a matter for His praise that the man suffers what he ought. The blame the man receives for not doing what he ought is nothing else than praise to the Creator to whom he owes the debt. If you are praised when you see what you ought to do, though you only see this in Him who is unchangeable truth, how much more should He be praised who has ordered you to will what you ought to do, and has given you the power to carry it out, and has not allowed you to refuse it unpunished!

If everyone owes that which he has received, and if man has been so made that he sins necessarily, then his duty is to sin.[41] Therefore, when he sins, he does what he ought to do. But if it is wicked to say this, then no one is forced by his own nature to sin, nor is he forced by the nature of anyone else. No one sins by suffering what he does not will. If he suffers justly, he does not sin by that which he suffers against his will; but he did sin by that which he willed to do, and by deserving to suffer thereby what he did not will. If he suffers unjustly, how does he sin? It is not a sin to suffer unjustly but to act unjustly. But if a man is compelled to sin neither by his own nature nor by that of someone else, it remains that he sins through his own will.

If you wish to attribute the sin to the Creator, you will clear the sinner because he did nothing against the ordinance of his Creator. But if your defence is sound, he did not sin, and there is nothing to attribute to the Creator. Let us then praise the Creator, if the sinner can be defended; let us also praise Him, if he cannot. If he is defended justly, he is no sinner, and so praise the Creator. If he cannot be defended, he is a sinner in so far as he turns away from the Creator, so praise the Creator.

Therefore, I can find no reason at all for attributing our sins to God, our Creator, and I assert that no such reason can be found, and indeed that it does not exist. I find that in these very sins He is to be praised, not only because He punishes them, but also because they are committed by departing from His truth.

E.—I accept most gladly what you say and approve it. I agree it is quite true that our sins can in no manner at all be rightly attributed to our Creator.

PERVERTED WILL IS THE CAUSE OF EVIL, AND IT IS USELESS TO LOOK FURTHER

17.47   But I should like to know, if possible, why that nature does not sin which God has foreknown will not sin, and why that nature sins which God has foreseen will sin. I do not now think that through God's foreknowledge the one is forced to sin and the other not to sin. Nevertheless, if there is no cause, rational creatures would not be divided into those which never sin, those which persist in sin, and those between these extremes who sometimes sin and sometimes turn to doing good. What cause is there for their division into these three classes?

I do not want you to reply that it is the will: it is the cause behind the will that I am asking about. There must be some cause which brings it about that some never will to sin, that others always do so, and that others do so on occasion, though all have the same nature. The one point which seems clear to me is that there must be a cause for this threefold division of will in the rational creature; but what the cause is I do not know.

48 *A.*—Since the will is the cause of sin, and you are looking for a cause of the will, if I can find this, will you not look for a cause of the cause I have found? What will satisfy these questions, what will put an end to our hesitation and discussion? You ought not to look further than the root. Do not suppose that anything can be truer than the sentence: *The desire of money is the root of all evil* [42]—that is, the desire for more than sufficiency. That amount is sufficiency which each nature demands for its preservation. Avarice—termed *philarguría* in Greek, which echoes better the origin of the word, for in olden times coins were made of silver or more frequently an alloy of silver —does not apply only to silver or money; but it must be understood to apply to everything which is desired to excess, whenever a man wills more than is enough. Such avarice is cupidity, and cupidity is perverted will. Perverted will, then, is the cause of all evil.

If the will followed nature, it would preserve, and would not harm nature, and so would not be perverted. Hence, we conclude, the root of all evil is not according to nature, and this is sufficient answer to those who would accuse nature. But if you look for the cause of this root, how can it be the root of all evil? Such cause would be the root cause, and if you found it, you will, as I said, look for a further cause, and the inquiry will be endless.

49 Now what could precede the will and be its cause? Either it is the will itself, and nothing else than the will is the root,[43] or it is not the will which is not sinful. Either the will itself is the original cause of sin, or no sin is the original cause of sin. Sin cannot be attributed to anything except to the sinner. It cannot rightly be attributed to anything except to him who wills it:[44] I do not know why you should wish to look for anything further.

Again, whatever is the cause of the will, is either just or unjust. If just, we shall not sin by submitting to it; if unjust, let us not submit to it, and we

18.50 shall not sin. But perhaps it uses compulsion and forces a man against his will? Need we repeat ourselves over and over again? Remember all that we said before about sin and free will. If it is difficult to keep it all in mind, do remember this summary. Whatever is the cause of the will, if we cannot resist it, we do not sin by yielding to it; if we can resist, we must not yield and we shall not sin. Perhaps it tricks us when off our guard? We must be careful not to be tricked. Or is the trickery such that we cannot possibly be on our guard against it? If so, there is no sin, for no one sins when he cannot guard against it. Yet sin is committed, and therefore we can guard against it.[45]

51   Nevertheless, some actions done in ignorance are judged to be wrong and in need of correction, as we read in the divine documents. For example, the Apostle says: *I obtained the mercy of God, because I did it ignorantly;* [46] and the Prophet says: *The sins of my youth and my ignorance do not remember.*[47] Actions done of necessity when a man wills to act rightly and cannot, are also judged wrong. Hence the words: *For the good which I will, I do not; but the evil which I will not, that I do;* and, *To will is present with me, but to accomplish that which is good, I find not;* [48] and, *The flesh lusteth against the spirit, and the spirit against the flesh; for these are contrary one to another, so that you do not the things that you would.*[49] But all this applies to men as they appear on the scene after the condemnation of death; for if this does not stand for man's punishment, but his natural condition, then there is no question of sin. If man has not lost his natural kind of being, and if he cannot become better, he is doing what he ought when he acts in this way. But if man would be good if he were constituted differently, and he is not good because he is in his present condition; if he has not the power to become good, whether because he does not see what he ought to be, or because he sees and yet cannot be what he sees he ought to be, then this is surely a punishment.

Now every punishment is a punishment for sin, if it is just, and is called a penalty; but if the punishment is unjust, since no one doubts it is a punishment, it is imposed on man by an unjust ruler.

But it would be folly to doubt the omnipotence and justice of God, and therefore this punishment must be just, and be exacted for some sin. No unjust ruler could have snatched man away from God without His knowledge or taken him by force against God's will, whether by threat or violence, in order to inflict torture on him as an unjust punishment. No one can frighten God, or struggle with Him. It remains, therefore, that this is a just punishment resulting from man's condemnation.

52   It is not surprising that man, through his ignorance, does not have free choice of will to determine what he ought to do; or that, through the resistance of carnal habits, which have become second nature as a result of the element of unrestraint handed on in human heredity, he sees what he ought to do and wills it, but cannot accomplish it. It is an absolutely just punishment for sin that a man should lose what he refuses to use rightly, when he could do so without any difficulty if he wished. Thus a man who knows what he ought to do and does not do it, loses the knowledge of what is right, and the man who has refused to act rightly when he could, loses the power when he wishes to have it.

Indeed for every sinful soul there are the two punishments, ignorance and difficulty. As a result of ignorance error shames us, and as a result of difficulty pain torments us. But to approve false for true, so as to err unwillingly, and to be unable to refrain from acts of passion on account of the resistance and pain of the bonds of the flesh, are

not natural to man in his original state, but are a
punishment after his condemnation. When we
speak of a will free to act rightly, we speak of the
will with which man was created.

19.53   Here that problem raises itself, which is often
brought up with murmurings and mutterings: men
are ready to accuse anything else for their sins
rather than themselves. Thus they say: If Adam
and Eve sinned, what have we unhappy people
done, to be born in the blindness of ignorance and
amid the torments of difficulty,[50] first to err not
knowing our duty, and then, when the commands
of justice begin to be revealed to us, to will to follow them, and to be powerless to do so because
some urge of fleshly concupiscence fights against
it?

My answer in brief is that these people should
keep quiet and cease to murmur against God.
They might perhaps be justified in complaining if
no one had ever conquered error and passion.
There is, however, everywhere present One who
in so many ways uses His creatures to call back the
servant who has abandoned Him, who teaches him
when he believes, consoles him when he hopes,
encourages him when he loves, helps him when he
strives, and hears him when he prays. It is not
counted to you as a fault that you are ignorant
against your will, but that you fail to seek the
knowledge you do not possess. Nor is it a fault
that you do not tend your wounded members, but
that you despise Him who wishes to heal them.
These are your own sins. No one is prevented

from knowing how valuable it is to seek the knowledge which it is valueless not to possess, and from knowing the duty humbly to confess his weakness, so that when he seeks and when he confesses he may be helped by Him who neither errs when He gives help nor becomes weary of giving it.

54 The wrong actions which are done in ignorance, and the right actions which cannot be done in spite of a good will, are called sins because they draw their origin from the first sin which was committed freely, and which brought about these effects as a due consequence.

By 'tongue' we mean not only the member we move in our mouth when we speak, but also the results of the movement of this member, namely, the form and connection of words. Thus we call one the Greek tongue and another the Latin tongue. In the same way by sin we do not only mean what is properly speaking a sin, a sin committed freely and deliberately, but also what is bound to follow as a punishment of such sin.

So too we use the word 'nature' properly speaking of the nature which men share in common, and with which at first man was created in a state of innocence. We also use nature to mean that nature with which we are born mortal, ignorant, and slaves of the flesh, after sentence has been pronounced on the first man. In the words of the Apostle: *We were by nature children of wrath, even as the rest.*[51]

20.55 God, the supreme Ruler of creation, justly decreed that from the first pair we should inherit ignorance, difficulty, and death, because they, as a result of their sin, fell into error, tribulation, and death. This was done that just punishment might be made manifest at man's first origin, and merciful deliverance at a later time. When the first man was condemned, he was not deprived of the happiness of having children. He was permitted to have descendants, though carnal and mortal, that the human race might in its own way be a beauty and honour to the earth. It was not equitable that the first man should beget children better than himself. But if his descendants converted to God, it was but proper that, showing this will, they should not be hindered, but receive aid in overcoming the punishment which the perversion of their origin had deserved. Thus too the Creator of things showed how easily man could have kept his first condition, if he had wished to do so, for his offspring was even able to rise above the state in which he was born.

56 Again, if only one soul was made from which are derived the souls of all men who are born, who can say that he himself did not sin when the first man sinned? If, however, a soul is created separately at the birth of each man, it does not seem wrong, but indeed quite reasonable and proper, that the evil merited by the earlier soul should belong by nature to the later, and the good merited by the later should belong by nature to the earlier. How was it unworthy of the Creator, if, in spite of all, He wished to show that a soul so far

surpasses a bodily creature in excellence, that the highest degree of the bodily creature only reaches the lowest degree to which the soul has fallen? For the sinful soul became involved in ignorance and difficulty, and this is rightly called punishment because the soul was better before the punishment. Even if, not only before sinning but from the very beginning of life, a soul should have that state of being to which another was reduced after living wickedly, it still has no small good for which to give thanks to the Creator, for even in its first beginning its state is better than any bodily thing however perfect. These are not ordinary blessings —not only that it is a soul, the nature of which is more excellent than any bodily thing; but, more than this, that it is capable, with the help of the Creator, of developing itself, and, if it does its duty earnestly, of acquiring and possessing the virtues which will free it from painful difficulty and blind ignorance.

If this is so, ignorance and difficulty will not be a punishment for sin to souls at their birth, but an encouragement to progress and a beginning of perfection. It is no small matter, before any meritorious action, to receive a natural power of judgment by which wisdom is preferred to error, and rest to difficulty, so that the soul may attain these ends not indeed at birth but as a result of effort. But if a soul refuses to do this, it will rightly be held guilty of sin, because it has not made good use of the power it received. Though born in a state of ignorance and difficulty, yet it is not forced by any necessity to remain in the state in which it was born. Only Almighty God, and no one else, could create such souls. For, though not loved by them He gives them being, and because He loves them He repairs their being,[52] and when loved by them He perfects their being. He who gives being to what has no being, gives happiness to those who love the author of their being.

57   If, however, souls pre-existing in some secret place assigned by God are sent to animate and govern the bodies of all the different persons who are born, they are sent for the following purpose. They are to govern rightly the body which is born subject to the punishment of the first man's sin, namely, liability to death, by using the virtues to keep it in check, and by subjecting it to a proper and lawful servitude, in order that they may prepare for it a place where in due order and time it may dwell incorrupt in heaven.

When these souls enter this life and endure the putting on of mortal limbs, they must also endure the forgetfulness of their former life and the toil of their present life. Ignorance and difficulty result,[53] which were the first man's penalty when death was laid upon him that he might realise the misery of his soul. These souls, however, find here a door to their work of restoring incorruption to the body. Thus, again, we only speak of this as sin because the flesh, derived from a sinful forefather, brings this ignorance and difficulty to the souls who enter into it. Neither they nor the Creator can be held responsible for these evils.

The Creator has given them the power to carry
out their burdensome duties well, and the path of
faith to guide the blindness arising from their lack
of memory.   Above all He has given them the
power to make the following judgment.   For
every soul agrees that it must strive to enlighten a
vain ignorance, and unceasingly endeavour to
carry the burden of its duty, to overcome the difficulty of doing right, and to implore the help of
the Creator in all its efforts.   Whether from without by law or from within by speaking directly to
the heart, He has ordered men to do their best.
He prepares the glory of the City of bliss for those
who vanquish him who led the first man into unhappiness, overcoming by wicked temptation.
Such men submit to this unhappiness in order to
conquer the devil by the excellence of their faith.
For there is no small glory in the struggle, if the
devil is conquered and submits to the very punishment by which he boasts he led man captive.   If a
man is induced by love of this life to give up the
struggle, he will have no right to attribute the
shame of his desertion to the command of his king.
Rather, the Lord of all will set him where the devil
dwells, whose shameful service he so loved that he
deserted his true camp.

58   But if souls existing elsewhere are not sent by
the Lord God, but of their own accord come to
dwell in bodies, we can easily see that whatever
ignorance and difficulty result from the action of
their own will, the Creator is in no way to blame.
Even if He had sent them Himself, since He did

not deprive them, despite their ignorance and difficulty, of their freedom to beg, and seek and strive, but was ready to give to those who beg, to show light to those who seek, and to open to those who knock, He would therefore be utterly without blame. To zealous souls of good will He would grant power to conquer ignorance and difficulty and to gain the crown of glory. To the negligent who wished to defend their sins on the ground of weakness, He would not impute their ignorance or difficulty. Because, however, they chose to remain in that state rather than by zealous seeking and learning and by humble confession and prayer to gain truth and strength, He would assign them just punishment.

21.59   There are these four opinions about the soul: that it comes by generation, that it is newly created when each person is born, that souls which pre-exist elsewhere are sent by God into the bodies of those who are born, or that they come down of their own will.[54] We should not lightly accept any of these opinions. Either this question has not yet been worked out and decided by Catholic commentators on Scripture, because of its obscurity and difficulty, or if this has been done, these works have not yet come into my hands.[55] At all events, our faith must keep us from holding anything about the substance of the Creator which is false or unworthy of Him. For we journey to Him by the path of pious devotion. If we hold any false opinion about Him, we shall be carried in the direction of vanity and not of happiness. If we hold any false opinion about a creature, provided we do not accept it as known for certain, there is no danger. We are not commanded to seek the creature in order to become happy, but the Creator Himself. If we hold any opinion about Him which is wrong or false, we are deceived by a pernicious error. For no one, if he journeys towards what does not exist, or towards what does not make him happy even if it does exist, can reach the life of happiness.

IT IS OUR FUTURE DESTINY WHICH IS IMPORTANT

60 For the contemplation of eternal truth, that we may be able to enjoy it and cling to it, a path has been provided through temporal things adapted to our weakness: we must believe past and future events, so far as is required by those who journey to the eternal. This discipline of faith is authoritative, being governed by divine mercy. Present events, so far as they concern creatures, are perceived as transitory, through the movements and changes of body and soul. We cannot have any knowledge of these things, except in so far as we experience them.

We should believe whatever we are told about past or future on God's authority, with regard to any creature. Some of these events happened before we could perceive them, some we have not yet perceived with our senses. Nevertheless we must believe them without any hesitation because they help greatly to strengthen our hope and excite our love, while they remind us of our salvation which God does not neglect throughout the ordered succession of temporal events.

If any error puts on the mask of divine authority, it can be refuted by the following test: is it proved to believe or affirm that any beauty, even though changeable, exists apart from God's creatures, or that any changeable beauty exists in the substance of God? Does it maintain that the substance of God is more or less than the Trinity? The whole energy of the Christian is at work with devotion and restraint to understand the Trinity, and all his progress is concerned with doing so. This is not the place to discuss the unity and equality of the Trinity, and that which is proper to each Person. To mention certain facts about the Lord God, the author of all things, the source of their forms,[56] and their governor, facts which pertain to sound faith and which form a useful support to the purpose of one who is a child in these matters and is only beginning to rise from things of earth to those of heaven—this is easy to do and many have already done it. But to cover the whole of this question, and so to treat of it that every human intelligence will, so far as is possible in this life, be satisfied with the clear reasoning, does not seem a task which we ourselves, or indeed anyone, would find easy, or lightly to be attempted even in thought and far less in word.

Now let us carry out our plan of discussion so far as God helps us and allows us to do so. With regard to creatures, we must believe without any hesitation whatever is told us concerning the past or is prophesied concerning the future, if this can foster sound religion and rouse us to sincere love of God and our neighbour. We must defend it against unbelievers, so that either their infidelity may be crushed by the weight of authority, or that they may shown so far as possible—first, that it is not foolish to believe these things, secondly, that it is foolish not to believe them. But we ought to refute false teaching not so much about the past and future as about the present, and especially about unchangeable realities, and, so far as possible, we ought to give clear proofs.

61   Certainly in the series of temporal events [57] we should prefer looking forward to the future to inquiry into the past. In the Divine Books too the story of past events prefigures, or promises, or witnesses to, the future. Indeed, even in matters which concern this present life, whether favourable or unfavourable, no one troubles about his earlier state, but all anxiety concentrates upon hopes for the future. As a result of some feeling in the depth of our natures, past events, being over and done with, are regarded as moments of happiness or misery, as though they had never occurred.

What disadvantage is it to me not to know when I began to exist, if I know that I exist now and hope to exist in the future? I do not trouble about the past, or think a false opinion about the past a disastrous error. I direct my course to my future, led by the mercy of my Creator. If, therefore, I be-

lieve or think falsely about my future state, or
about Him with whom I shall be in the future, I
must be most careful to guard against this error.
The danger is that I may not make the necessary
preparation, or may be unable to reach the end I
have in view, if I confuse one thing with another.

If I were buying a coat, it would not affect me
adversely to have forgotten last winter, but such
would be the case, were I not to believe that cold
weather will be coming on. So too it will be no
hindrance to my soul if it forgets what it may have
endured in the past, provided it keeps carefully in
mind all for which it is urged to prepare in the
future. If, for example, a man was sailing for
Rome, it would not matter if he forgot the land
from which he set sail, so long as he knew whither
to steer from the place at which he was. It would
not help him to remember the land from which he
set out, if he made a mistake about the port of
Rome and was wrecked. In the same way it will
do no harm to me to forget the beginning of my
life, if I know the end where I can find rest. It
will not help me to remember or to guess the beginning of my life, if I have an unworthy notion
of God Himself who is the sole end of the soul's
labours, and run upon the reefs of error.

62   These words should not make anyone think that
we are warning competent critics against consult-
ing the divinely inspired Scriptures—whether soul
is generated from soul, or whether each soul is created separately for the person whom it animates,
or whether souls are sent by divine command from

elsewhere to govern and animate a body, or whether they put themselves there by their own will. To examine an important question, reason may demand that we consider and discuss these things, or else leisure from more important matters may be granted for study and research in these fields.

I have mentioned this rather to prevent, on so grave a question, unreasonable exasperation against those who question one's opinion through doubt which is perhaps too human. Also, if anyone can find any clear evidence, he should not suppose another person has abandoned hope of the future, because he has forgotten his origins in the past.

22.63 Whatever the truth about this matter, whether we must leave it aside altogether, or whether we must put off its consideration to another time, we are not prevented from seeing the answer to the problem under discussion. We see that souls pay the penalty for their sins, and that the majesty and substance of the Creator remains unimpaired, just, unshakeable, and unchangeable. Sins, as we have already explained, are to be attributed to nothing but to their own wills, and we must not look for any further [58] cause of sins.

64 If, however, ignorance and difficulty are according to nature, the soul starts from this condition to advance and move towards knowledge and a state of rest, until it reaches perfection in the life of happiness. If of its own will it neglects its progress in the study of higher things and in devotion, though the opportunity for this is not denied it, it

is justly precipitated into worse ignorance and difficulty, which is already punishment, and is placed among lower beings by a right and proper disposition of affairs.

A soul is not held guilty if its ignorance and incapacity result from its nature, but only if it does not attempt to acquire knowledge, and if it makes no sufficient effort to gain the power to act rightly. It is natural for a child not to know how to speak and to be unable to do so. Its ignorance of, and difficulty in, speaking are no crime against the laws of grammar; we even regard such things with pleasure and affection. The child did not fail to gain this power through any fault, nor did it possess this power and then lose it through any fault. If our happiness consisted in eloquence, and it were a crime to make a mistake in speaking, in the same sense as in life certain actions are sinful, no one would be blamed for childhood, because that was the starting point in the acquirement of eloquence. Clearly, however, he could be justly blamed if through perversity of will he fell back into childhood or remained in it.

So too if ignorance of the truth and difficulty in doing right are natural to man, and if this is the condition from which he starts in his progress to the happiness of wisdom and the state of rest, no one has any right to blame happiness for its natural origin. Yet, if a man refuses to make progress or wilfully falls back from progress, it is right and just that he should be punished.

65   The Creator of the soul always deserves praise,

for endowing it from its first beginning with the capacity of gaining the supreme good, for helping it to advance, for finishing and perfecting its progress, for justly condemning it according to its deserts when it sins, that is, when it refuses to raise itself from its original state to its perfection, or when it falls back again after it has made progress.

The fact that at first it was not as perfect as it received the power to become at a later stage, does not mean that it was created evil. All the perfections of bodily things are far inferior to the soul in its first condition, though a sound judgment would count even these praiseworthy in their own way. The fact that the soul does not know what it ought to do arises from the fact that it has not yet received this knowledge; but it will receive this, if it makes good use of what it has already received; and it has been endowed sufficiently to seek devoutly and diligently if it wills to do so.

If through ignorance of what it ought to do it is unable at present to fulfil its duty, this also is a perfection it has not yet been granted. One part of it has advanced to the higher stage of perceiving the good it ought to do,[59] but another part is slower and carnal and is not prevailed upon to share this judgment. Thus difficulty itself urges the soul to pray for help in the work of perfection from Him who, it realises, caused the work to begin. Thus it loves Him more, since not by its own strength but by the mercy of Him whose goodness gave it existence, it is raised to enjoy happiness. The

more it loves the author of its being, the more
firmly it rests in Him, and the more plentifully it
enjoys His eternity.

If the young plant of a tree should not be called
barren, though for some summers it bears no fruit
until in due time it becomes fruitful, why should
not the Creator of the soul be praised with due
devotion, if He has granted it an early period during which by zeal and progress it may come to bear
the fruit of wisdom and justice, and if He has be-
stowed on it the honour of having the power, if it
wills, to tend towards happiness?

THE SUFFERINGS OF YOUNG CHILDREN

23.66   Those who do not understand these matters like
to bring forward the deaths of young children and
the bodily suffering with which we frequently see
them afflicted, as a means of discrediting the above
argument. What need was there of the child
being born, they ask, since it has departed from life
before it could gain any merit in life? How is it
to be counted in the judgment to come, seeing that
it neither finds a place among the just, having performed no good action, nor among the wicked,
having committed no sin?

We reply as follows. In relation to the whole,
to the ordered connection of all creation in space
and time, no one whatever can be created without
a purpose. Not even the leaf of a tree is created
without a purpose. It is, however, purposeless to
ask about the merits of one who has gained no

merit. We need not fear that there may be a life halfway between virtue and vice, a sentence of the Judge halfway between reward and punishment.

67   In this connection, too, people will raise the question: What benefit do children gain from the sacrament of Christ's baptism, since they often die after receiving it and before they can derive any knowledge from it?

About this there is a good pious belief that the child is benefitted by the faith of those who bring it for baptism. This belief is supported by the salutary authority of the Church, so that we may all realise what benefit we have in our own faith, seeing that it [60] can be used to do good to others who do not yet have faith of their own. What benefit did the widow's son gain from his own faith, since, being dead, he had none? Yet the faith of his mother helped to bring about his resurrection.[61] How much more probable is it that the faith of another can help a child, whose lack of faith cannot be imputed to it!

68   A more serious objection on the ground of cruelty is often raised concerning the bodily sufferings of children who have never committed sin during their lives. If the souls which animate them had no existence prior to their becoming human beings, the question is asked, what evil they have done to deserve suffering. As though innocence could have any merit before a person has power to do wrong!

But God does good in correcting adults when their children whom they love suffer pain and death. Why should not this be done, since, when

the suffering is past, it is as nothing to those who
have endured it? Those, on the other hand, for
whose sake this has happened, will either be better
men if they make use of their temporal ills and
choose to live better lives, or they will have no
excuse when they are punished at the future judgment, if in spite of the sufferings of this life they
refuse to turn their hearts to eternal life.

Moreover, when the hearts of parents are soft-
ened by the sufferings of children, or when their
faith is stirred, or their pity roused, who knows
what ample compensation God reserves for these
children in the secret of His judgments? They
have not, it is true, performed right actions; yet
they have suffered without having sinned. Nor is
it to no purpose that the Church urges us to honour
as martyrs the children who were slain when
Herod sought the life of the Lord Jesus Christ.

THE SUFFERINGS OF ANIMALS

69   Those who put these specious questions, guided
by no zeal to examine such problems, but raising
trouble from the sheer desire to talk, will also disturb the faith of the more simple by questions
about the pain and distress of animals. They ask
what wrong animals have committed, to deserve
such evils, or what good they can hope for, when
they are afflicted in this way.

They say this or have such thoughts because
they have no sense of justice in these matters.
They cannot appreciate the nature or the excel-

lence of the supreme good, and want everything to correspond with their notion of what it is. Apart from the highest celestial bodies which are subject but little to corruption, they have no idea of a supreme good. Therefore they make the unreasonable demand that the bodies of beasts shall suffer neither death nor corruption, as if they were not mortal, though they are in the lowest rank, or were evil because the heavenly bodies are better.

Moreover, the pain suffered by animals enables us to see a power in the souls of beasts, which is in its way wonderful and admirable. It shows us how their souls strive for unity in governing and animating their bodies. For what else is pain but a feeling which resists division or corruption? Hence it is clearer than day that such a soul craves for unity and is tenacious of it throughout the whole of its body. Neither willingly nor with indifference, but reluctantly and with a struggle, it meets bodily suffering, and is distressed by the collapse of its unity and soundness. Only the pain of beasts makes us realise the striving for unity in the lower living creatures. If we did not realise this, we should not be sufficiently reminded that everything is constituted by that supreme, sublime, and ineffable unity of the Creator.

70 Indeed, if you consider the matter reverently and with care, all beauty and every movement in the creature claiming the attention of the human mind, speaks to us and instructs us. With its various movements and tendencies, as with many dif-

ferent tongues, it hails us on all sides and bids us recognise the Creator.

Of all the things that have no sense of pain or pleasure, there is none that does not acquire through a certain unity the beauty characteristic of its type, or at least in some degree stability of its nature. So too of the things that are sensitive to the annoyance of pain or the attraction of pleasure, there is none that does not by the very act of avoiding pain and seeking pleasure, confess that it shuns division and seeks unity. In rational souls every desire of knowledge, in which their nature takes pleasure, refers all it perceives to the test of unity, and, when shunning error, shuns nothing else than confusion and meaningless inconsistency. What is it that troubles us in inconsistency but that it has no sure unity? Hence it is clear that everything, whether it inflicts harm or suffers harm, whether it causes pleasure or is given pleasure, suggests and proclaims the unity of the Creator.

But if ignorance and difficulty with which this life must necessarily begin, are not natural to souls, it follows that either they have been undertaken as a duty or imposed as a punishment. Now I think we have sufficiently discussed this subject.

THE FIRST MAN'S SIN

24.71 It is more important to inquire in what state the first man was created than how his descendants have been propagated.

Those who put the problem as follows think

they are framing it very cleverly. If the first man was created wise, how was he seduced? If he was created foolish, why is not God the cause of vice, since folly is the greatest vice? As if human nature might not receive some condition midway between folly and wisdom, which could be called neither folly nor wisdom! Only then does a man begin to be foolish or wise and really deserve to be called one or the other, when it becomes possible for him to possess wisdom and when his will is guilty of wicked folly if he neglects to gain it.

No one is so stupid as to call an infant foolish, though it would be more absurd to want to call it wise. An infant can be called neither wise nor foolish, though it is already a human being. Hence it is clear that human nature receives a middle state which cannot rightly be called either folly or wisdom. And thus if anyone were born in the same state as those have who lack wisdom through their own neglect, no one would be right in calling him foolish, seeing that it was due to nature and not to vice.

Folly is not any kind of ignorance of what we should seek and what we should avoid, but it is vicious ignorance. We do not call an irrational animal foolish, because it has not been given the power to become wise. Often, however, we apply terms in a similar, but not in the same, sense. Blindness is the worst affliction of the eye, but it is not an affliction to young puppies, and blindness is not the right term to use.

72   If, therefore, man was created such that, al-

though he was not yet wise, he could yet be given a command with the obligation of obeying it, it is not surprising that he could be led into sin. Neither was it unjust that he should be punished if he disobeyed the command, nor is His Creator the cause of his vices, because the absence of wisdom was not yet a vice in man, if he had not yet received the power to possess it.

Nevertheless man had the means by which, if he used them well, he could rise to what he did not possess. To be rational is different from being wise. By reason every man is made able to recognise the command to which he ought to be faithful and so carry out what is commanded. As reason of its very nature makes us recognise the command, so the observance of the command makes us gain wisdom; and what nature does in making us recognise the command, this will does in making us observe it. As the rational nature is, in a sense, the merit of receiving the command, so observance of the command is the merit of receiving wisdom.

Now, from the time when man begins to be capable of receiving the command, from this time he begins to be capable of sinning. He sins in two ways before he becomes wise, either by failing to make himself fit to receive the command, or by not observing it when he has received it. When he is wise, a man sins by turning away from wisdom. As a command is not received from him to whom the command is given but from him who gives the command, so wisdom is not received from him who is enlightened but from him who gives the enlightenment.

So, why should not man's Creator be praised? Man is something good. He is better than a beast because he is capable of receiving a command. Man is still better when he has already accepted the command, and better again when he has obeyed it. He is best of all when he is happy with the eternal light of wisdom.

The evil of sin consists in neglect either to grasp the command, or to observe it, or to practise the contemplation of wisdom. Hence we can understand how the first man could be led into sin even though he was created wise. Since this sin arose from free will, punishment followed by a just law of God.[62] Thus too the apostle Paul says: *Professing themselves to be wise, they became fools.* For pride turns from wisdom, and folly follows from this. Folly is a kind of blindness, as the same says, *. . . and their foolish heart was darkened.*[63] And how is it darkened, if not by turning away from the light of wisdom? How does it come to turn away, except because man, whose good God is, wills to be his own good as God is His own good? Therefore Scripture says: *My soul is troubled within myself,*[64] and, *Taste, and you shall be as gods.*[65]

73　Some who consider this matter are troubled by this question—did the first man fall from God through folly, or was he made foolish by falling? If you reply that folly made him fall from wisdom, he will appear to have been foolish before he fell

from wisdom, so that folly was the cause of his
falling. Again, if you reply that he was made
foolish by falling, they ask whether he was foolish
or wise in causing himself to fall. If he was wise
in doing so, he acted rightly and committed no sin;
if he was foolish, folly, they say, possessed him already and made him fall. Without folly he could
not act foolishly.

Hence it is clear that there is a state between
those two by which a man passes from wisdom to
folly; and an act done in this state cannot be called
an act either of folly or of wisdom. In the present
life man can only understand this through what
contradicts it. For no mortal man becomes wise
unless he passes from folly to wisdom. If he makes
this passage foolishly, it would be most absurd to
call it a good action, while if he makes it wisely, it
is also absurd to say that he already possessed wisdom before he passed to wisdom. Hence we see
that there is a state between the two which can be
described in neither way. Thus when the first
man left the citadel of wisdom and passed to folly,
the passage was neither foolish nor wise. We find
something similar to this in sleep and waking: to
go to sleep is not the same as to be asleep, nor is to
begin to wake up the same as to be awake, but
there is a passage from one to the other. There is
this difference, however, that the latter actions are
for the most part involuntary, while the former is
always voluntary. It is for this reason that it justly
deserves punishment.

25.74 The will is not drawn to perform an action except when an object is perceived. We have it in our power to accept or reject something, but we have no power to decide what the eye shall light on. We must agree that the soul comes into contact with both higher and lower objects in such a way that a rational person takes what it chooses from both, and deserves unhappiness or happiness in accordance with its choice.

Thus in Paradise among the higher objects perceived was the command of God, among the lower objects, the temptation of the serpent. It was not in man's power to determine what the Lord should command, or what the serpent should suggest as a temptation. But if he is established in the sound state of wisdom, he is unshackled by any bond of difficulty and free not to yield to the seduction of the lower object perceived. We know this because the foolish themselves conquer such temptations when they are about to pass over to wisdom, even though it is painful to renounce the deadly pleasure of wicked habits.

THE DEVIL'S SIN

75 The question may be asked at this point: If two objects were presented to man's consciousness on either side, one the commandment of God, the other the temptation of the serpent, how did the suggestion come to the devil himself to do the wrong which brought about his fall from his place on high? Had no object appeared to his sight, he would not have chosen to do what he did. If no

such idea had occurred to his mind, he could not
possibly have turned his thoughts to wickedness.
Wherefore, how did that thought, whatever it
was, come into his mind, of striving for what was
to change him from a good angel to a devil? The
will, if it wills at all, must will some object. It cannot do this unless the object is presented from outside through the bodily senses, or comes into the
mind in some hidden way.

Therefore, we must distinguish two kinds of
objects which are perceived. One comes from the
persuasion of a will, as when man sinned by consenting to the devil; the other comes from things
which are presented in the natural course to the
attention of the soul, or the bodily senses. If we
ask what is presented to the attention of the soul,
it is not the unchangeable Trinity, for this cannot
be subject to examination but rather transcends the
mind. First, the soul itself is presented to the
attention of the soul, and so we become conscious
that we are alive. Secondly, the body, which the
mind governs, is presented; and that is why for any
action the soul moves the required member at the
required time. Finally, bodily things of every sort
are presented to the bodily senses.

76   The soul in contemplating supreme wisdom—
which, being unchangeable, cannot be identified
with the soul—also looks at its changeable self and
in some sense comes into its own mind. The reason
is simply that it is distinct from God, and yet is
something capable of causing itself pleasure after
God. It is better if it forgets itself through love

of the unchangeable God, or despises itself utterly in comparison with Him. But if, so to speak, it goes out of its way to produce a false imitation of God, and to will to take pleasure in its own power, then the greater it wishes to become the less it becomes in fact. And that is *pride, the beginning of all sin;* and *the beginning of the pride of man is to fall off from God.*[66]

The devil added malevolent envy to his pride when he persuaded man to share his pride, through which he knew he was damned. Hence it was that man suffered a punishment designed to correct him rather than to destroy him, so that while the devil showed himself a model of pride, the Lord should show Himself a model of humility, through whom we are promised eternal life. Thus the blood of Christ having been offered for us after unutterable distress and pain, we ought to follow Our Saviour with such love, and be so enraptured by His brightness, that no lower object may detach us from so sublime a spectacle. If our attention should be distracted by any lower desire, the everlasting damnation and torment of the devil ought to call us back.

THE SUPREME WORTH OF JUSTICE, TRUTH, AND WISDOM

77   So beautiful is justice, so delightful is eternal light, that is to say, unchangeable truth and wisdom, that, even though we were permitted to abide in it only for one day, for this alone it would be

right and proper to despise countless years of this
life, though filled with pleasures and abundant
temporal goods. Real truth and feeling are expressed in the words, *Far better is one day in
Thy courts above thousands.*[67] They may also be
taken in another sense: a thousand days might
mean time and its changes, while one day means
unchangeable eternity.

I do not know whether I have failed to answer
any of your questions, so far as the Lord has
deigned to grant me power. Even if anything
occurs to you, the limits of this book compel me
to come to an end and to take some rest after our
discussion.

APPENDIX

ST. AUGUSTINE'S REVIEW (A.D. 427) OF *THE PROBLEM OF FREE CHOICE*

Retractations bk. 1 ch. 9

While we were still staying at Rome, we wished to debate and trace out the cause of evil. Our plan of debate aimed at understanding by means of thorough rational inquiry—so far as, with God's help, discussion should enable us—what we believed about this question on divine authority. After careful examination of the arguments we agreed that evil occurred only through free choice of will, and so the three books resulting from this discussion were called *The Problem of Free Choice*. I finished the second and third of these books, as well as I could at the time, in Africa, after I was ordained priest at Hippo Regius.

2. In these books we discussed so many problems that some questions arose, which either I could not solve, or which required long consideration before they could be decided, and these we put off. But whatever the answer to these questions, or even if there were many answers, when it was not clear where the truth lay, the conclusion nevertheless came to this, that, whatever the truth, rightly and obviously praise should be given to God. We undertook this discussion because of those who deny that evil is due to free choice of will and who maintain that God, if this is so, deserves blame as the Creator of every kind of thing. Thus they wish in their wicked error—they are

the Manichees—to introduce a being, evil in nature, which is unchangeable and coeternal with God. As this was why we raised the problem, these books contain no reference to God's grace, by which He has predestined His elect in such a way that He Himself makes ready the wills of those among them who are now making use of free choice. When there was any occasion for mentioning this grace, it was mentioned in passing, not defended by careful reasoning as if it was the main subject. It is one thing to inquire into the cause of evil, another to inquire how we can return to our former good, or reach one that is greater.

3. Hence the recent Pelagian heretics, who hold a theory of free choice of will which leaves no place for the grace of God, since they hold it is given in accordance with our merits, must not boast of my support. I said much in these books in defence of free choice, which was called for by the purpose of the discussion. In the first book I said indeed that 'wrongdoing is punished by God's justice,' and added, 'it would not be punished justly, unless it were done wilfully' [1.1.1]. Again, when I showed that a good will was so great a good that it was rightly preferred to all bodily and external goods, I said: 'I think you now see that it lies in the power of our will whether we enjoy or lack this great and true good. What is so fully in the power of the will as the will itself?' [1.12.26]. And in another place: 'Then what reason is there for doubting that, even though we were never wise before, yet by our will we deserve, and spend, a praiseworthy and happy life, and by our will a life that is shameful and unhappy?' [1.13.28]. Again, in another place: 'Hence it follows that whoever wishes to live rightly and virtuously,

if he wishes so to wish in preference to goods which are
but passing, will acquire this great possession with such
ease, that to wish for it will be the same as to possess what
he wished' [1.13.29]. Again, I said elsewhere: 'The eternal law, to the consideration of which it is now time to
return, has settled this with unchangeable firmness; it has
settled that merit lies in the will, while reward and punishment lie in happiness and misery' [1.14.30]. And in another place: 'We have agreed that it lies in the will what
each man chooses to seek and attach himself to' [1.16.34].
And in the second book: 'Man himself is something good
in so far as he is man, for he can live rightly when he so
wills' [2.1.2]. In another place I said 'that we could not
act rightly except by this free choice of will' [2.18.47].
And in the third book: 'What need is there to ask the
source of that movement by which the will turns from the
unchangeable good to the changeable good? We agree
that it belongs only to the soul, and is voluntary and
therefore culpable; and the whole value of teaching in this
matter consists in its power to make us censure and check
this movement, and turn our wills away from temporal
things below us to enjoyment of the everlasting good'
[3.1.2]. And in another place: 'The voice of truth speaks
clearly in what you say. You could not be aware of anything in our power, if not of our actions when we will.
Nothing is so fully in our power as the will itself, for it is
ready at once and without delay to act as we will' [3.3.7].
Again in another place, 'If you are praised when you see
what you ought to do, though you only see this in Him
who is unchangeable truth, how much more should He be
praised who has ordered you to will what you ought to
do, and has given you the power to carry it out, and has

not allowed you to refuse it unpunished!' Then I added, 'If everyone owes that which he has received, and if man has been so made that he sins necessarily, then his duty is to sin. Therefore, when he sins, he does what he ought to do. But if it is wicked to say this, then no one is forced by his own nature to sin' [3.16.46]. And again: 'Now what could precede the will and be its cause? Either it is the will itself, and nothing else than the will is the root, or it is not the will which is not sinful. Either the will itself is the original cause of sin, or no sin is the original cause of sin. Sin cannot be attributed to anything except to the sinner. It cannot rightly be attributed to anything except to him who wills it' [3.17.49]. And a little later: 'No one sins when he cannot guard against it. Yet sin is committed, and therefore we can guard against it' [3.18.50]. Pelagius used this evidence of mine in a book of his. When I answered this book, I chose for the title of my book, *The Problem of Nature and Grace*.

4. In these and similar statements of mine I did not mention God's grace, as this was not the subject I was then dealing with. Hence the Pelagians think, or may think, that I held their views. They are wrong, however, in thinking so. It is the will by which we sin and by which we live rightly, as I explained in these passages. Unless, therefore, the will itself is set free by the grace of God from that slavery by which it has been made *a servant of sin*, and unless it is given help to overcome its vices, mortal men cannot live upright and devout lives. If this gift of God, by which the will is set free, did not precede the act of the will, it would be given in accordance with the will's merits, and would not be grace which is certainly given as a free gift. I have dealt sufficiently with this subject in

other small works of mine, in which I have refuted these recent heretics who oppose this view of grace. Yet even in this book, *The Problem of Free Choice*, which was not written against them at all, but against the Manichees, I was not entirely silent about this grace of God, which they attempt with unspeakable wickedness to deny. In fact I said in the second book that, 'not to speak of great goods, not even the least can exist except as coming from Him from whom come all good things, that is, from God.' And a little later I stated: 'The virtues by which we live rightly are great goods, but all kinds of bodily beauty, without which we can live rightly, are the least goods. The powers of the soul, without which we cannot live rightly, are the middle goods. No one uses the virtues wrongly, but anyone can use the other goods, the middle and the least, wrongly as well as rightly. No one uses virtue wrongly, because the work of virtue is the good use of those things which we are capable of using wrongly. No one makes a bad use when he makes a good use. Hence the magnificent abundance of God's goodness has furnished us not only with great goods, but also with the middle and the least. His goodness should be praised more highly for great than for middle goods, more for middle than for least, but for all more than if He had not given all' [2.19.50]. And in another place: 'Only keep firm your sense of reverence towards God, so that no good may occur either to your senses, your intelligence, or your thoughts in any way, which you do not acknowledge to be from God' [2.20.54]. I also said in another place: 'But, though man fell through his own will, he cannot rise through his own will. Therefore let us believe firmly that

God's arm, that is, Our Lord Jesus Christ, is stretched out to us from on high' [*ibid.*].

5. In the third book after the words which, as I have mentioned, Pelagius quoted from my works—'No one sins when he cannot guard against it. Yet sin is committed, and therefore we can guard against it'—I added at once: 'Nevertheless some actions done in ignorance are judged wrong and in need of correction, as we read in the divine documents. For example, the Apostle says: *I obtained the mercy of God, because I did it ignorantly;* and the Prophet says: *The sins of my youth and my ignorance do not remember.* Actions done of necessity when a man wills to act rightly and cannot, are also judged wrong. Hence the words: *For the good which I will, I do not; but the evil which I will not, that I do;* and, *To will is present with me, but to accomplish that which is good I find not;* and, *The flesh lusteth against the spirit, and the spirit against the flesh; for these are contrary one to another, so that you do not the things that you would.* But all this applies to men as they appear on the scene after the condemnation of death; for if this does not stand for man's punishment, but his natural condition, then there is no question of sin. If man has not lost his natural kind of being, and if he cannot become better, he does what he ought when he acts in this way. But if man would be good if he were constituted differently, and he is not good because he is in his present condition; if he has not the power to become good, whether because he does not see what he ought to be, or because he sees and yet cannot be what he sees he ought to be, then this is surely a punishment. Now every punishment is a punishment for sin, if it is just, and is called a penalty; but if the punishment is unjust, since none

doubts it is a punishment, it is imposed on man by an unjust ruler. But it would be folly to doubt the omnipotence and justice of God, and therefore this punishment
must be just, and be exacted for some sin. No unjust ruler
could have snatched man away from God without His
knowledge, or taken him by force against God's will,
whether by threat or violence, in order to inflict torture
on him as an unjust punishment. No one can frighten
God, or struggle with Him. It remains, therefore, that
this is a just punishment resulting from man's condemnation' [3.18.50 f.]. And in another place I said: 'To approve false for true, so as to err unwillingly, and to be
unable to refrain from acts of passion on account of the
resistance and pain of the bonds of the flesh, are not natural to man in his original state, but are a punishment after
his condemnation. When we speak of a will free to act
rightly, we speak of the will with which man was created'
[3.18.52].

6. Thus, long before the Pelagian heresy arose, we debated as though we were already debating against them.
For we stated that all good things come from God—the
great, the middle, and the least goods; among the middle
goods is found free choice of will since we can use it
wrongly, but yet it is such that we cannot live rightly
without it. To use it well is at once virtue, and virtue is
found among the great goods which no one can use
wrongly. Because all good things, as I have said—great,
middle, and least—come from God, it follows that from
God comes the good use of free will, which is virtue and
is counted among the great goods. Then I spoke of the
misery, justly inflicted on sinners, from which the grace
of God frees them, because man could fall of his own

accord, that is, by his free choice, but could not rise in this way. The misery, to which we are justly condemned, involves ignorance and difficulty, which every man suffers from the moment of his birth, nor is anyone delivered from this evil except by the grace of God. The Pelagians refuse to attribute this misery to a just condemnation, since they deny original sin. Yet, even though ignorance and difficulty were the original and natural state of man, we ought not on this account to blame God, but to praise Him. We argued this in the same third book. This discussion is to be regarded as aimed against the Manichees, who do not recognise as Sacred Scripture the Old Testament, where the story of original sin is told. What we read in the Apostolic Epistles they have the dreadful effrontery to claim is a falsification of Scripture and not the genuine record of the Apostles. But against the Pelagians we have to defend both deposits of Scripture, which Scripture they profess to accept. This work begins with the words, 'I should like you to tell me: is not God the cause of evil?'

NOTES

LIST OF ABBREVIATIONS

ACW   Ancient Christian Writers (Westminster, Md.–London 1946–).

CSEL   Corpus scriptorum ecclesiasticorum latinorum (Vienna 1866–).

DTC   Dictionnaire de théologie catholique (Paris 1903–).

Green TN   W. M. Green, 'Textual Notes on Augustine's *De libero arbitrio,' Revue de philologie de littérature et d'histoire anciennes* 28 (1954) 21–29.

PL   J. P. Migne, Patrologia latina (Paris 1857–66).

Thonnard   F. J. Thonnard, Bibliothèque Augustinienne, *Oeuvres de Saint Augustin,* 1re Série, Opuscules 6: *Dialogues philosophiques* 3. *De l'âme à Dieu* (Paris 1941) 123 ff.

INTRODUCTION

[1] *Retract.* 1.9.1 f. (cf. the Appendix).

[2] *Ibid.* 1.9.2.

[3] *Contra Secundinum* 11: 'The less anything is, so much the nearer it is to nothing. When these defects are due to free will, they are rightly blamed and called sins. But when these voluntary defects are followed by misfortune, trouble, grief, and pain, all of which we suffer against our will, sins are rightly punished by penalties, or washed away by devout practices. If you are willing to consider this calmly, you will cease to accuse the natures of things, and to make a charge against the substances themselves. If you wish for a fuller or more complete discussion

of this matter, read my three books which have the title, *De libero arbitrio:* you can find them at Nola in Campania, in the hands of the excellent servant of God, Paulinus.'

[4] This account is taken from F. C. Burkitt's chapter 14 in *The Cambridge Ancient History* 12 (Cambridge 1939) 504–514: 'Mani and the Manichees.' See also, among others, H. C. Puech, *Le Manichéisme, son fondateur, sa doctrine* (Paris 1949).

[5] G. Bardy, 'Manichéisme,' DTC 9.2 (1927), 1841–95.

[6] *Contra Faustum Manichaeum* (CSEL 25,1.249–797). On Manichaeism and Augustine as its onetime ardent disciple, see the chapters by J. J. O'Meara, *The Young Augustine* (London 1954) 61–115.

[7] Cf. R. Hedde–É. Amann, 'Pélagianisme,' DTC 12.1 (1933) 675–715.

[8] Cf. É. Amann, 'Semi-Pélagiens,' DTC 14.2 (1941) 1796–1850.

[9] See *Retract.* 1.9.2–6.

[10] J. Burnaby, *Amor Dei. A Study of the Religion of St. Augustine* (London 1938) 184.

[11] See Augustine, *Ep.* 31.7.

[12] Augustine, *Ep.* 166.7—cf. also below, n. 54 to the third book.

[13] J. H. S. Burleigh, *The City of God. A study of St. Augustine's Philosophy* (London 1949) 72.

[14] Cf. *De dono perseverantiae* 26 f. (written 428–29): 'I argued against them [the Manichees] in my book about free choice, and hence they think they have a complaint to make against me. When the authority of Scripture was unavailing against such perversity, I did not wish to give a complete solution to the very difficult questions which occurred, for fear that the work should be too long. I was able to prove by unanswerable arguments (I actually did so, without definitely using Scripture, leaving aside the truth of any part of it), that God should be praised in all things, and that there was no need whatever to believe, as they wish to do, that there are two coeternal substances of good and evil confounded together.

'Then, in the first book of the *Retractations,* a work of mine which you have not yet read, when I came to review my book, *The Problem of Free Choice,* I wrote as follows [extracts follow from *Retract.* 1.9] . . . . This I said in the first book of the *Retractations,* when I reviewed my book on free choice. Nor did I only say what I have quoted about this book, but much more, which I felt unnecessarily long to insert in what I am writing for you. This, I think, will be your judgment when you have read it all. So in the third book about free choice I argued in such a way about children that, even though the Pelagians were right in saying that ignorance and difficulty, without which no man is born, belonged to our original nature and were not punishments, nevertheless the Manichees would be refuted who wish to hold that there are two coeternal natures of good and evil.'

[15] Cf. *Confessions* 9.17; also the note to the same and to 8.15 by J. Gibb—W. Montgomery, *The Confessions of Augustine* (Cambridge 1908) 252, 218.

[16] *Ibid.* 9.31.

[17] These letters are the following numbers in the Augustinian collection: Evod. to Aug.—158, 160, 161, 163; Aug. to Evod.— 159, 162, 164, 169.— H. Pope, *St. Augustine of Hippo* (London 1937) 121 f. (omitting some of the references), writes: 'His [Evodius'] devotion to Augustine is touching. He writes him long letters on doctrinal subjects and Augustine takes it for granted that he has copies of his works such as the *De Vera Religione*, *De Quantitate Animae*, *De Libero Arbitrio*, etc. In fact in the two last-named Evodius was one of the disputants, as Augustine reminds him: "You ask a lot of questions of a very busy man, and what is worse, you seem to think the answers to such questions can be dictated off-hand, though the problems presented are so difficult that even when carefully dictated or written the answers can hardly be brought within the grasp of even such a mind as yours. . . . But if you will but recall points that you know well, or at least, unless I am mistaken, did once know well, though you may possibly have forgotten the discussions we had together and which I committed to writing, whether *De Quantitate Animae* or *De Libero Arbitrio*, you will find there the answer to your questions" (*Ep.* 162.2, A.D. 415). Only with an intimate friend could Augustine have indulged in the above ironical remark about Evodius' intellectual capacity; only to one knit to him in the closest friendship could he have said: "See what (a long letter) a busy man like me has contrived to write to a lazy man like you!" (*Ep.* 169.12).

'Evodius was certainly not dull-witted. For when trouble arose in a certain monastery owing to the failure of the monks to understand Augustine's teaching on grace and predestination the Abbot, Valentinus, wrote to Evodius for counsel. . . . He also had the privilege of a quasi martyrdom, for the Council held at Carthage on June 26, 404, sent him and Theodosius to Rome to state the Catholic case against the enormities perpetrated by the Donatists, and a later Council sent them on the same errand. Petilian inveighed against these ambassadors . . . , but he was careful not to say that his fellow Donatists had scourged and grievously wounded them both on their return from their embassy in A.D. 408.'

On Evodius see also J. M. Colleran's introduction to his translation of Augustine's *De quantitate animae:* ACW 9.4 f.

TEXT: BOOK ONE

[1] C. J. Perl, *Aurelius Augustinus: Der freie Wille* (Paderborn 1947) 189, calls attention to the abrupt, almost brusque, character of the question which introduces the present inquiry. Presupposed, so he states, are many detailed discussions of the Manichaean theory—that evil is an independent principle, eternally existent and unchangeable in the presence of the good. Presupposed is the denial and refutation of such dualism—there is only one original and eternal principle, the good, God, the Creator of all. Evil originated, physical and moral evil: it originated in the free will of man. But the free will of created man was created by God; and at this stage of the discussion the Manichee, in the words of Evodius, is prompted to ask the fateful question: Did not God, therefore, the Creator of *all* things, also cause and create evil—sin?

[2] This is the first of the considerable number of passages in the *De libero arbitrio* which Augustine quotes (*Retract.* 1.9.3) as claimed by the Pelagians in support of their doctrine.

[3] We have used 'teaching' to translate the Latin *disciplina,* which is derived from *discere,* to 'learn.' The dictionary gives for *disciplina,* as its primary meaning, 'instruction, tuition, teaching, in the widest sense of the word,' and as a secondary meaning, 'learning, knowledge, science, discipline.' The literal translation of this sentence is, 'teaching (*disciplina*) is only derived from learning (*a discendo*),' but if we use 'teaching' for *disciplina,* we cannot bring out the meaning in English in a literal translation.

The argument of this passage is more easily understood if we realise that *disciplina* means teaching in the widest sense, and is therefore almost equivalent to education. We then understand that it stands for something which is plainly good, and which Evodius at once recognises to be a good. Moreover we must remember that St. Augustine considered evil to be at root a defect or failure, in itself negative rather than positive, and therefore in so far as teaching is positively given, he can argue that it must be good, since teaching of evil would really be a failure to teach.

⁴ Isa. 7.9, according to the Septuagint reading.

⁵ This is the main problem with which the *De libero arbitrio* deals: we have to try to understand what we believe about the origin of evil.

In many places throughout his works St. Augustine repeats in one form or another the advice that we should believe first in order to understand. The emphasis he lays on this principle, and the influence it had on succeeding generations, e.g. on St. Anselm, who also laid great stress on it, obliges us to examine its meaning. At first sight it looks paradoxical, and has often been misunderstood. Are we urged to a blind faith, unsupported by evidence?

(1) The first point we should notice is that St. Augustine certainly does not recommend a blind faith, when he says we should believe in order to understand. He fully acknowledges that evidence is, and should be, required, before the assent of faith. This is plainly shown in many passages in his writings, and a few examples may be given. 'Far be it that God should hate that in us wherein He has created us higher than other living things. Far be it, I say, that we should believe so as not to find the reason or to seek it, since we could not ever believe, unless we had rational souls. . . . If then it is reasonable that faith should precede reason in regard to those great facts which we cannot yet grasp, without doubt some degree of reason which makes us act in this way, also precedes faith' (*Ep.* 120.1.3). Again: 'Understand, therefore, that you may believe: believe that you may understand. I tell you shortly how we carry out both without contradiction. Understand my word, in order to believe it; believe the word of God, in order to understand it' (*Serm.* 43.7.9). Again: 'We believe those things which our senses do not perceive, if the evidence for them seems adequate. . . . We are right in saying we know not only those things which we have seen or now see, but also those things which we believe, persuaded by evidence or by witnesses suitable in any case' (*Ep.* 147.2.7–3.8). Many other passages might be quoted (See E. Portalié, 'Augustin (Saint),' DTC 1.2 [1903] 2338 f.), but these are sufficient to show that St. Augustine required rational evidence to justify belief. In

the *De libero arbitrio*, when in the second book he sets out to prove the existence of God, he starts from the fundamental truth of our own existence. Étienne Gilson points out that St. Augustine's purely philosophic refutation of scepticism implies that in his view reason can attain certain truths without the help of faith (*Introd. à l'étude de S. Augustin* [2 ed. Paris 1943] 41).

(2) Yet faith is the essential means, according to St. Augustine, even for knowledge, if it is to have real value. We shall appreciate this, if we follow his teaching about wisdom (*sapientia*). Wisdom is the only kind of knowledge which is ultimately valuable, because wisdom alone will lead us to the perfect happiness of the Beatific Vision. Thonnard (486 f.) gives a clear and useful summary of his teaching.

In the *De Trinitate* (cf. esp. 12.15.25, 13.19.24, 14.1.1–3) St. Augustine tells us that knowledge (*scientia*) is the work of the lower reason, which looks at things from the temporal and human point of view. By itself knowledge tends to make us enjoy creatures as an end in themselves, and thus is a source of evil: it leads to pride which is the primary sin. On the other hand, wisdom is the work of the higher reason, and judges from the point of view of the eternal types, the divine ideas. It is the fruit of illumination given by the Word, and so implies absolute detachment from self and creatures. The soul, however, which possesses wisdom, does not give up knowledge, for we need knowledge to guide us through temporal things on our way towards eternal life. It is normally through the study of creatures that we reach contemplation of the eternal truths, and thus knowledge acquires a true value if it is used as a means to wisdom. In addition to wisdom and knowledge there is spiritual understanding, which lies between the other two, though nearer to wisdom. Spiritual understanding perfects faith, and gives a true, though imperfect, understanding of revealed truth. For it gives us the whole truth, but in an obscure and veiled form. Spiritual understanding and wisdom reveal to us its meaning, the first rather in a speculative form, the second in a fuller way, since it is inspired by charity and unites us to God.

Thus St. Augustine teaches us to believe in order to understand, because he means by understanding that grasp of truth which is finally perfected in the Beatific Vision. 'It is never to be forgotten that the Augustinian "intellect" is not the discursive reason but the mind at worship': thus J. Burnaby, *Amor Dei*,

A Study of the Religion of St. Augustine (London 1938), 155.
A merely human and temporal understanding he regards as of
little value, because it does not lead us to the ultimate truth
wherein our final happiness lies. The faith which St. Augustine
refers to when he speaks of belief in this connection, is faith accompanied by charity and involving a moral and spiritual purification. We must distinguish between the early stage of faith in
which the believer sees for certain that what he believes is true,
but does not yet understand at all clearly what it means, and the
later stage when he gains a fuller understanding. 'For faith has
its eyes by which in some way it sees that to be true which it
does not yet see, and by which it sees most certainly that it does
not yet see what it believes' (*Ep.* 120.2.8). Gilson puts this
clearly. To St. Augustine, he states (46), it is faith which tells us
what there is to understand, and faith which purifies the heart
and renders reason able to understand what God reveals. When
St. Augustine speaks of understanding, he always means the result of a rational activity to which faith opens the door. 'Understanding is the reward of faith. Therefore do not seek to
understand that you may believe, but believe that you may
understand' (*In Ioan. Evang.* 29.6). Again: 'Our hearts are
cleansed by faith that they may be able to be fit to see. For we
walk now by faith, not yet by sight' (*Enarr. in Ps.* 123.2).
Finally, there is a well-known passage in which St. Augustine
sums up his teaching on this subject: 'Who does not see that
thought precedes belief? No one believes anything unless he has
first thought it should be believed. . . . Yet belief itself is nothing else than thought accompanied by assent. For not everyone
who thinks believes; many think so as not to believe. But everyone who believes thinks, and thinks by belief and believes by
thought' (*De praed. sanct.* 2.5).

(3) We must remember throughout that St. Augustine does
not use the terminology developed by the later theologians.
Thus St. Thomas makes a clear distinction between human faith
based on the authority of men, and supernatural faith based on
the authority of God, who reveals truths necessary for eternal
life. St. Augustine does not distinguish explicitly between these
two kinds of faith, but passes from one to the other without
clearly expressing the difference. He writes in this way in the
De magistro, for example, and also in the *De utilitate credendi*,
where he refers to the natural belief children have that their

parents are really their parents, a belief based on evidence but not on personal knowledge, and so goes on to argue the necessity of divine faith before we can understand the things of God (see Thonnard 484 f.).

(4) We should notice also that when St. Augustine discusses the relation between faith and reason, he does not have in mind precisely the same problems as are usually referred to in modern discussions on this subject. Gilson points this out (*op. cit.* 41). St. Augustine, he says, certainly agreed that there were truths, such as the truths of mathematics, which could be known by reason and not only by faith, but this was not quite the kind of problem he had in mind when he discussed the relation between belief and knowledge. Nor had he in mind the problem of the precise degree and kind of certainty which should accompany faith, in the form in which it is discussed at the present day.

(5) This brings us to the question which is often asked, and which follows from the considerations just mentioned: does St. Augustine have a system of philosophy to teach apart from a system of theology? St. Thomas distinguishes philosophy as a discipline which works on purely rational evidence, from theology which works from revealed truth. To St. Augustine, however, philosophy is love of wisdom, and its object is the possession of that wisdom which will lead us to supernatural happiness. Reason by itself, he maintains, cannot achieve this. He does not make a distinction explicitly between the two disciplines; he is thinking nearly always of the problem of human knowledge from the supernatural standpoint. Nevertheless his writings contain many arguments which are based on purely natural reasoning, and we can, if we like, pick them out, and compose a philosophy of the natural, as opposed to the Christian and supernatural order, even though St. Augustine did not do this himself. To help us to understand St. Augustine's attitude we may take an example from that part of the *De libero arbitrio* in which he is discussing the proof for the existence of God. Evodius first suggests the evidence from Scripture for God's existence as sufficient proof. Augustine accepts this, though he goes on to argue from reason alone. What he seems to imply is that faith in God, based on the evidence from Scripture, is reasonable, but that by examining the purely rational argument we shall deepen our understanding of what is involved (cf. Thonnard 499). Thus it is not only in regard to such doctrines as that of

the Trinity that faith precedes understanding, but even such a doctrine as that of the existence of God, for which there are rational grounds apart from faith, may be rightly accepted first by faith. In short, St. Augustine has in mind the individual in real life whose happiness consists in the attainment of supernatural wisdom based on faith, but whose beliefs are partly based on reason alone. For him in practice there is no separate domain where only natural reason presides, although it is possible for him to compose a system of natural reasoning, and to reckon up the truths which can be accepted on this kind of evidence and apart from faith.

F. Copleston, *A History of Philosophy* 2 (Westminster, Md., 1950) 48 f., sums up the position as follows: 'It is not that Augustine failed to recognise, still less that he denied, the intellect's power of attaining truth without revelation; it is rather that he regarded the Christian wisdom as one whole, that he tried to penetrate by his understanding the Christian faith and to see the world and human life in the light of the Christian wisdom. He knew quite well that rational arguments can be adduced for God's existence, for example, but it was not so much the mere intellectual assent to God's existence that interested him as the real assent, the positive adhesion of the will to God, and he knew that in the concrete such an adhesion to God requires divine grace. In short, Augustine did not play two parts, the part of the theologian and the part of the philosopher who considers the "natural man"; he thought rather of man as he is in the concrete, fallen and redeemed mankind, man who is able indeed to attain truth but who is constantly solicited by God's grace and who requires grace in order to appropriate the truth that saves.'

⁶ We have translated the Latin *libido* by 'passion,' as perhaps the nearest English equivalent, though 'passion' may suggest a merely passive state whereas *libido* implies a positive and active force. This latter characteristic is made clear in the following: 'There is, first of all, a factor in the soul which Augustine calls *libido* or *cupiditas*. It is the source of appetition, of desire in general; it may even designate the act of desire. Care should be taken, by those who are accustomed to some other type of psychology, not to confuse this *cupiditas* with either sensual appetite or intellectual appetite exclusively. It is not a faculty, at least not in the precise Aristotelico-Thomistic sense, and it is not called into play

by sensory perception alone, though it errs by choosing the things of the senses rather than higher goods. In this respect Augustine now unifies the appetitive part of the soul and uses the term will (*voluntas*) to designate it' (V. J. Bourke, *Augustine's Quest of Wisdom* [Milwaukee 1945] 91 f.).

To St. Augustine *concupiscentia* and *libido* 'signified a desire already disordered and perverted, the flesh in revolt against the spirit' (cf. Burnaby, *op. cit.* 59). It is clear that St. Augustine is not here using *cupiditas* exclusively in a bad sense, since below, in 1.4.10, he says that wrong actions are wrong because they are done through *libido*, and adds that *libido* is a blameworthy *cupiditas*.

[7] The argument is that, just in so far as the murder is committed from the desire to live without fear, the motive is good, though murder will not achieve this desire. Evil desire is not the direct motive of this murder, because the desire which is its direct motive is good. It is not *libido* or passion which makes an action wrong. If this were so, there might be a murder which was not a sin, since a murder might be committed from some motive other than evil desire.

[8] In the Benedictine edition there is a note to say that in previous editions confusion had occurred in some places in assigning the text to the speakers. Here—in these editions—Augustine continued to 'by killing a man,' while Evodius began again at 'I agree,' and then Augustine again at 'Answer this question.' Such mistakes were rectified by reference to the MSS.

[9] This point is never in fact dealt with.

[10] Here again there was a mistake in the earlier editions. The whole passage down to 'does not seem to me to be a law' is assigned to Evodius, and Augustine continues 'I see pretty well' until the beginning of § 13. The sense and the MSS are against this arrangement. Here, as in § 9 above, Perl, *op. cit.*, follows the earlier tradition.

[11] The word, translated here by 'subjects,' is *populus*. *Populus* or 'people' is used by St. Augustine in this and other similar passages for the people as a social body, and in contrast to the government. See Thonnard 492, who refers to the *De civitate Dei* (esp. 2.21.2), where St. Augustine defines *populus* in this way.

[12] In the earlier editions: E. I find it much harder. . . . A. No law may find them guilty. . . . E. So I think that that law. . . .

[13] These remarks of St. Augustine on popular government raise

the question of his political theory. He never wrote a special work on this subject, but the circumstances of his life compelled him to deal from time to time with particular aspects of it. From these partial discussions it is possible to gather a fairly complete general notion of his theory, with its emphasis on authority as the foundation of society, on law and justice, on the relations between Church and State. He was much influenced by Cicero, whose *De legibus* he had carefully studied, but he did not merely repeat Cicero's teaching; he adapted it to his Christian outlook. God is the source of order and law not only in human life but throughout the universe, and He gives to each thing its nature and the opportunities it has to develop, directing it by means of the temporal law, which may change, being adapted to changing things, and which depends for its force on the unchanging eternal law (see Thonnard 492 f.).

Thus we can see what was the place in St. Augustine's scheme for a Christian state, but the question may be asked: how does all this apply if the state is not Christian? We must not suppose that in Augustine's eyes the non-Christian state is outside God's purpose altogether. To quote Copleston, *op. cit.* 2.89: 'This does not mean, of course, that in Augustine's eyes the State exists in a non-moral sphere: on the contrary, the same moral law holds good for States as for individuals. The point he wants to make is that the State will not embody true justice, will not be a really moral State, unless it is a Christian State: it is Christianity which makes men good citizens. The State itself, as an instrument of force, has its roots in the consequences of original sin and, given the fact of original sin and its consequences, is a necessary institution; but a just State is out of the question unless it is a Christian State.' See also W. Cunningham, *St. Austin and His Place in the History of Christian Thought* (London 1886) 192 f.; Gilson, *op. cit.* 229 f.; J. Mausbach, *Die Ethik des Heiligen Augustinus* (2 ed. Freiburg i. Br. 1929) 1.326–50.

[14] The supreme type or reason which governs things: their exemplar cause. The Latin word is *ratio*, for which there is no satisfactory English equivalent, covering all its different shades of meaning. St. Thomas, *Summa theol.* I–II Q. 93 art. 1., after referring to this passage in the *De libero arbitrio*, says: 'As there pre-exists in any artist the type (*ratio*) of those things which are made by his art, so too in any ruler there must pre-exist the type of the order of those things to be done by the subjects of his rule.

As the type of the things to be made by an art is called the art, or exemplar, of the things to be made, so too the type in the man who rules the acts of his subjects acquires the character (*ratio*) of law, if the other conditions are observed which we mentioned above about the character of law in Q. 90. But God by His wisdom is the Creator of all things; to them He has the relation of the artist to the work of art, as was explained in I Q. 14 art. 8. He is also the ruler of all the acts and movements to be found in each creature, as was also explained in I Q. 103 art. 5. Hence, as the type of the divine wisdom, in so far as through it all things are created, has the character (*ratio*) of an art or exemplar or idea, so the type of the divine wisdom, moving all things to their due end, acquires the character (*ratio*) of law. Thus the eternal law is nothing else than the type of the divine wisdom, so far as it directs all acts and movements.'

[15] We have translated *beatus* as 'happy,' but it should be remembered that *beatus* does not mean 'happy' in any restricted sense; it means 'happy' in the fullest and highest sense. Cf. Augustine's own *De beata vita*, and Gilson, *op. cit.* 1–10; also B. Roland-Gosselin, 'St. Augustine's System of Morals,' in *A Monument to St. Augustine* (London 1945) 228–33.

[16] This phrase, *impressa nobis*, should be noticed in connection with St. Augustine's theory of knowledge which will be discussed later on (see 245 n.2).

[17] Prof. Green TN 23 reads *eminuit*, 'as has appeared clearly,' instead of *emicuit*.

[18] Reading with the manuscripts and Prof. Green PN 23: '*quoniam* scire' for '*quam* scire.' For the distinction between St. Augustine's use of knowledge and of understanding see notes 5 and 19; also note 2 to Book 2.

[19] St. Augustine does not usually regard the soul's faculties as distinct from the soul itself: he finds an image of the Trinity in the soul because memory, understanding, and will make up one single soul (*De Trin.* 10.11.18). Yet he has to distinguish different functions of the soul, and his use of terms is not always clear. Thonnard (493 f.) suggests the following classification:

First, there is the distinction between the vital principle which St. Augustine simply calls *vita* or life, and which is common to all living things on every level, and the two kinds of soul, *anima* and *animus*, the first being common to man and animals, the second peculiar to man. This last, the soul capable of reasoning, has a higher part where wisdom resides and which is called *mens* or mind. *Anima, animus,* and *mens* correspond roughly in Plotinus to lower soul or 'nature,' higher soul, and intellect. The line between the last two is sometimes so sharply drawn in Plotinus as to make the intellect hardly part of our personality at all, but elsewhere the distinction almost disappears. Further, Augustine notes four degrees of knowledge. First, there are the external senses which act by means of physical sense organs. Secondly, the inner sense whose work is to direct the activity of the external senses, and which is part of the *anima* since it exists in animals as well as men. Thirdly, there is reason in the strict sense, that is, the lower reason, which has the work of arranging things in classes. Fourthly, there is the higher reason, the understanding, *intellectus* or *intelligentia,* by which the soul contemplates the eternal types or ideas and God Himself—the faculty of wisdom.

Corresponding to these two higher levels of knowledge there are concupiscence which follows lower reason, and will which follows higher reason, and where resides the love of God.

I may quote here from an earlier translator and commentator in the series—J. J. O'Meara, *St. Augustine, Against the Academics:* ACW 12. 169 n. 6:

'In general he [St. Augustine] speaks of the *anima* (soul) as that which with the body makes up the human composite (*C. Acad.* 1.9; *De ord.* 2.6, 19); of the *animus* (spirit) as the intellectual, as opposed to the sensitive or vegetative, part of the *anima* (*De ord.* 2.6); of the *mens* (mind) as a faculty of the *animus* (*Epist.* 3.4), which is capable of a lower discursive function (*De ord.* 2.30, 38, 40, 50) called *ratio* (reason), and a higher intuitional function (*De ord.* 2.17, 19, 41–42; *Epist.* 3.4; 8.2) called *intellectus* (intellection).'

[20] In earlier editions Evodius continues until '. . . does not exercise its control.' Then Augustine begins, 'Please do this yourself . . . ,' and goes on, 'at least you can easily remember. . . .'

[21] This refers to §§ 16 and 17.

[22] One of the earlier editions has 'they are not in control,' in the plural. The singular, however, gives better sense: 'it (the mind) is not in control.'

[23] 'Whatever kind of being': the Latin is *natura,* a word which St. Augustine uses fairly frequently later in the dialogue. He

explains (3.13.36): 'By *nature* I mean what we usually call *substance*.'

[24] The question of the origin of souls is discussed later on (3.20.56–22.63).

[25] This is one of the sentences which, as St. Augustine tells us in the *Retractations* (1.9.3), was claimed by the Pelagians as supporting their view. They took it to mean that the will could choose good or evil entirely of its own power, without the need of grace.

Notice the argument here. Augustine shows Evodius that he has a will, and a good will, and that this is of supreme value. Then he goes on to argue that it lies in the power of the will whether we possess the supreme good or not, because nothing is so fully in the power of the will as the will itself.

It may be well to keep the following distinctions in mind:

1. Will in a general sense is common to all living things, since they all tend to act in their characteristic way, and make every effort to do so.

2. When this effort is not impeded by any obstacle, the will can be called free, but we must remember the sense in which we are using the word 'free.'

3. The will of a rational being, who is conscious of himself, controls his action in a far more complete way than does the will of an animal, even though no choice is being made. This is another sense in which we can call the will free.

4. The will may be free in both these two senses, and yet not free in the sense that it has the power of choice. If an intellectual being attains the supreme good which satisfies all its desires, its will is free in the sense that no obstacle impedes its action, and also in the sense that it is the conscious master of its action, but it is not free in the sense of having the power of choice, because, having every desire satisfied, there is no scope for choice. Thus the blessed in heaven are supremely free, but without choice as to the primary object of their conduct. Thus another sense in which the will can be called free is the sense in which it has the power of choice.

Now St. Augustine does not explicitly make these distinctions. However, he uses will to mean that power by which we as rational beings and as Christians can love God and rejoice in Wisdom, and therefore he is always speaking of the will of a man who is free in the sense of conscious of his own act and of the object to which that act tends. Hence he is justified in saying: 'What is so fully in the power of the will as the will itself?' For a will in the sense he means must have the power of choice if confronted with the possibility either of good or evil conduct.

[26] Plato classified the virtues into wisdom, fortitude, temperance, and justice. Aristotle described these same four virtues, though with additions of his own. Cicero adopted the same list. The first Christian writer to do so was St. Ambrose, who uses (cf. *Exp. Evang. Luc.* 5.50, 62) the term 'cardinal virtues.' St. Augustine speaks of prudence instead of wisdom, but the meaning is the same: 'the knowledge what to seek and what to avoid.'

[27] Prof. Green reads *tribuimus* instead of *tribuamus:* 'why do we not grant him fortitude?' instead of 'why should we not . . .?'

[28] Prof. Green TN23 reads *iniquum* instead of *inimicum: iniquus* in the sense of 'opposed, hostile, unfavorable' (properly= *inimicus*) is found in Christian as well as classical authors.

[29] St. Augustine notes in the *Retractations* (1.9.3) that this sentence was claimed by the Pelagians as supporting their view.

[30] Another sentence appealed to by the Pelagians.

[31] So too with this sentence.

[32] St. Augustine's views on material goods and their use, on wealth and poverty, find very frequent expression, especially in his sermons: cf. Mausbach, *op. cit.* 1.284 ff.; O. Schilling, *Reichtum und Armut in der altkirchlichen Literatur* (Freiburg i. Br. 1908) 167–77.

[33] Another passage quoted by the Pelagians for their teaching.

BOOK TWO

[1] Another passage claimed by the Pelagians, as St. Augustine tells us in the *Retractations* (1.9.3).

[2] This phrase, 'the truth within you, which is the source of all instruction,' raises the question of St. Augustine's theory of knowledge, so important in connection with his argument for the existence of God.

We may begin by noticing the principal other passages in the *De libero arbitrio* which state his theory:

'The notion which is impressed on us of eternal law' (1.6.15).

'By what idea or image do we see so sure a truth [i.e. of mathematics] so confidently throughout innumerable instances, unless we do it by an inner light, unknown to the bodily sense?' (2.8.23).

'So, as, before we are happy, the idea of happiness is nevertheless impressed on our minds—for through the idea we know and say confidently and without any doubt that we wish to be happy —so too, before we are wise, we have the idea of wisdom impressed on the mind' (2.9.26).

'The very light of wisdom, in which these things can be seen and grasped, may be one light shared in common by all wise men' (2.9.27).

'So too a strong, vigorous, mental gaze, when it sees with certainty many unchangeable truths, turns to the truth itself in which all things are shown' (2.13.36).

'If you are praised when you see what you ought to do, though you only see this in Him who is unchangeable truth. . . .' (3.16.46).

St. Augustine was interested in the problem of knowledge from a particular point of view; it was with a particular aspect of the problem of universals that he was mainly concerned. This problem—at the centre of all philosophical thought—considers the question: how are we to explain the unchanging and necessary character of the universal ideas we use when the objects around us, which we express by means of universals, are changing and contingent? What is the source from which we obtain our ideas? St. Augustine was especially interested in the source of mathematical laws and of moral principles, as we can see in this part of the *De libero arbitrio*. He did not, however, regard the problem from the point of view of pure philosophy, and was not writing a technical treatise on the subject, but was concerned with theology. He discussed the question in the *De magistro*, which he wrote in 387, and never changed his theory: he taught that we cannot learn these ultimate principles from a human master, but that we see them by an inner light.

This brings us to the difficulty in his theory: what exactly did he mean by comparing truth to the light, and how did he conceive that the action of God takes place when we see the truth? We must remember the history of St. Augustine's intellectual development. He adapted the Platonic philosophy which had so deeply influenced him, and therefore approached the question of our knowledge by way of a theory of illumination. Plato had described the idea of good as the sun of the intelligible world (*Rep.* 517 b), and St. Augustine followed in his steps with suitable modifications. 'I call upon thee, O God, Truth, in whom and for whom and through whom shine to the understanding all things which so shine' (*Solil.* 1.1.3). Again he speaks of God and truths of human learning as related in a similar way to the light and the earth which it illumines, and goes on to say that these human truths cannot be understood, 'unless they are illumined by something else as by their sun' (*Solil.* 1.8.15). E. Portalié, *art. cit.*, DTC 1.2.2334, gives a number of texts to show the doctrine, and he stresses that St. Augustine compares the need of the intelligence for God's light which is truth to the need of the will for grace. According to St. Augustine man acquires wisdom through illumination by divine truth; the eternal types or ideas which are the object of wisdom, cannot be derived from a reality perceived by the sense, nor from the soul which is limited by ignorance and doubt. The human intelligence must participate in some way in the subsistent truth in which the world of ideas is fully realised. The divine action, which is simply creative for other beings, is illuminative in regard to the intelligence, and this is the explanation of the absolute and universal character of our judgments (see Thonnard 477).

What, then, does St. Augustine mean by this illumination of the human intellect? We can leave aside any pantheistic explanation because it is clear that his system is not pantheistic. The chief theories are the following:

1. That we see the divine ideas directly in God Himself; this is to hold that St. Augustine is an ontologist. Portalié (*ibid.* 2335) gives two arguments against this:

(a) St. Augustine makes it clear that man does not enjoy the direct vision of God in the present life, with the possible exceptions of Moses and St. Paul.

(b) God, regarded as the sun in relation to the soul, is not an object of our knowledge but is the agent producing in the soul that by which we have knowledge. The sun of truth impresses on the soul the image of truth, as the seal is impressed on the wax.

Gilson says ('The Future of Augustinian Metaphysics,' in *A Monument to St. Augustine* 307): 'Whatever, then, the letter of St. Augustine may be . . . , it cannot signify ontologism unless it implies the negation of the entire thought of St. Augustine: the doctrine of divine illumination is not the vision of the First Cause, but the induction of the First Cause, starting from an effect, namely truth.'

He also points out (*Introd. à S. Augustin* 110 f.) that the metaphors of St. Augustine, however expressive they may be, remain metaphors. If we had the direct vision of God, we should not need to ask for any other proof than this of His existence. In fact, St. Augustine gives a proof for the existence of God in several places, and especially in the long argument in the *De libero arbitrio* (2.3.7–2.15.39). Copleston (*op. cit.* 2.61 f.) argues as follows: 'Now, how can St. Augustine have supposed that such a man beholds the essence of God, when in his spiritual doctrine he insists so much on the need of moral purification in order to draw near to God and is well aware that the vision of God is reserved to the saved in the next life? . . . Happily we have to help us such texts as the passage of the *De Trinitate* (12.15.24) where the Saint says that the nature of the mind is such that, 'when directed to intelligible things in the natural order, according to the disposition of the Creator, it sees them in a certain incorporeal light which is *sui generis*, just as the corporeal eye sees adjacent objects in the corporeal light." These words seem to show that the illumination in question is a spiritual illumination which performs the same function for the objects of the mind as the sun's light performs for the objects of the eye: in other words, as the sunlight makes corporeal things visible to the eye, so the divine illumination makes the eternal truths visible to the mind. From this it would appear to follow that it is not the illumination itself which is seen by the mind, nor the intelligible Sun, God, but that the characteristic of necessity and eternity in the necessary and eternal truths are made visible to the mind by the activity of God. This is certainly not an ontologistic theory.' Nevertheless we must remember that St. Augustine says in the *De libero arbitrio* (2.13.36) that, just as men with healthy eyes can look at the sun itself, so men with a strong mental gaze can turn to the truth itself.

2. The scholastic explanation, following St. Thomas. According to this view to call God the light of the soul is simply to say that He is the creative cause of the intelligence and the source of all truth. It must be borne in mind that the Thomists, basing themselves on Aristotle, hold that the soul has a power, the *intellectus agens*, which acts upon the object presented by the senses and abstracts the intelligible element, i.e., the universal, unchanging idea. Hence it is this power in particular which,

according to their interpretation of St. Augustine, participates in the divine light.

Portalié argues that this explanation is unsatisfactory, because St. Augustine did not confine himself to so vague a theory. If it were true, it would mean that St. Augustine never really dealt with the problem of knowledge at all, though in fact it seems to have been one of his main interests. According to this view all St. Augustine is saying is: 'We know, because all knowledge is an image of the divine ideas, and God has given us intelligence to know them.' But the question is: how do finite creatures perceive eternal truth? Plato says, by memory; Aristotle, by abstraction; others, by innate ideas. St. Augustine would say nothing.

Gilson also maintains (*Introd*. 113 f.) that the theory of St. Augustine is quite opposed to Aristotelian abstraction: the two views explain differently the matter on which the intellect operates. The soul, as having sense perception, is not, according to Aristotle, higher than the body in so far as the body is perceived by the senses, and therefore the body can act on the soul, and produce the *species* from which the soul abstracts the intelligible element. St. Augustine, on the other hand, holds that the soul transcends the body, and he cannot therefore admit that what is perceived by the senses is received as an object in the soul. St. Augustine has no need in his theory for an *intellectus agens*, like that of St. Thomas.

Copleston (*op. cit.* 2.63–65) criticises this theory, but does so from a slightly different angle. 'It hardly seems possible, therefore, to reduce the illumination-theory to nothing more than a statement of the truth that God conserves and creates the human intellect and that the natural light of the intellect is a participated light. . . . To say that St. Augustine was wrong in postulating a special divine illumination and that St. Thomas was right in denying the necessity of such an illumination is an understandable attitude; but it seems to be carrying conciliation too far, if one attempts to maintain that both thinkers were saying the same thing, even if one affirms that St. Thomas was saying clearly and unambiguously what St. Augustine had said obscurely and with the aid of metaphor. . . . If the illumination has an idiogenetic function, as I believe it to have in St. Augustine's view, then this function has reference not to the content of the concept, as if it infused that content, but to the quality of our judgment concerning the concept or to our discernment of a character in the object, its relation to the norm or standard, which is not contained in the bare notion of the thing. If this is true, then the difference between St. Augustine and St. Thomas does not so much consist in their respective attitudes towards abstraction (since, whether Augustine explicitly says so or not, his view, as interpreted above, would at least demand abstraction in some form) as in the fact that Augustine thought it necessary to postulate a special illuminative action of God, beyond His creative and conserving activity, in the mind's realisation of eternal and necessary truths, whereas St. Thomas did not.'

3. Portalié (*art. cit.* 2336) argues that the true interpretation of St. Augustine is the following. The soul grasps intellectual truths, because God produces in it an image of them. In Scholastic language this theory attributes to God the part which the Aristotelian theory attributes to the *intellectus agens*, but of course, it does not attribute the knowledge to a separate intelligence. The view is claimed to be supported not only by St. Augustine's words, but also by his general theory, in which the illumination of the intelligence is compared to the influence of grace on the will.

Gilson (*op. cit.* 117 n. 2) criticises this view of Portalié on the ground that the Aristotelian doctrine of abstraction is quite foreign to St. Augustine's theory, and therefore that no question of an *intellectus agens* can arise. We may add that the view seems to suffer from the very defect which Portalié urges against the Scholastic interpretation; it does not make clear the precise relation between God's action and that of the creature.

4. Gilson himself (*op. cit.* 123 f.) reaches a different conclusion. There is nothing, he says, empirical about the origin of the notions which we owe to illumination. These notions have no other content than the judgment by which they are expressed, e.g. justice is to render each man his due; wisdom is to prefer the eternal to the temporal. St. Augustine often calls these notions 'rules' according to which we judge. To say this is to go as far as the writings of St. Augustine will take us, and, if we go further, we must not make St. Augustine responsible for our theories.

Such, then, are the main explanations given of St. Augustine's theory of knowledge. The very fact that there is so much disagreement supports Gilson's cautious conclusion. It seems that we must be content not to know how St. Augustine would have dealt with many of the questions that can be asked about his theory. At the same time the following points may be mentioned. The root difficulty in this matter is that we are aware of certain aspects of reality which seem to belong to God, such as necessity and freedom from change, and yet we do not know God directly. Some theories try to escape the difficulty by saying that these aspects of reality can be found in the finite world, others that we know God directly. These theories, however, seem to many minds unsatisfactory. Now we become in a true sense what we know, and in a true sense what we know we are. Therefore the problem is nothing else than the problem of the relation between creature and Creator. If we agree that we know God by natural knowledge in this life just in the way in which He is present to us as cause, that is, if we agree that we simply know God as cause, no more and no less, then, it may be suggested, this makes possible a clear interpretation of St. Augustine, even though it is not how St. Augustine himself put it. God illumines our intellects by being present to us as cause; we know the finite world not merely by itself alone, but as dependent on its cause. We have an indirect and inadequate, but a real, idea of God, that is, of absolute truth, derived from our awareness of the cause as present to its effect. Truth is reality as known, and the light of truth in which we know finite things is nothing else than the cause which gives them being. Thus it is not true to say that we only see objects in the light of truth, and not the sun which gives them light. We do not see the sun directly or adequately, but we do see it indirectly and inadequately; we see the Creator indirectly as cause, and we see creatures directly as the effects of the cause. For further literature on the subject see Gilson, *op. cit.* 332–35.

[3] Apparently all MSS read *animae*= 'soul' for *homini*= 'man' of the editors since 1506. Green TN 25 points out that in Biblical (and Christian) Latin *anima* commonly= *homo*.

[4] Ps. 52.1.

[5] That is, in 1.2.4.

[6] Isa. 7.9, according to the Septuagint. The words have already been quoted in 1.2.4. The Vulgate has 'If you will not believe, you shall not continue.' In the *De doctrina christiana* (1.12.17) Augustine quotes both versions.

[7] John 17.3.

[8] Matt. 7.7.

[9] To appreciate St. Augustine's argument for the existence of God, the reader should have in his mind the philosophic background of St. Augustine's thought. After Plato's death the school of philosophy he had founded deteriorated, and, neglecting his idealism, it came to deny the possibility of knowledge altogether and to hold that only probability was possible. A period of eclecticism followed: an inner light was regarded as the guide to truth. Then Neo-Platonism arose at Alexandria, its chief exponent being Plotinus, who greatly influenced St. Augustine. Plotinus (205–270 A. D.) apparently was an Egyptian of Latin name and Greek speech, trained at Alexandria under Ammonius Saccas, and later teaching at Rome. After his death his disciple, Porphyry, edited his writings, arranging them in six books, or *Enneads*, each of nine treatises.

Plotinus (for the following see especially A. H. Armstrong, *An Introduction to Ancient Philosophy* [Westminster, Md., 1949] 175–96) regarded the cosmos as having two movements, one of outgoing or descent by which the higher produces the lower, and another of ascent and simplification by which the soul passes up through all the stages of being to final union with the First Principle. This First Principle stands at the head of Plotinus' system; it is transcendent, and is called the One, or the Good, or occasionally God. Exactly what Plotinus meant is not altogether clear, but the One or Good is beyond Mind and beyond Being, and is the source of the Divine Mind, together with the World of Forms which the Divine Mind contains. For Plato the One or Good was itself a Form and a substance, containing all other Forms, but for Plotinus it was transcendent and 'other.' The lines of thought which led him to this conclusion are various. As to the human soul's relation to the One, the passages in which he suggests that it will become identified with the One are very few, and his usual teaching is opposed to this.

The process by which the higher produces the lower is automatic and necessary. Contemplation is the primary activity, but production is the necessary reflex action of contemplation. The product is always lower than the producer; the producer loses nothing by giving forth the product. Plotinus usually describes this process as emanation or radiation. It should be understood that the two movements of outgoing and return are timeless and simultaneous.

Plotinus' World of Forms differs a good deal from Plato's. Its organic character as a single living reality is greatly stressed, and there are Forms of individuals. The World of Forms contains the archetypes of all individual things, past, present, or future. In the Divine Mind-World the Forms are themselves living intelligences, and so know and become one another without separation or division. The Forms are part of the Divine Life, and not static objects of contemplation. The Divine Mind is ourselves at our highest: we are only fully ourselves when we escape from our limited ego, and pass beyond Soul to realise we are Divine Mind in all its multiplex universality.

Soul emanates from Mind, as Mind emanates from the First Principle, and Mind is the source of Soul's reality and of all that is good and beautiful and intelligent in it. Mind receives the First Principle, the One, according to its capacity, and this involves a descent towards multiplicity. So too Soul receives Mind according to its capacity. Mind is the realm of intuitive thought, and soul of discursive thought, in which truths are known by a process of reasoning. Soul is the link between the intelligible and the material worlds, and is present in both, while material things are only represented in the intelligible world by their archetypes.

The relation of Universal Soul to individual souls is obscure, but it seems that in some sense individual souls are part of Universal Soul, and can become universal by contemplation. The soul is in the body by a law of the universe, not owing to a fall. If the particular soul narrows itself to the selfish interests of a particular body, it sinks down, but it can on the other hand rise to the universality of transcendent Soul, and pass beyond Soul altogether to its rightful place in the world of the Divine Mind. Plotinus' levels of being are not rigidly separated, but are stages in the unfolding of a single life.

The lower Soul or Nature, Soul immanent, is Soul at the lowest level. It produces the immanent forms of bodies, and Plotinus describes these much as Aristotle describes his immanent forms. But in Plotinus matter remains unchanged by the forms imposed on it. Matter is evil; it is the principle of negation. Yet the material universe is not evil, for it is the work of the higher soul, being ruled by Nature which is its principle of order. It is the best possible material universe. Material evil and suffering result inevitably from the conflict whereby a degree of order is introduced. The wise man is beyond the reach of suffering because he is detached, but the foolish only get what they deserve.

St. Augustine first came to know the works of Plotinus at Milan just before his conversion, when he read parts of the *Enneads* in a Latin translation. He was deeply influenced, and in particular it was Plotinus who helped him to free himself from Manichaean materialism: he came to realise that beings might exist which were immaterial, and that God was altogether immaterial. He thought, though mistakenly, that Plotinus' teaching about the Divine Mind was the same as that of St. John about the Divine Logos. Cf. P. Henry, *Plotin et l'Occident* (Louvain 1934) 89 f., and *passim* for the preceding.

St. Augustine adopted much of the philosophy of Plotinus, but modified it to fit the Christian faith. He got rid of its pantheistic tendencies, and rejected the view of Plotinus that God's existence was immediately evident, and needed no rational proof. See J. J. O'Meara, *The Young Augustine* (London 1954) 131–55; the same, 'Neo-Platonism in the Conversion of Saint Augustine,' *Dominican Studies* 3 (1950) 334–43.

[10] St. Augustine starts his argument with the consciousness we have of our own existence, because this is clearer than anything else. The present passage is not the only place where he makes this the foundation of certainty; he says in the *De Trinitate* (15.12.21): 'One who does not exist cannot be deceived, and therefore, if I am deceived, I exist.' We are reminded of the *cogito ergo sum* of Descartes, and there is a real resemblance between St. Augustine and Descartes in so far as they both find in the same fact a truth which can be known directly and without reference to sense experience. Yet there is a difference between them. Descartes regards this as typical of a clear and distinct idea, innate, and given us by God. St. Augustine regards it as one among other truths which are not innate but seen by the light in which we see all truths that we see. The truths of number and the principles of wisdom, he goes on to explain, do not depend on consciousness of the thinking self, but are also seen clearly and independently. St. Augustine bases his philosophy on the existence and perfection of the world as perceived by the senses, and on the existence of the soul as knowing the external world and also itself. See Thonnard 500 f. On St. Augustine's conviction that we *can* attain certainty regarding certain facts (his victory over Academic scepticism he expressed especially in

his *Contra Academicos*), and his explanation of '*how* it is that we are able not only to know with certainty eternal and necessary truths, but also to know them as eternal and necessary truths' (theory of divine illumination), see also Copleston, *op. cit.* 2.51–67; Gilson, *op. cit.* 103–130, *passim;* M. C. D'Arcy, 'The Philosophy of St. Augustine,' in *A Monument to Saint Augustine* 180–83; R. Jolivet, 'La doctrine augustinienne de l'illumination,' in *Mélanges augustiniens* (Paris 1931) 382–502.

[11] Following the weight of the manuscript evidence (Green TN 25), *fidere* for *figere* (= 'by which we can *establish* that. . . .'

[12] Some MSS have: 'Just as the inner sense judges whether our sight is too weak or sufficiently strong, so too the sight itself judges. . . .'

[13] At this point of the argument we should notice how in certain important respects St. Augustine modified the theory of Plotinus. Augustine added to the grades of being as described by Plotinus, and maintained that all beings of every grade, and not only the highest, are created by God and by God alone, instead of each emanating from the grade above it. This was clearly demanded by the Christian faith. Moreover, St. Augustine introduced a new principle of distinction between the grades. Evodius argues that existence, life, and understanding are in ascending order of importance because life includes existence, and understanding includes existence and life. St. Augustine then proposes a new principle by which the higher can be distinguished from the lower: that which judges another is higher. The reason he introduces this principle is that the inner sense requires a standard by which we may be able to classify it: the standard by which we recognise that what contains more is higher than what contains less, does not help us here. This new development is important because it implies in our knowledge, not only sensible but more especially intellectual, a certain participation in the divine exemplar ideas or types which govern created things. These ideas have a twofold effect, one creative and the other formal, guiding created things to their natural ends. Our ideas and judgments participate only in this second effect. We impose on lesser things a certain kind of order when we judge them, but we cannot affect their existence. This new principle is the means St. Augustine uses to argue to the existence of God, because it enables him to show that there is something

eternal and unchangeable which is higher than our reason, since it governs our reason. See Thonnard 502 f.

[14] St. Augustine does not make it altogether clear what he means by these words, yet at the end of the argument (2.15.39) he repeats: 'For if there is anything more excellent, it is this which is God, but, if there is nothing more excellent, then truth itself is God.' F. Cayré, in his book, *Dieu présent dans la vie de l'esprit* (Paris 1951) 123 f., has an interesting comment. He says St. Augustine's attitude is at first sight surprising, and different explanations have been given. The simplest is that of P. Thonnard (503–505), who sees in the answer of Augustine a sort of argument *ad hominem*. Cayré, however, maintains the answer is provisional until Evodius understands from the argument which follows that, if there is a being above our reason, that being is God, because that being must be above all others. We must not, he says, forget that the *De libero arbitrio* is a dialogue, and that St. Augustine is a supremely skilful writer. He wishes to present Evodius with a certain mystery so as to stimulate discussion. In the end the matter will become clear of itself; it will be enough to show that unchangeable Truth exists and is above our reason, for this can be nothing else than God. Augustine is setting himself to find in man something so great that what is above it can only be God, and in doing this he replies to the objection of Evodius. Thus the solution of this difficulty is to be found in the whole argument that follows, which is an indirect, but effective, answer to Evodius. Cayré refers to Gilson (*op. cit.* 17), who points out that the whole discussion leads up to a necessary, unchangeable, eternal Being, who must be greater than all others, and must therefore be God. To show this, it is not enough to reach a being above man, but we must show that there is something in man of such a kind that what is beyond it can only be God, and we find this in the Truth.

This explanation seems confirmed if we reflect on St. Augustine's words shortly before, in the same section: 'But I ask you: if you find there is nothing above our reason except the eternal and unchangeable, will you hesitate to call this God?' By showing that above our reason there is the eternal and unchangeable, he shows that there can be nothing else still greater, for the eternal and unchangeable must necessarily be supreme.

[15] What does St. Augustine mean when he says the same food is wholly taken by each of us? He has said above: 'We can both

taste the same honey or any other food or drink,' and: 'Though we both breathe the same air with our nostrils, or take the same food when we taste it, yet I do not draw in the same part of the air as you, nor do I take the same part of the food as you.' He seems to mean, therefore, that the same food is wholly taken by each of us, in the sense that it is wholly the same kind of food, wholly, honey, for instance.

¹⁶ Prof. Green reads *unusquisque nostrum sibi* instead of *unicuique nostrum soli*: 'that which each of us is for himself.'

¹⁷ This shows that St. Augustine's theory of knowledge is not one of intellectual abstraction, requiring an active power, the *intellectus agens*, to abstract the idea from the object as received by the senses—cf. § 22.

¹⁸ Another reading is: 'nature of number' instead of 'truth of number.'

¹⁹ The literal translation of these last few words is: 'whatever the number may be, counting from the beginning, the whole after it is its double.' In view of what precedes the meaning must apparently be that, whatever the number may be, if we add to it the units of which it is made up, the total which results is its double. The passage is recognised to be difficult.

²⁰ Eccles. 7.26 (Sept.). The Vulgate has: *I have surveyed all things with my mind, to know, and consider, and seek out wisdom and reason.*

²¹ Following, with Green TN 26, the difficult variant *pulchra* for the better attested, but even more difficult *plura*.

²² Burnaby, *Amor Dei* 157, calls attention to St. Augustine's 'acute sense of the beauty of nature.' For Augustine the beauty of earth, sea, air, heavens, stars is 'almost unspeakable,' 'filling with awe everyone who contemplates them' (*Enarr. in Ps.* 144. 15). The master Craftsman and Designer of the world has set all its greatness and beauty before us that 'seeing what we can see, we may love Him whom we cannot see, in order that one day through the merit of our love for Him we may be enabled to see' (*ibid.* 103.1.1). That the saint's interest in nature may have been stimulated by his early study of Vergil, is observed by J. P. Christopher, ACW 2.115 n. 113.

²³ The following remarks may be helpful at this point.

1. First let us summarise this part of the argument. Augustine wishes to show that there is something above our reason, not changed by our knowing it. Evodius suggests the law and truth

of number, among many other examples that might be given. Augustine agrees, but asks whether numbers might not be in some sense images of visible things and perceived by the senses. Evodius replies that seven and three must always be ten, whereas bodily things change. Again Augustine agrees, and gives another argument in support. All numbers consist of so many units, but no bodily thing is perfectly one since it has parts, that is to say, is extended in space. Yet we know what perfect oneness is, or we should not be able to say that it is not to be found in bodily things. Moreover we know that certain laws hold good for number even in instances when we cannot verify them. Such truths we must recognise 'by an inner light, unknown to the bodily sense' (2.8.23). There are many other such truths, and wisdom is the truth in which we see the supreme good. The 'principles and illuminations in which the virtues appear' (2.10. 29) are the concern of wisdom.

2. It may be well to explain a little more fully the argument that no bodily or physical things are perfectly one, since this is one aspect of a principle which is central to all later Scholastic thought—indeed to all philosophical thought. Being and one are at root the same, merely emphasising different aspects, because a thing is a thing in so far as it is one thing—in so far as a thing exists or has being it exists as one thing. That which is perfectly one exists perfectly, and is without limitation or defect: it is the infinite, God. For every dependent thing, since it is dependent, that is, a creature, might cease to exist, or else it would be self-existent. If it is liable to cease to exist, it cannot at any given moment have all its possible existence, and therefore its existence is not an absolute unity, not possessed all together without any distinction. Only God, the creator and source of all dependent things, is perfectly one, being absolutely independent and self-existent.

How, then, does it come about that creatures can be called one in any sense at all, if they are not perfectly one? The precise way in which we shall answer this question will depend on the detailed theory of metaphysics we accept, but, since existence and oneness are at root the same, and since created things certainly exist, though in an imperfect and dependent manner, it is plain that a created thing, even a bodily thing, is in some sense one, not perfectly one, but imperfectly. Thus one is used 'analogically' of creatures and the Creator, partly in the same sense and partly in a different sense. The creature 'participates' in the oneness of God. To put the matter in the way it has just been put, is not to put it in St. Augustine's way, but it may help to bring out the problem with which he was dealing.

3. The eternal truth of such a fact as that seven and three make ten is another aspect of this same central philosophical problem. As St. Augustine insists, it is only one example out of many which show that we have some knowledge of the eternal and unchangeable. Indeed every fact is eternally true; even the most trivial fact which will never be repeated is eternally true. Every created thing, even the lowest, participates in some way not only in the being and oneness but also in the truth of the eternal God. It should be noticed that it makes no difference to this argument whether we interpret our knowledge that seven and three make ten as analytic or as synthetic, since in either case we reach a truth which is unchangeable and therefore, as St. Augustine argues, a truth which, in so far as unchangeable, cannot be derived from changing things. This is not quite the case with his other example, that of mathematical principles which apply even when we cannot verify them. St. Augustine's point here is that such principles cannot be taken from bodily things. But if the application of such principles can be explained because the same pattern is seen to exist in countless different sets of numbers, what we know is always the same pattern, and the problem might be partly avoided. However, here too we should in any case be confronted with an unchanging truth.

24 St. Augustine's fascination for number and his frequent attribution of a sacred or mystical signification to certain numbers is well-known. These play a particularly prominent role in his sermons: see the numerous entries (for numbers from '1' to '144,000') in M. Pontet, *L'exégèse de S. Augustin prédicateur* (Paris 1944), in 'Index des symboles' *s. v.* 'Nombres' (607 f.). Cf. also A. Schmitt, 'Mathematik und Zahlenmystik,' in M. Grabmann—J. Mausbach, *Aurelius Augustinus: Die Festschrift der Görres-Gesellschaft zum 1500. Todestage des hl. Augustinus* (Cologne 1930) 353–366; also ACW 5.203 f.; 15.202 f., 229 f.

25 Wisd. 8.1.

26 Instead of *infra nos esse cernimus* Prof. Green TN 26 reads with certain MSS *cernimus, putamus etiam ipsos numeros infra nos esse:* 'on which we see numbers impressed, and think that the numbers themselves are below us.'

27 The earlier editions (e. g. Erasmus) have: 'if an eye, able to

discern it, seeks for it.' Prof. Green reads *id cerni possit inquirat* instead of *cerni possit inquirit:* 'but it would demand an eye capable of discerning it.'

[28] In §§ 15–19 of this second book.

[29] Ps. 36.4.

[30] This is one of the chief passages which might be claimed to show that St. Augustine was an ontologist, since he speaks of those with strong eyesight who are ready to gaze at the sun itself. We have already mentioned reasons for not regarding St. Augustine as an ontologist in any unorthodox sense (see n. 2 above). For an account of the history of ontologism, beginning with V. Gioberti (1801–1852), see especially A. Fonck, 'Ontologisme,' DTC 11.1 (1931) 1000–1061; for Augustine claimed (with St. Bonaventure) by the ontologists as their principal authority, cf. *ibid.* 1003–1009; for the principles condemned by the Holy See in 1861, *ibid.* 1046 ff.

[31] John 8.31 f.

[32] Perl in his running commentary (214 f.) remarks that St. Augustine's discussion has by now lost its character of dialogue and that the long passage bears the traits of a lyric or hymn to truth. Note the same encomiastic writing in the following paragraph, which Gilson (*Introduction* 20 n. 1) terms the classical text illustrating Augustine's view that 'the truth is independent of the mind which it orders and which it transcends.'

[33] To appreciate St. Augustine's argument for the existence of God the following may be found useful:

1. What is the connection between the earlier part of the argument in the *De libero arbitrio* and the final claim that truth itself is God? Augustine believed that God is the direct Creator of every grade of being: why did he not argue at once to the source of even the lowest grade, without taking us up through the lowest grades to the higher grades, and then declaring that we could find God in truth itself? It was because in the eternal truths as we perceive them there is a clearer image of God, and Thonnard suggests (503) that it may also have been that he doubted whether we could rise directly from the sensible world to God. Plotinus held that the higher level explained the lower level which was derived from it, and St. Augustine perhaps saw no clear refutation of this, though he did not admit it. We can, however, see a continuous thread running through the argument. We start from the fact that we exist and know that we exist.

This leads to the distinction between existence, life, and consciousness. Then the inner sense is discovered, and, in assigning to it its place, the principle is found that what judges is higher than what is judged. This principle is employed to show that truth is higher than our reason, though reason is our highest power. Then comes the claim that in seeing truth we are aware of the eternal truth which is God. It is at this last stage that we are carried at once from the recognition of truth as higher than ourselves to recognition of God as the source of truth, without any clear definition of the relation of participated truth to its source. But the thread running through the argument is there, and we can see that each stage contributes to the whole, from the certainty expressed of our own existence to the final conclusion.

2. The argument which St. Augustine gives us here for the existence of God is plainly not systematic in the sense that the Thomist proofs are systematic, and a number of questions are left unanswered which a modern discussion of the subject would wish to find discussed. We must be content not to know precisely how St. Augustine would have dealt with these questions, and be satisfied with what he does tell us. The central part of the argument is this. Reason is the highest element in man's nature. Above our reason is truth, because truth is eternal and unchangeable, and because we judge according to the truth, but never judge the truth itself. The supreme good is known and grasped in the truth which we perceive. If there is anything higher than truth it is God, but, if there is not, then truth itself is God. Undoubtedly for St. Augustine the eternal and unchanging truth is God.

We note that St. Augustine does not clearly and explicitly distinguish here between the truth in which we participate and the source of truth which is God; he does not explicitly argue from effect to cause, but, having led us on and prepared the way, he claims that in knowing the truth we are aware of God. We should like to ask what exactly is the relation between truth as we know it and the absolute truth which is God, but he does not satisfy us. Thonnard (504 f.) explains that by an act of intuition, without dwelling on the process of thought which would take us from participated truth to its source, St. Augustine asserts the existence of God. The image of God is so clearly reflected in the principles of wisdom and number that we see both source and participation at a single glance. The method here described by which God's existence is known does not exclude the process of reasoning from participated truth to its source. Indeed, when he has finished his main argument, and goes on to show that all that is good comes from God, Augustine says: 'Nothing can give its form to itself. . . . So we conclude that body and soul are given their forms by a form which is unchangeable and everlasting' (2.17.45). This is not intended as a necessary supplement to the main argument, but at least it shows that the more direct approach does not exclude the argument from effect to cause. Thonnard (505) refers to *De musica* 6.12.36 (written 387–389): 'What, then, must we believe is the source from which the soul receives that which is eternal and unchangeable but the one eternal and unchangeable God?' On the other hand, Cayré (*op. cit.* 134 f.) argues that St. Augustine's final assertion of the existence of God is not intuitive in this sense, but is a conclusion from the fact that our knowledge of the truth has been shown to be inexplicable as derived from ourselves. Yet this seems hardly satisfactory in view of the language St. Augustine uses.

Perhaps the solution, which allows for a measure of truth in both views, is that St. Augustine means his argument to be a process of analysis which proceeds by the laws of reason, but which brings out gradually the full implication of what we are aware of from the beginning in a more or less confused way; that we do not start from a premise and then go on to find something in no way included in the original premise, but that we make explicit what was originally implicit. If this is correct, Augustine does use the method of intuition, but in a special sense; he does argue from effect to cause, but in the sense that we find that what we were at first aware of contains both effect and cause. This seems borne out by St. Augustine's own words: 'So, as, before we are happy, the idea of happiness is nevertheless impressed on our minds—for through this idea we know and say confidently and without any doubt that we wish to be happy—so too, before we are wise, we have the idea of wisdom impressed on the mind' (2.9.26).

3. We should notice the distinction between St. Augustine's argument and the ontological argument as used by St. Anselm. St. Anselm argues that we can conceive of that than which nothing greater can be conceived; that that than which nothing greater can be conceived must have existence or it would have

something still greater than itself, and therefore that God must exist. St. Augustine, it is true, agrees that God must be greater than anything we can conceive, but he does not argue that therefore God must exist; he sets out to show that such a being must exist because we are aware of truth.

[34] Wisd. 6.17. This passage of Wisdom describes how wisdom is easy to find, if it is sought for. St. Augustine does not follow the literal sense when he speaks of the works of Providence as means used by wisdom to reveal herself to us, though the general sense is the same (see Thonnard 508). Cf. below, § 45.

[35] St. Augustine's first treatise, it will be remembered, dealt with beauty—De pulchro et apto. It was written during his Manichaean years, when he was twenty-six or twenty-seven and teacher of rhetoric at Carthage. It has been lost; in fact, around the year 400 Augustine himself no longer had a copy of it (cf. Conf. 4.13.20). For the Christian Augustine's 'laws of beauty' (pulchritudinis leges), his thoughts on human reason conforming to eternal, divine norms in its judgments on beauty, see his De vera religione 29.52–43.81 (written ca. 390). Cf. Mausbach, op. cit. 1.94–96; Perl 216–218.

[36] Some MSS and the earlier editions have indignum, unworthy or undeserving, instead of indigum, poor or in want.

[37] It may be useful here to give some explanation of the meaning of form. In Greek philosophy the word (ἰδέα) came to be used to answer the question: 'What kind of thing is it?' Thus it came to mean the nature or essence of a thing. Everything was considered to have a 'form' because everything is some definite kind of thing. Gilson (Introd. 260) says that fundamentally the words idea, forma, species, and ratio all have the same meaning for St. Augustine. Things, he explains, always exist according to St. Augustine in at least two different ways, in themselves, that is, in their own nature, and in God, that is, in their eternal types or ideas, and this double existence is simultaneous.

First, as to their existence in God. Plato in his theory of ideas had thought of a 'form' primarily as a perfect type or example to which imperfect individual things on earth attain in a greater or less degree. Cf. e.g. Armstrong, op. cit. 36–41. Here Copleston, op. cit. 59 f., offers the link to St. Augustine: 'The same question which could be raised in regard to the Platonic theory recurs again . . . in regard to the Augustinian theory, namely, "Where are these ideas?" (Of course we must remember, in regard to both thinkers, that the "ideas" in question are not subjective ideas but objective essences, and that the query "where?" does not refer to locality, since the ideas are *ex hypothesi* immaterial, but rather to what one might call ontological situation or status.) Neo-Platonists, seeing the difficulty in accepting a sphere of impersonal immaterial essences, i.e. the condition *apparently* at least assigned to the essences in Plato's published works, interpreted the Platonic ideas as thoughts of God, and "placed" them in Nous, the divine mind, which emanates from the One as the first proceeding hypostasis. (Compare Philo's theory of the ideas as contained within the Logos.) We may say that Augustine accepted this position, if we allow for the fact that he did not accept the emanation theory of Neo-Platonism. The exemplar ideas and eternal truths are in God. "The ideas are certain archetypal forms or stable and immutable essences of things, which have not themselves been formed but, existing eternally and without change, are contained in the divine intelligence" ' (for the text quoted cf. Augustine, *De div. quaest.* 46.2). See also C. Boyer, *L'idée de vérité dans la philosophie de saint Augustin* (Paris 1921) 71–79; L. F. Jansen, "The Divine Ideas in the Writings of St. Augustine," *The Modern Schoolman* 22 (1945) 117–31.

Then, as to the existence of things in their own nature. Thonnard (508 f.) notices the following points. In works later than the *De libero arbitrio* St. Augustine distinguishes in God's action on the world a twofold effect: creation, and the giving of forms —information. God draws the formless matter out of nothing, and then gives it a form or particular perfection. There is no temporal, but only a logical, priority of the one over the other. The precise relation between the two is disputed.

A. Gardeil, *La structure de l'âme et l'expérience mystique* (Paris 1927) 313–25, says that creation consists in the production of formless matter which alone is taken from nothing, while the real thing, constituted with its form and rendered intelligible, is due to its participation in the ideas in God's mind. Gilson (*op. cit.* 253–67), however, holds that the divine act of creation is indivisible, but consists in the production of two effects: it gives the formless matter, and at the same time it gives the form.

This latter view appears to be supported by Augustine's statement in the present paragraph, that a changeable thing would fall back into nothing without a form. When God gives a living thing its form, He makes the thing participate in the exemplar ideas or types in His mind, and exercises that kind of causality which is exemplar. From this it follows that Augustine does not think of the giving of a form merely as the reception of form in matter. To him the giving of a form implies creation and participation in the idea in God's mind. Thonnard goes so far as to translate *forma* by perfection, because by receiving its form a thing receives its perfection through participation in the divine idea, and this is the same as creation. The originality of Augustine's theory consists, he says, in combining in the notion of participation that causality by which the form is given—exemplar causality, and that causality by which the thing is created—efficient causality.

[38] Ps. 101.27 f.

[39] Wisd. 7.27.

[40] Instead of *intulissem* Prof. Green reads *retulissem*: 'I argued in return.'

[41] Another passage which, St. Augustine tells us in the *Retractations*, the Pelagians claimed as supporting them.

[42] Ps. 13.1.

[43] Cf. Matt. 10.30.

[44] Literally: 'In the same way that we know by reason all those things which we know so as to satisfy knowledge (*ad scientiam*).'

[45] These 'illuminations of the virtues,' *lumina virtutum*, are the exemplary ideas by which we should direct our lives; cf. 2.10.29. Cf. Gilson, *Introduction* 169.

[46] This is directed against the Manichaean view that evil is an independent principle. Cf. R. Jolivet, *Le problème du mal d'après saint Augustin* (Paris 1936), 28 ff.

[47] Some of the MSS and the older editions lack the words, 'not even a trace,' *non quidem nonnihil sed. . . .*

[48] St. Augustine comes to one of the most crucial points of his argument here—the question: How can sin consist in a movement away from God, since every movement is caused by God? There can be no argument for God's existence which does not depend in some form or other on the principle of causality, and if we are to say that the creature can act without its action being caused by God, does not the whole theistic position fall to the ground? The more general objection which is often made against free will, that if an action is free it must in the last analysis be without any motive at all, is really the same difficulty.

Augustine's solution, which is an application of the principle that evil as such is not positive but is a defect, has not perhaps been given sufficient weight by later Scholastic philosophers over the whole field of the problem of free will in relation to God. If we can show—and a good case can be made for doing so—that every choice lies between a better and worse line of conduct, then freedom of choice can be explained without denying the law of causality. We can say it consists in following the highest motive or in following other motives which in varying degrees are defective in comparison with the highest. Thus there is always a positive motive for whatever action is chosen, but the motives may vary in degree of perfection from the most ultimate good which may involve a painful act at the moment to the most immediate good which, though pleasant at the moment, may lead to ultimate pain. Choice is possible, and yet God determines all that is positive in the act. He permits the will to fail in varying degrees to correspond with the varying degrees of imperfection in possible motives. In so far as the will fails there is no cause; it is just a lack of cause, a defect when it follows a lower motive. Hence it is not a question of the will moving in one of two different and equally positive directions, but of the will acting up to its full power or failing so to act in varying degrees, and there is always a cause to account for its action so far as the action is positive and not defective. There seems no reason why we should not admit a negative priority on the part of the creature over God's causality upon its conduct, since there is no before or after in God. Cf. M. Pontifex, *The Existence of God. A Thomist Essay* (London 1947) ch. 5, where this theory is defended.

It is surprising that St. Augustine did not apply this principle even more fully than he did, and use it, for example, when he discussed the foreknowledge of God in the third book. There is no doubt, however, that it was always in his mind. In the *City of God* (12.6 f.) he expresses it very clearly:

'If the further question be asked, what is the efficient cause of evil will, none is found. It is the will itself which makes the action evil, but what is it that makes the will evil? And thus evil will is the efficient cause of the evil action, but of the evil will there is no such cause. . . . Let no one, therefore, look for the efficient cause of the evil will; for it is not efficient, but deficient: this will is not productive of an effect, but it is a defect. Defection from that which supremely is, to that which is in a less

degree, this is the beginning of an evil will. But to seek to discover the causes of these defections—causes, as I have said, not
efficient, but deficient—is tantamount to endeavouring to see
darkness or hear silence.'

⁴⁹ One of the passages mentioned in the *Retractations* (4) by
St. Augustine as showing his teaching on grace even at the time
when he wrote the *De libero arbitrio*, and as refuting the Pelagian
theory.

BOOK THREE

¹ We are brought back again to the question which was discussed at the end of the second book. It was argued there that
a defect as such can have no cause, but Augustine does not refer
again to this argument. Now he sets to work to show that, since
an evil act is culpable, it must be due to the free will of the sinner,
and therefore that no one else is responsible. This argument
does not contradict the previous argument, but supplements it.

² Evodius is trying to get out of his former words, 'I do not
know whether this is any fault,' by claiming to have spoken
ironically. In fact, it seems, he had meant his words seriously,
and during Augustine's reply he thinks of yet another answer,
namely, that the movement deserves blame, but that the soul itself does not. We may perhaps see in this passage a record of
the actual discussion; it seems hardly possible that such a subtle
incident would have been invented.

³ Prof. Green reads *iam animo* instead of *in animo*: 'now I see
it is in the soul.'

⁴ The reference is to 1.11.21.

⁵ There is another reading, 'love (*diligat*) the lower,' instead of,
'choose (*deligat*) the lower.'

⁶ This is another passage mentioned in the *Retractations* (1.9.3)
as claimed by the Pelagians to support them.

⁷ The meaning of the passage seems to be that if the movement of the will were not voluntary, it would, so to speak, swing
loosely as on a hinge. It is curious that Augustine uses the
phrase 'when he turns the hinge of his will,' since the point is
that the agent would not control the movement.

⁸ Pulsasti vehementer: misericordia Dei adsit (*var.*: Pulsasti
vehementer misericordiam Dei. Adsit) aperiatque pulsantibus.

⁹ Prof. Green reads *aut* instead of *alii*: 'Or they are glad. . . .'

¹⁰ The reference is to 2.17.45, and to the passage which follows.

[11] Ps. 40.5.

[12] There is another reading, 'more capable of living (*ad viven-dum*), instead of, 'more capable of seeing (*ad videndum*).'

[13] These words were claimed in their favour by the Pelagians.

[14] There is another reading, 'we live (*vivimus*) of necessity.'

[15] Prof. Green TN 26 f. restores this second example: *aut, non voluntate infirmamur, sed necessitate.*

[16] It seems worthwhile to give some consideration to Augustine's discussion of the problem of God's foreknowledge of the creature's freely chosen acts in the light of the two chief lines of solution which have been proposed by Catholic theologians since his time.

First, there is the Thomist theory. This theory, as its chief feature, emphasises the absolute dependence of the creature on God, and, working from this side, tries to find a place for free choice of the creature's will. It holds that God premoves man's will with absolute certainty to the course He designs for it, but it combines with this the claim that, since God's power is infinite, He can do so in such a way that the mode of man's action is free. In this system there is no difficulty about God's foreknowledge of the future, but it is hard to see, as has often been pointed out, how man can remain free if God premoves his will with absolute certainty. Is it not of the essence of freedom of choice that it shall not be thus premoved?

The Molinist system, first advocated by Molina (1535–1600) and developed by Suarez (1548–1617), seeks to avoid this difficulty, and starts from man's freedom and then tries to fit in God's causality. Its explanation is that God knows all the ways in which a creature would act freely in every conceivable set of circumstances, and hence what a creature would freely choose to do if given a particular set of circumstances. How does God have foreknowledge of this? There are three ways, the Molinists say, in which God has knowledge of the acts of creatures: by 'simple intelligence,' by which He knows things merely as possible, by the 'knowledge of vision,' by which He knows what will actually happen, and by 'middle knowledge,' *scientia media*, by which He knows what would occur if certain conditions were fulfilled. The Molinist theory, therefore, is that man is free, but that this does not contradict God's supreme authority, because God, knowing what each man would freely do in any circumstances, brings about the circumstances and gives His concurrence as He Himself sees fit, and consequently His providence remains supreme. It may be objected that man's freedom is scarcely safeguarded if he will infallibly act in a particular way in given circumstances, and that it is difficult to understand what can be meant by saying that God knows how a man would freely choose to act in circumstances which have not actually arisen, because, if the choice is free, it is only determined when it is in fact made and not before.

G. H. Joyce, *Principles of Natural Theology* (London 1951) 544, puts the theory in a form which meets some of the objections: 'Where . . . the acts of free agents are concerned, the case is different: for the Divine decree must be such as to allow for liberty of choice. Here recourse is had to *scientia media*. God foresees the alternatives presented to the created will in each individual contingency, and foresees likewise which alternative the creature will freely choose, provided the choice be rendered possible by the concurrence requisite for its realization. That particular concurrence, and not another, He has decreed from all eternity to give. He would have decreed otherwise, had His foreknowledge shown Him that the created agent's choice would take another direction. The future free volition of the creature determines which shall be the concurrence destined for it. Yet we may say with truth that when the moment for action comes, God offers to the will a concurrence for any one of the various possible alternatives. Did He not do so, it would not be really capable of taking any other course than that which it actually chooses.'

Would St. Augustine agree with either of these theories? He argues that man's will is free, in the sense that God is in no way responsible for causing evil acts, but that God foreknows how man will act. He reconciles the two statements by arguing that foreknowledge does not imply that God is the cause of sin, since it would be impossible to foreknow a sin: it would not be a sin if it was caused by being foreknown. To some extent, therefore, St. Augustine would seem to tend towards the Molinist view, in so far as he affirms man's freedom of choice and denies that God's foreknowledge takes away this freedom. But Augustine was forced by the Pelagian controversy to work out his ideas on the subject more fully than was the case when he wrote the *De libero arbitrio*. Thonnard (510) points this out, and shows that St. Augustine's theory of grace took him in the opposite direction from Molinism. St. Augustine came to hold that freedom is never so perfect as when it is entirely under the creative influence of God: 'What will be freer than the free will when it cannot serve sin?' (*De corr. et grat.* 32). Here, however, as in other places, he seems to make no clear distinction between freedom of will in the sense of choice between more than one possible line of action, and freedom of will in the sense of absence of any obstacles to the action desired. But in any case Augustine's theory, as it developed, tended to emphasise God's providential control of man's action, and to start from this side of the problem, as does the Thomist theory.

It is perhaps surprising, as has already been pointed out, that St. Augustine did not make more use of the important principle which he advocated at the end of the second book. There he dealt with the question, what causes an evil movement of the will, and he replied that, since in so far as evil it is nothing but a deficiency, in so far as evil it has no cause. This seems relevant to the problem of God's foreknowledge if taken in conjunction with another point which though well known to all schools of theology, deserves more emphasis than is usually given it. Speaking strictly there can be no foreknowledge in God because in Him there is no before or after but only one indivisible act, the eternally present. God sees temporal things as successive, but sees them all together in the single moment of eternity. This surely gives a key to the problem. Man sins by free choice, and God is not responsible; God sees this sin from eternity, and yet by seeing it does not cause it. He sees and permits the defect in the creature, which has no cause outside the creature because it is negative and not positive; God limits His creative act in regard to the creature according to the defect which He sees and permits.

[17] In § 9 Evodius asked three questions: how it could be just to punish sins which are bound to occur, or how future events if foreknown are not bound to occur, or why the Creator is not responsible for what is bound to occur. Augustine has dealt with the first two questions, and now turns to the wider question of God's providence.

St. Augustine's teaching on providence was largely influenced by the teaching of Plotinus. Plotinus maintained that we should not try to judge things by taking any one thing in isolation from the rest, but that they must each be taken in their relation to the whole, when we shall see that the defects of individual things do not prevent their harmonising with the beauty of the whole. The hierarchy of beings which exist has the same effect of producing beauty in the whole. If there were no variety but all were equal, the universe would be less well governed. Even the wicked have their place and their beauty in relation to the whole, just as in a play each character is given his part by the author in order to make up the beauty of the whole play.

Although St. Augustine was much influenced by Plotinus, he did not merely repeat his views, but adapted them to the Christian faith. Providence to Plotinus was the work of the Logos which was an emanation from God, while to St. Augustine it was the work of the Three Persons of the Trinity performed in creation. Again, Plotinus held that unhappiness on earth was due to the misdeeds of souls in a former existence, and this was of course denied by St. Augustine. Again, Plotinus rejected any idea of the Redemption, since justice, he supposed, acted like a natural force and could not be frustrated by any act of free will. Hence for Plotinus prayer and the grace of God play no part in man's salvation: in so far as this is not already eternally achieved (man's highest self, his νοῦς, does not 'come down' but remains eternally in its state of perfection), man must work it out for himself by his own efforts; no additional help will be given beyond the divinity already in him by nature. So the only kinds of prayer which Plotinus can recognise are purely contemplative prayer with no element of petition in it, or a magical operation (to which alone he gives the name 'prayer' though it is not really prayer in our sense at all) which produces an automatic, unwilled response from inferior divinities within the visible cosmos in virtue of the universal sympathy. Such a theory made it hard to explain moral evil. Augustine, as against this, firmly maintained the freedom of the will and its responsibility, basing on man's freedom his explanation of the existence of sin. Thus he did not have to deny the presence of moral evil, but, while recognising it, yet detached it from any causality on the part of God. In spite of the presence of evil, praise—he maintained—is due to the Creator for all things. Providence is the work of God, carried out through the Redemption by which man is saved from his sins. See Thonnard 511–14; also R. Jolivet, *Le problème du mal d'après Saint Augustin* (Paris 1936) appendix: 'S. Augustin et Plotin' (esp. 149 ff.).

[18] Instead of *regula illa pietatis facile commovebit*, Prof. Green prefers the reading *regulam illam pietatis facile non movebit*, 'will not easily disturb that rule of piety. . . .'

[19] Augustine says, 'For whatever reason shows you with truth to be better, be assured that God has made this.' He is applying his theory that we know truth by divine illumination, and argues therefore that what we see clearly by divine illumination to be true must actually exist, and have been created by God. We have seen how St. Augustine was influenced by Neo-Platonism in his teaching on providence, and here we have another manifestation of the same influence. Thonnard says (514) that St. Augustine gives us in these words the formula of a philosophical optimism, that is to say, that St. Augustine teaches that the actual world is the best possible realisation of such a thing as our world. St. Augustine does not suggest that the world is the best possible in the sense that God could not have made anything better of a different kind, but only that it is the best realisation of the particular purpose aimed at in the creation of the world. He recognises that God did not create the world from any necessity but of His free will, and therefore that we cannot look for any further cause for its creation beyond God's will to create it. The world is one possible form of creation out of other possible forms, and God was not bound to create the most perfect thing possible—indeed no most perfect thing in the absolute sense is conceivable.

Thus the explanation of this sentence in which Augustine says that whatever we can truly conceive as better must exist, depends on the theory of exemplar ideas in the mind of God: 'You cannot conceive anything better in creation, which has escaped the Creator's thought. The human soul is by nature in contact with the divine types on which it depends. When it says, "This would be better than that," it sees this in the type with which it is in contact, provided it tells the truth and sees what it says it sees' (later in this same section). These exemplar ideas or types are not merely models, but through them God exercises creative as well as formal causality on everything in the world. They are also the source of all intelligibility of things. We can start from the perception of these exemplar ideas, and thus deduce what must actually exist; for, according to St. Augustine, what we conceive as better must be created in actual fact.

[20] Another reading is: 'you would not wish this to be heaven' (*caelum* for *solum*).

[21] The arguments with which St. Augustine meets objections to the doctrine of eternal punishment may be summed up as follows:

1. Sin which deserves eternal punishment is committed by the free choice of the sinner, and God is in no way responsible. 'What cause can be found in our sins to blame Him, when there is no blame for our sins which is not praise for Him?' (3.13.37). The nature which God creates is good, and any defect arising in it is due solely to the free will of the creature. 'If this is unjust, you will not be unhappy; but if it is just, let us praise Him by whose law this will be the case' (3.6.19).

2. Souls, even when they are sinful, are higher than the highest things which do not have life. 'Our soul, though corrupted with sin, is higher and better than if it were changed into the light seen by our eyes' (3.5.12); and, 'The soul is always superior to the body' (3.5.16).

3. The perfection of the whole is realised, provided none of the souls that are required for it are lacking. 'Provided that souls themselves are not lacking, whether those which are made unhappy when they sin or those which are made happy when they do right, the whole, having beings of every kind, is always complete and perfect' (3.9.26). 'You will find the unhappiness which grieves you has this value: that those souls which have rightly become unhappy because they willed to be sinful, are not lacking to the perfection of the whole' (3.9.25).

4. Therefore, in spite of the state of unrepentant sinners, the whole is perfect. 'When sinners are unhappy, the whole is perfect in spite of this' (3.9.26); and, 'Such is the generosity of God's goodness that He has not refrained from creating even that creature which He foreknew would not only sin, but remain in the will to sin' (3.5.15). This is true because punishment sets right the ugliness of sin. 'For sin and the punishment of sin are not themselves substantial things (*naturae*), but they are states (*affectiones*) of substantial things, the former voluntary, the latter penal. Now the voluntary state when sin is committed is a shameful state. Therefore to this is applied a penal state, to set it where such may fitly be, and to make it harmonise with the beauty of the whole, so that the sin's punishment may make up for its shamefulness' (3.9.26). Also, 'He created them not that

they might sin, but that they might add beauty to the whole, whether they willed to sin or not' (3.11.32).

What are we to think of these arguments? We can agree that if the responsibility rests with the man who by his free will has chosen to sin, and if he deserves such punishment, then no objection can be raised on the score of justice. But the rest of the argument seems less convincing. It depends on two contentions—that the important thing for the perfection of the whole is the presence of the full number of souls required, and that the infliction of punishment on guilty souls restores their harmony with the beauty of the whole. The difficulty here is to see how a sinful soul can be anything else than ugly and a blot on the beauty of the whole—*corruptio optimi pessima.* The fact that the guilty soul is punished does not seem to make it cease to be ugly; all it seems to do is to prevent it from enjoying a happiness or beauty to which it has no right. Perhaps the heart of the difficulty is to see how the souls of the blessed can be utterly happy when they are aware of other souls who are tragic failures, and, however justly, are unhappy and ugly. Does not complete happiness require awareness of nothing that is not completely happy and beautiful? This is presumably, from one point of view, the difficulty St. Augustine had in mind, since he seeks to show that the whole is perfect and beautiful in spite of sinners. It may be questioned whether his solution is satisfactory.

It is of interest in this connection to read the long discussion of eternal punishment in the 21st book of the *De civitate Dei.* There St. Augustine says that Scripture compels us to accept the doctrine of eternal punishment, but that, without necessarily agreeing, he will not oppose those who think the punishment of hell may through God's mercy be made less than is deserved (cf. ch. 24; also *Enchir.* 29.112, with note to same in ACW 3.144 n. 370).

²² This alludes to Manichaeism. See above, the Introd. § 2.

²³ *Semper,* omitted by Prof. Green.

²⁴ See Burnaby, *op. cit.* 37: 'For Augustine, creation *de nihilo* is simply creation, and creatureliness means a being which is not God's and therefore not unchangeable. His whole conception of moral good and evil is dynamic: man's soul is in the making and cannot stand still. Righteousness is its movement towards integration, sin its movement towards disintegration—a verging *ad nihilum,* an "unmaking." Change is the rule of temporal exist-

ence, changelessness is the quality of the eternal, the limit towards which the creature may approximate.'

²⁵ Perl (231) rightly terms this entire section with its fiction of a debate on suicide 'a masterpiece of psychology.' The theological aspects of suicide, even its sinfulness, are left aside: self-destruction involves an illusion and mistake, a wrong evaluation of existence and non-existence, a misinterpretation of natural feeling (*sensus*) and opinion (*opinio*). Better known is St. Augustine's broader treatment of the problem of suicide in the light of pagan and Christian morality, in the first book of the *City of God:* 1.16–27 (cf. also 19.4, refutation of the Stoic teaching on the matter). Besides adducing celebrated examples among the ancient Romans—Lucretia, Cato—he adverts to Christians, virgins who chose suicide to preserve their chastity in times of persecution and, as was charged by the opposition, in some instances were venerated in the Church as martyrs. While he refrains from passing judgment on such persons, he is uncompromising in rejecting suicide in any case whatsoever. See V. J. Bourke's presentation of the subject: *Augustine's Quest of Wisdom* (Milwaukee 1945) 251 f. For further patristic material, also on suicide in time of persecution, see A. Michel, 'Suicide,' DTC 14.2 (1941) 2739–49; C. Schneider, *Geistesgeschichte des antiken Christentums* (Munich 1954) 1.503.

²⁶ Prof. Green reads *quam* instead of *qua:* 'since he wishes a thing not to exist, which he is forced to praise, though lower.'

²⁷ 1 Cor. 6.3.

²⁸ Luke 20.36.

²⁹ This means that those who through vainglory desire equality with the angels do not desire to be raised to the level of the angels, but desire that the angels should be lowered to their level.

Prof. Green TN 27 omits *angelos in 'non ideo volunt aequales esse angelis, sed angelos sibi'*: the difficult *'sed sibi'* is found suggestive of *'sed sui iuris esse.'*

³⁰ Matt. 25.41.

³¹ Ps. 18.13 f.

³² St. Augustine's teaching on the devil's rights should be noticed. He says it would have been unjust that the devil should not rule over his captive, that the devil claimed all the descendants of Adam by lawful right, but that when the debt was paid, justice required that he should let them go.

These thoughts of the devil having rights and of a debt paid to him bring to mind much modern discussion of a formidable body of patristic antecedents in the matter. First, there is the 'rights' theory which finds in some of the Fathers, with Irenaeus the first to offer it, an ascription to the devil of rights of possession over captured humankind—rights either freely conceded to him by God after man's fall, or acquired and held by him even in strict justice. Conjoined with this is the 'ransom' theory, based primarily on language in Origen and claiming full expression in the redemptive theology of the Origenist St. Gregory of Nyssa. This theory sees in Christ's redemption of mankind a ransom of our souls from the captivity and bondage of Satan. The theory as proposed by certain authors in the nineteenth century finds in the Fathers the concept of Christ's ransom developed to the full and extreme—of a contract entered into by God and the devil, whereby the soul and blood of Christ were surrendered to the devil as a pawn or price for giving up captive mankind. It was, therefore, to the devil, not to God, that Christ offered the supreme sacrifice on the Cross!

For a brief on these theories and an appraisal of the relevant patristic texts (as found also in Sts. Basil, Gregory Nazianzen, Ambrose, Jerome, etc.), cf. J. Rivière, *The Doctrine of the Atonement* (tr. by L. Cappadelta, London-St. Louis 1909) 2.111 ff.; also, for Irenaeus: F. Vernet, 'Irénée (Saint),' DTC 7.2 (1923) 2479–81; J. Lawson, *The Biblical Theology of Saint Irenaeus* (London 1948) 197 f.; for Origen: R. Cadiou, *Origen. His Life at Alexandria* (tr. by J. A. Southwell, St. Louis-London 1944) 300 f.

As for St. Augustine, besides the reflections already seen and remaining to be seen in *De libero arbitrio*, there are scattered throughout his works a number of other reminders of his wrestling with the traditional rights-and-ransom speculation on the defeat of Satan through the Saviour's redemption of man. What is perhaps his most 'suspicious' statement occurs in his work *On the Trinity*, in a lengthy discussion (13.12.16–15.19) of the Redeemer's deliverance of man from the power of the devil. The sentence reads (§ 19): '*In hac redemptione tanquam pretium pro nobis datus est sanguis Christi, quo accepto diabolus non ditatus est, sed ligatus: ut nos ab eius nexibus solveremur, nec quemquam secum eorum quos Christus ab omni debito liber indebite fuso suo sanguine redemisset, peccatorum retibus involutum traheret ad secundae ac sempiternae mortis exitium.*' However much this passage may smack of the old ransom idea, it is rightly emphasised by E. Portalié, 'Augustin (Saint),' DTC 1.2 (1903) 2371 f., that it must be studied and weighed in its entire context (note in the sentence itself the use of the word *tanquam*='as it were'!). Such study of the entire discussion, Portalié finds, shows: '1. The devil has no right over us, and what is styled his right was merely a permission granted by God to punish sinners; he was the executioner, not the master. 2. Hence, no ransom was due to him, and God's forgiveness of our sins immediately resulted in our being set free. 3. This forgiveness might have been granted gratuitously without any reparation, but it was more seemly that Divine Justice should be fulfilled and that the devil should lose his power through his injustice; such was the plan of the Passion' (tr. by Cappadelta, *op. cit.* 149 f.).

These conclusions are further borne out and amplified in numerous passages elsewhere in Augustine. He knows of no pact or negotiation between God or Christ and the devil, but only of Christ mediating between man and His Divine Father: cf., e.g., *Enchir.* 28.108; *De praed. sanct.* 30.15; *De nat. et grat.* 2.2. Fallen man was delivered from the power of the devil, not because the devil was in some way bargained with and placated or satisfied, but because Christ satisfied God and reconciled us with Him: cf. *Enchir.* 14.49; *De civ. Dei* 1.22; *De Trin.* 4.13.17; *Serm.* 26.3; etc. If in the passage cited above Augustine states equivalently that Christ redeemed or ransomed us from the devil, he elsewhere too says in figurative and dramatized language that Christ redeemed us from the slavery of sin (*Serm.* 30.1), that He redeemed us from hell (*Serm.* 314.4), from death (*De nat. et grat.* 24.26), etc.; cf. Portalié, *loc. cit.*; also Rivière, *Le dogme de la rédemption chez Saint Augustin* (3. ed. Paris 1933); Thonnard 516 f.

Rivière, *Doctrine of the Atonement* 150 f., observes regarding the soteriological language here used by Augustine—and his language certainly deserves very special attention in his discussions of these matters—that 'Saint Augustine is inclined to use the common vocabulary associated with the ransom theory. In this he was not only making a concession to the received language, he was also endeavouring to explain it away. He retains indeed the traditional expressions, but only after having first emptied them of their contents and explained them in accordance with his own system. His only reason for thus paying any attention to the old theory was that it was widespread in the Christian community; his intention was, not to adopt but to adapt it.'

[33] Cf. John 1.3 and 14.

[34] In the phrase 'from whom and through whom and in whom all things have been made' St. Augustine alludes to the Three Persons of the Trinity. 'From whom,' *a quo*, refers to God the Father considered as the ultimate cause of creation; 'through whom,' *per quem*, refers to God the Son, the Word, considered as the means through whom all has been done; 'in whom,' *in quo*, refers to God the Holy Spirit, considered as the sanctifier in whom the union of all with their cause takes place. Thonnard (517) suggests the paraphrase: '. . . of Him by the power of whom, according to the wisdom of whom, in the goodness of whom all has been made.'

[35] Five of the early MSS read 'whatever their function' (quantilibet *muneris*).—Occasionally among the Fathers, including St. Augustine, we find speculation regarding the number of angels. They are very numerous (Dan. 7.10, Luke 2.13, etc.), but can an approximation be made of their great number? Some, interpreting the parable of the lost sheep (Matt. 18.12–14, Luke 15.3–7), identify the single lost sheep with fallen man, and the ninety-nine that had not strayed, with the angels. This proportion of 99:1 is thought of by St. Hilary, *Comm. in Matt.* 18.6; by St. Ambrose, *Exp. Evang. Luc.* 7.210; and so too by St. Augustine, *Coll. c. Max.* 9. Again, some writers proposed that the chosen among men were to fill the places left by the fallen angels: see Augustine, *Enchir.* 9.29 (= ACW 3.37; cf. 123 n. 73), and *De civ. Dei* 22.1. Augustine grants, *Enchir. ibid.*, that the men saved may exceed the vacancies they fill. Gregory the Great, on the other hand, equates the number of the elect with that of the faithful angels: cf. *In Evang. hom.* 34. Concerning the subject, cf. G. Bareille, 'Ange d'après les Pères,' DTC 1.1 (1903) 1205 f.

[36] Here the sense requires omission of the words '*qui non possunt*,' a late interpolation carried by the Maurist editors (Green TN 27 f.).

[37] This refers to Manichaeism.

[38] 1 Cor. 3.17.

[39] Augustine's etymology of *vituperare*, *vituperatio*, as consisting of *vitium+parare*, 'preparing (= charging, imputing) a fault (defect, vice, etc.),' still appears as acceptable as any: cf. A.

Walde, *Lateinisches etymologisches Wörterbuch* (3. ed. Heidelberg 1954) s. v.

[40] Thonnard (522) explains the connection of thought here as follows. The idea of a debt suggests to Augustine the idea of what is due in justice, and hence he considers providence in its relation to evil from a fresh point of view. The thought is threefold. First, there is the point that temporal things when they decay, do not fail to give what they owe because decay is natural to them. Secondly, there is the point that a creature with free will, when it does what is right, pays what is due and praise should be given to the Creator. Thirdly, if it does not do what is right, by its punishment justice is fulfilled and again praise is due to the Creator. Thus Augustine reaches the general conclusion, aimed at in this part of the book, that God deserves praise in all circumstances, even though creatures choose to sin.

[41] Another sentence claimed in their favour by the Pelagians.

[42] 1 Tim. 6.10.—In the following St. Augustine hints at the very obvious etymological sense of the Greek word φιλαργυρία (φιλεῖν = to love + ἄργυρος = silver) = 'love of silver.' When in the following lines he describes the Latin *avaritia* as an 'excessive desire' of anything, he reflects the root meaning: *av-ere* = to 'desire vehemently.'

[43] Prof. Green reads *recedetur* instead of *receditur:* '. . . and nothing else than the will *will be* the root.'

[44] Another sentence which the Pelagians claimed in their support.

[45] Yet another sentence which the Pelagians claimed.

[46] 1 Tim. 1.13.

[47] Ps. 24.7.

[48] Rom. 7.19 and 18.

[49] Gal. 5.17.

[50] 'Difficulty' is perhaps the nearest equivalent to the Latin *difficultas,* but it is not wholly satisfactory. The word implies here the presence of obstacles to a moral agent.

[51] Eph. 2.3.

[52] The words, 'and because He loves them He repairs their being,' are found in the earlier editions, but apparently not in the MSS.

[53] Instead of *consequitur* Prof. Green reads *consequetur:* 'will result.'

[54] Certain questions with regard to the origin of men's souls

puzzled St. Augustine throughout his life, and he never became convinced what was their true solution. Let us start with what seemed quite clear to him. He had no doubt that the soul cannot be an emanation from the divine substance, that no soul can be derived from a body or from an animal soul (this applying to the souls of Adam and Eve as well as to the rest of mankind), that any theory is false which speaks of a former life in which souls, pure spirits, have for their sins deserved to be exiled in human or animal bodies, that is to say, any theory of metempsychosis; and, finally, that neither the soul of Adam nor of his descendants can come from an immaterial substance created on the first day. The problem which puzzled him was concerned, not with the soul of Adam, but with the souls of Adam's descendants. If a man's soul came by propagation from his parents, how are we to explain individual personality, while, if each soul is created by a separate act, how can we explain its contraction of the guilt of original sin? If each is created separately, is it created when each body is formed? If so, how are we to account for the words of Genesis in which God is described as resting on the seventh day, since on this theory creation would go on during the whole course of human history? If each soul was created at the beginning of the world and united by God to the body at the appropriate time, or if each was created at the beginning of the world and is united by its own act to the body, what is its state before it joins the body?—Regarding the problem and the principal passages see Portalié, DTC 1.2.2359–61; Gilson, *op. cit.* 66–68, 94–96 (pre-existence); Copleston, *op. cit.* 2.79 f.

The origin of the souls, besides occupying Augustine on numerous occasions, is treated by him in a separate work of four books: *De anima et eius origine* (written ca. 419, or perhaps as late as 423/24—so H. Pope, *Saint Augustine of Hippo* [London 1937] 380). Particularly interesting and instructive is a long letter (= *Ep.* 166) to St. Jerome of the year 415, bearing the title, *De origine animae hominis*—a veritable treatise on the problem. In this letter (§ 1) Augustine, 'an old man,' approaches the 'much older' man for light on the problem whose solution he has sought over many years and the principal burden of which is stated clearly. It is extracted briefly here.

'Some years ago,' writes Augustine (7), 'I wrote certain books on *The Problem of Free Choice*. These went forth into the hands of many, and many have them now. There I brought up

four views on the soul's incarnation: 1) that all other souls are
generated from the one given to the first man; 2) that for each
and every person a new soul is made; 3) that souls already in existence somewhere are sent by God into the bodies, or 4) enter
them of their own will. I thought it necessary to treat these
views in such a way that, regardless of which of them might be
true, I was not to be hindered in my purpose to oppose with all
my might those—the Manichaeans—who attempt to lay upon God
the responsibility for a nature ruled by its own principle of
evil. . . .'

Jerome apparently held the second view, that God creates each
soul for each newborn individual (8). But he has not solved
for Augustine the difficulty in Genesis, of God resting on the
seventh day. Jerome, in turn, has sent enquirers to Augustine to
seek solution of the problem, which is still full of difficulties for
Augustine (9): for instance (10), if souls are individually created, day after day, whence the sin of infants that they should
require remission of it in baptism? These souls, post-created,
are tied to flesh derived from the vitiated flesh of the first sinner
Adam: is it just on the part of the Creator to expose them and to
deliver them over to condemnation on such basis of guilt?
Thousands of infants die without baptism—is their condemnation
on such ground just?

Some objections to creation of the soul at birth, Augustine explains (11–15), can be met. 'But when I am confronted by the
penal problem of the little ones, I am embarrassed, believe me,
by great difficulties, and I am utterly lost for an answer.' And
here it is not merely the eternal punishments of infants in the
afterlife, but the sufferings and miseries that are theirs in the few
days they live, that disconcert Jerome's enquirer (16). Further,
there are those who never attain to the use of reason—idiots or
imbeciles: if individual souls are created for such, how are we to
reconcile with divine justice the transference to these of the
primeval penalty (17)?

Augustine continues for some paragraphs more on the subject
of infants suffering in this life (present to his mind, we must not
forget, is the uncertain lot of infants in antiquity—the practice of
infanticide and exposition of infants, the tragic fate of the offspring of slaves, etc.) and the fate of infants dying unbaptized.
He quotes at some length (18) from a passage in the *De libero
arbitrio* (3.23.68) which we shall read some pages farther on:

here he had suggested that we do not know 'what ample compensation God reserves for these children in the secret of His judgments.' But Augustine admits to Jerome (20) that this is only a conjecture and at best a partial answer, certainly not applying to the great numbers who die without baptism. Regarding these—'if by a separate creative act of God each receives his soul at birth, why are they doomed to punishment if they die in infancy without the sacrament of Christ? That they are doomed if they so leave the body, is testified both by Holy Scripture and by the Holy Church' (25).

We know from the *Retractations* (2.45) that St. Jerome, pleading lack of leisure, did not make answer to St. Augustine's difficulties. Some few years before his death, in the same *Retractations* (1.1.3), Augustine confessed: 'As regards its (the soul's) origin, by which it comes to be in the body, whether it is from that one man who was first created, when *man was made into a living soul* (1 Cor. 15:45), or whether in like manner for each individual an individual soul is created, I neither then knew, nor do I know now.'

[55] St. Augustine held that no error was possible in the Bible: if a reader thinks he has found a false statement, either the reading is wrong, or the interpretation is wrong, or the text is wrongly understood (*C. Faust. Man.* 11.5). He admits that forgetfulness may occur in the writer and one name may be confused with another (*De cons. Evang.* 3.7.30). As to the authority of the different versions, he considers the Septuagint inspired, and both Hebrew and Greek texts inspired even in the parts which one or other lack (*De civ. Dei* 18.42 f.). He claimed liberty of discussion in regard to the Latin texts: he often quotes the so-called Itala, often the ancient African texts, sometimes St. Jerome's Vulgate. Concerning the interpretation of Scripture his principles were: first, prudence, so that he denounced rash interpretations which would bring the word of God into ridicule; secondly, that every meaning which is found by a reader and is good and true, even though not intended by the writer, is the intention of the Holy Spirit (*De doct. Christ.* 3.27.34). See Portalié, DTC 1.2.2342 f.; for extensive study, M. Pontet, *L'exégèse de S. Augustin prédicateur* (Paris 1944) 1–383.

[56] The Latin word here translated 'source of their forms' is *formator*.

[57] There is another reading, 'in the misery of temporal events' —*miseria* for *serie*.

[58] Another reading has 'deeper cause'—*interior* instead of *ulterior*.

[59] Instead of *quod recte faciat* Prof. Green TN 28 prefers the reading *recti facti*: '. . . the good of right action.'

[60] Following Prof. Green (28) who excises *aliena* (= the faith 'of another'), an early interpolation, between *potest* and <*ac*>-*commodari*.

[61] Cf. Luke 7.12–15.

[62] Instead of *iusta divina lege poena consecuta est* Prof. Green TN 29 reads *iustam divina lege poenam consecutam*: 'From this it is understood that . . ., and (that) since this sin was done in free will, by divine law a just penalty followed after it.'

[63] Rom. 1.22 and 21.

[64] Ps. 41.7.

[65] Gen. 3.5.

[66] Ecclus. 10.15 and 14.

[67] Ps. 83.11.

INDEX

INDEX

ANCIENT CHRISTIAN WRITERS
The Works of the Fathers in Translation
Edited by
J. QUASTEN, S. T. D., and J. C. PLUMPE, Ph. D.